The Freckleton,
England, Air Disaster

The Freckleton, England, Air Disaster

*The B-24 Crash That Killed
38 Preschoolers and 23 Adults,
August 23, 1944*

JAMES R. HEDTKE

3-27-2014

Dear Ellin,

You were one of the best student
I had the opportunity to teach!
Thank you for all you and your family
do for Cabrini College.

Best wishes

Jim Hedtke

McFarland & Company, Inc., Publishers
Jefferson, North Carolina

LIBRARY OF CONGRESS CATALOGUING-IN-PUBLICATION DATA

Hedtke, James R.
   The Freckleton, England, air disaster : the B-24 crash
that killed 38 preschoolers and 23 adults, August 23,
1944 / James R. Hedtke.
       p.   cm.
   Includes bibliographical references and index.

   ISBN 978-0-7864-7841-5 (softcover : acid free paper) ∞
   ISBN 978-1-4766-1362-8 (ebook)

   1. Aircraft accidents—England—Freckleton—History—20th
century.   2. Disasters—England—Freckleton—History—20th
century.   3. B-24 (Bomber)—History.   4. Airplanes, Military—
England—Lancashire—Flight testing—History—20th century.
5. United States. Army Air Forces—History—World War, 1939–
1945.   6. Aircraft accident victims—England—Freckleton—
History—20th century.   7. Freckleton (England)—History—
20th century.   8. Freckleton (England)—Biography.   I. Title.

TL553.53.G7H43 2014
363.12'409427662—dc23   2014000028

BRITISH LIBRARY CATALOGUING DATA ARE AVAILABLE

On the cover: American GIs, medics and MPs, as well as British
first responders, sifted through the rubble of the infants' wing for
survivors. Only three of the 41 children from this section of Holy
Trinity School lived through the carnage. The survivors, Ruby
Whittle, George Carey and David Madden, were badly burned
and endured years of painful surgeries (courtesy of BAe Systems
Heritage Division); clock (iStockphoto/Thinkstock); background
smoke (Zoonar/Thinkstock)

Manufactured in the United States of America

McFarland & Company, Inc., Publishers
  Box 611, Jefferson, North Carolina 28640
  www.mcfarlandpub.com

To the children of Freckleton, past,
present and future, and to the
children and grandchildren of the
Hedtke and Martin families.

Table of Contents

Acknowledgments

In 1958, nine-year-old Judy Ivers from Springfield, Pennsylvania, thought it would be fun to have a pen pal. She read an advertisement in *Ingénue*, a magazine aimed at pre-teen girls, for an agency that would provide American girls with a pen pal in England. Judy Ivers seized the moment. She sent the required 15 cents in stamps to the agency and received back the name of Jackie Whittle, an English girl who lived on Kirkham Road in the village of Freckleton. A 54-year friendship commenced with the first letter. Over half a century later, the two have remained steadfast friends and continue to write letters, send e-mails and visit each other on a regular basis.

I married Judy Ivers in 1971. Throughout the years she has been my best friend, a loyal confidante, and the source of my inspiration. Almost from the day I met Judy, she told me stories about Jackie and her family. In 1987, Judy and I took our first trip to England. One of our destinations was the village of Freckleton. After 29 years of trans–Atlantic correspondence, Judy and Jackie finally met face to face. The meeting was a truly emotional experience that solidified nearly three decades of friendship that had developed through the written word. Since that inaugural visit, the Hedtke and Martin families have exchanged several visits and attended the weddings of each other's children.

It was on our first visit to Freckleton in 1987 that Jackie and her husband, Peter Martin, told us the story of the air disaster in the village and took us to visit the communal grave in Holy Trinity Cemetery. I immediately became fascinated with the accident and became determined to be one of the voices to tell the victims' story. Without Judy's and Jackie's friendship, I never would have known about the tragic events of August 23, 1944. I will always be grateful that their friendship led me to this compelling story of love, sorrow, compassion, and hope.

Jackie and Pete Martin are more than friends. They have served as a liaison between the survivors of the crash, many of the victims' families and me. They have also provided photographs and news articles on the accident. Their untiring efforts and commitment to this project have turned my interest in the air disaster into a completed work.

Peter Shakeshaft's and Richard Spencer's works on Freckleton were extremely helpful in developing a synopsis of the history of the village prior to World War II. Harry Holmes' two excellent books on the U.S. Army Air Force Base Air Depot (or BAD2) disaster provided a solid background about the American base at Warton. David Mayor's article on the air disaster, which first appeared in *BAD News* in March 1979, provided a starting point for most of the research on the tragedy.

I am deeply indebted to the survivors of the crash for their courage and willingness to tell their stories. I would specifically like to thank Ruby Currell, Joan Richardson, Irene Cottam, Valerie Whittle, Barbara Hall, Bill Bone, Jack Nichol, Brenda Sidebottom and Elsie Dollin for the interviews and letters that form the focal point of the work. I would also like to thank the members of the BAD2 Association who provided me with letters, testimony and documents concerning the tragedy. Without the help of Ralph Scott, Thomas Miller and Ernest Bloemendal, the book would have remained a work in progress.

My colleagues at Cabrini College have been very supportive of my research endeavors. I would like to express my appreciation to Jolyon Girard, Darryl Mace and Jonnie Guerra for their advice and their confidence in me. Don Dempsey provided technical assistance in preparing the photographs used in this book for publication. For forty years it has been an honor to be a member of the Cabrini College faculty and to be part of the college community's commitment to provide each of its students with an education of the heart.

An author is always dependent on talented librarians and researchers. I would like to thank the staff of Cabrini College's Holy Spirit Library, especially the late Cory Salazar, for procuring primary and secondary resources for my research. Lawral Wornek provided invaluable help in tracking down photographs for the book. I also want to thank Robert Jolly, Library Frontline Assistant at the Harris Library in Preston, UK, for helping me find and obtain local news stories on the disaster. Myrna Barnes, director of the Morton County Historical Society Museum, provided useful information on pilot Burtie Orth. The U.S. Air Force Historical Research Agency at Maxwell Air Force Base in Alabama provided the official records and testimony necessary for the success of this work. Keith Spong and Colin Charnley of BAe Systems

Heritage Division procured photographs of BAD2 and the crash site and secured the permission to use them in this work. Kathy McCrea, Catherine Arnesen, Shannon Tinney and Patti Stocker provided technical aid in the preparation of the manuscript.

I am pleased to include David Carr's poem about the air tragedy in the work. It is a fitting tribute to David's uncle, who was lost in the fire in the infant's room, and to his grandparents, who suffered one of the worst tragedies in life, the loss of a child.

Finally, I would like to remember the 61 victims of the Freckleton air disaster. The sacrifice and loss of their lives was part of the price of the freedom and liberty we enjoy today as American and British citizens. Though their lives abruptly ended, their legacy never will.

Preface

"What's past is prologue"—William Shakespeare, *The Tempest*

When dawn broke on Freckleton on the morning of August 23, 1944, the United Kingdom had been at war with Nazi Germany for almost five years. The small village of Freckleton, situated in northwest England, had not endured the terrors and ravages of the "blitz" because of its geographic position. The village, however, contributed its fair share of husbands, sons, brothers and sweethearts to the struggle against fascism and oppression. The war also affected Freckleton in another way. In the adjacent village of Warton, the American Eighth Air Force operated a Base Air Depot known as BAD2. The depot assembled, repaired and refurbished aircraft for the "Mighty Eighth." Servicemen were billeted around Freckleton and Warton and the locals soon called the area "Little America." The drone of aircraft arriving and leaving BAD2 constantly reminded the villagers that the war continued to rage on in Europe and the Pacific.

In many respects, Wednesday, August 23, 1944, should have been a day of celebration for the Allies in their struggle against the Axis powers. On the eastern front in Europe, Soviet forces cut off 12 divisions of the German 6th Army in Romania. The defeat of the German forces signaled an imminent peril for its Axis ally, Romania. On August 23, the Romanian government accepted Soviet armistice terms and dropped out of its alliance with Germany. Romania's withdrawal hurt the German war effort by depriving Germany of the third largest military force in Europe and the loss of needed oil and food supplies.

On the western front, the liberation of Paris had begun. With Allied armies moving closer to the city, the people of Paris rose up against the Germans on August 19, 1944. At 6:30 a.m. on August 23, units of the French 2nd Armored Division entered the suburbs of Paris. American soldiers in the

Fourth U.S. Infantry Division, commanded by General Barton, attacked Paris from the east. On August 25, the Germans in Paris surrendered and Allied forces officially liberated "The City of Light."

In New Guinea on August 23, American forces overcame the last Japanese resistance on the island of Numfoor. With New Guinea secured, the Americans redeployed most of their forces to continue the relentless island-hopping campaign toward Japan. On this date as well, senior Allied representatives met at Dumbarton Oaks to discuss post-war security. These discussions eventually led to the creation of the United Nations.

In the early morning of August 23, there were no omens to warn the inhabitants of Freckleton about the tragedy that was about to befall the village that day. It seemed to be just another ordinary day in very extraordinary times. Children ate their breakfast anxiously awaiting their second day of school after the summer break. Teachers assiduously reviewed their lesson plans in final preparation for the school day. Patrons and employees in the Sad Sack Café discussed the war in Europe and the inevitable liberation of Paris. Mothers and wives stared at the vacant chairs at the breakfast table and offered a solemn prayer that their loved one would safely return home from the war. Even the weather report suggested an ordinary day, "some early sunshine and light cloud followed by rain showers later in the morning."

It appeared to be another ordinary day as well for the men stationed at BAD2. Servicemen like Thomas Miller and Ralph Scott continued to work at a hectic pace to repair and refurbish aircraft so that the Eighth Air Force could maintain air superiority over the skies of Western Europe and relentlessly batter Nazi assets on the ground.

First Lieutenant John Bloemendal of Minnesota finished his breakfast and assumed his duties as Officer of the Day. He was scheduled to take a B-24 Liberator on a test flight at 8:30 a.m. Routine duties as Officer of the Day sidetracked Bloemendal and delayed takeoff of the test flight until 10:30 a.m. This delay sealed the fates of both First Lieutenant Bloemendal and the citizens of Freckleton.

At 10:30 a.m., the control tower at the Warton airfield cleared two B-24s repaired at BAD2 for takeoff on a test flight. Bloemendal, a veteran test pilot, flew a repaired B-24 nicknamed the *Classy Chassis II* and First Lieutenant Peter Manassero commanded the other aircraft. At almost the same time as takeoff, a quick moving, severe thunderstorm arrived in the area of Freckleton. Upon receiving warning of the approaching thunderstorm from the weather station at Burtonwood, the Warton control tower recalled the two airplanes. In the midst of the raging storm, Bloemendal tried to land the

Classy Chassis II at the Warton airfield. Manassero decided not to land his B-24 at Warton because of the weather conditions and instead decided to fly northward to escape the storm.

As Bloemendal continued his approach to the runway at Warton, he realized he was not going to make a successful landing at the field. He tried to retract his landing gear and fly around the field to follow Manassero's path out of the storm and to safety. It was too late! When Bloemendal attempted to bank his turn, he lost control of the aircraft and it barreled into the village of Freckleton. Along its downward path the *Classy Chassis II* clipped the tops of trees and demolished three houses and the Sad Sack Café. The B-24 then somersaulted down Lytham Road. Fuel from the plane's ruptured tanks spewed into the Holy Trinity School's infant wing and immediately engulfed the building, teachers and students in flames.

The final death toll from the crash of the *Classy Chassis II* was 61 people killed, including 38 children. This crash was the single greatest civilian air disaster suffered by the Allies in World War II. In a fireball that lasted minutes, an English village lost an entire generation and was left with a legacy of loss that continues to the present day.

August 23, 1944, turned out not to be an ordinary day for the people of Freckleton and the servicemen stationed at the American air base. It was a tragic day of tremendous loss, horrific suffering and unspeakable pain. August 23 would never be an ordinary day in Freckleton ever again. Each year the people of the village remember the anniversary of the crash with ceremonies that memorialize the 61 victims.

The story of the Freckleton air disaster is not just a tale of loss, suffering and pain. It is also the story of courage, love, compassion and reconciliation. The story reminds us that life's journey is filled with happiness and sorrow, despair and hope, life and death. Through all of their suffering and sorrow, the people of Freckleton have honored the past while building a brighter future. The following narrative is the story of their journey.

Note on Sources: *Chapter 5. The Crash and Chapter 8. The Investigation quote from the same testimony because eyewitnesses gave only short statements to the U.S.A.A.F., and in most instances the statement consisted of only two or three sentences. The two chapters use the same testimony for two different purposes. Whereas in Chapter 5 eyewitness accounts are used to describe the crash, Chapter 8 examines why the crash occurred and here the testimony is used to support or challenge the various theories of the crash and the official U.S. version of what happened that tragic day.*

1

Freckleton Before World War II

"Village of flower and music"—Freckleton organization website

The village of Freckleton is located in Lancashire, England, near the junction of the Dow and Douglas Rivers on the South Fylde Coast. The Fylde is a square shaped, coastal plain peninsula bounded by the Irish Sea to the west, Morecambe Bay to the north and the River Ribble estuary to the south. Freckleton is also part of the Fylde Borough, the local government for the southern portion of the Fylde peninsula. Today the population of Freckleton is more than 6,000 persons, nearly six times the population of the village when World War II commenced in September 1939.

Geologists and archeologists contend that Freckleton is over 2,000 years old.[1] Roman history substantiates this claim. When the Romans invaded the British Isles, the 20th Legion marched to northwest England and established a garrison at Chester. From Chester, the Romans advanced to the Fylde peninsula and built a fort at what is the present-day village of Kirkham. The Romans used the port of Freckleton to supply and reinforce their troops at Kirkham.[2]

The appearance of Freckleton in recorded English history does not occur until the publication of the *Domesday Book* in 1086. William the Conqueror commissioned the book in December 1085. The purpose of the work was to survey and assess the land and resources owned by the English south of the Rivers Ribble and Tees. Another important reason for the land survey was to establish the extent of taxes William could raise in the kingdom. The two-volume work published in August 1086 contained records for 13,418 English settlements. The hand-recorded volumes contained the names of landowners and tenants, census figures, landownership records, available resources, and the customary dues/taxes paid to the king. The *Domesday Book* did not receive its name until the 12th century when the English people compared the book to the last judgment, doomsday, in the New Testament of the Bible.

The English sarcastically likened the comprehensive scope and irreversible nature of the *Domesday Book* to the "book of life" God will use at the last judgment to separate saints from sinners. Today, the original *Domesday Book* is housed in the National Archives in Kew, London.

In the *Domesday Book*, the name of the village appears as Frecheltun. The origin of the village's name is uncertain. Local historian Peter Shakeshaft, who wrote the *History of Freckleton*, believes the origin of the village's name is Anglo-Saxon.[3] He contends that the modern word *freckle* derives from the Anglo-Saxon words *frecel* and *welle* meaning *dangerous pool*. Shakeshaft suggests that *freckle* could also derive from the personal Anglo-Saxon name Frecla. Whatever the meaning and derivation of *freckle*, we know that it was coupled with the old English word for settlement, *tun*, which eventually evolved into *ton*. The *Domesday Book* put the size of "Frecheltun" at 400 acres and stated that the land in the region was arable.[4]

At the time the authors wrote the *Domesday Book*, agriculture was the village's main source of income. Agriculture remained the area's staple economic paradigm throughout the millennium until the onset of World War II. In the 18th century, agriculture in Freckleton was quite different from the norm in the rest of England. There was no lord of the manor in Freckleton and individuals privately owned the small farms in the area.[5] Freckletonians communally managed the excellent grazing on the marshes on the north bank of the River Ribble. The villagers developed an intricate system of sharing the rights for the pasturing of farm animals. This communal system still operates in virtually the same manner today.[6] The lack of gentry had a dramatic impact on the politics of the village. In an era when the landed aristocracy dominated British politics, the citizens of Freckleton generally governed their community themselves.

At the beginning of the 13th century, Sir Richard Freckleton built a water mill on the River Dow to grind grain. The mill soon made Freckleton the agricultural center of the Fylde region. In 1615, the owners built a new mill and house. The Earl of Derby purchased the mill in 1669. His heirs sold the property to the Clifton family in 1850. The Spencer family was the last full-time millers until the facility went out of business in 1915. Farmers in the area used the Freckleton mill to grind corn for market. For most of the time it operated, the mill depended on the tidal water of the River Dow to function. The Spencer family finally built a dam and this freed the mill's operation from the forces of nature, allowing the millers to use the mill at any time of day. In the winter, the mill became a popular attraction for the villagers. When the dam pond froze over, Freckletonians would lace on their skates and glide over the ice. Local musicians often produced melodies to accompany the skaters as they playfully navigated the pond.[7] Unfortunately for posterity, the water mill was demolished in 1968.

Local farmers grew corn and raised livestock such as poultry, cattle and sheep. Dairy farmers produced not only milk but also renowned cheeses and butter. Local families like the Sudells, Carters, and Masons consistently won prizes for their dairy products at agricultural shows throughout the region.[8] In the 1930s, there were 85 Freckleton families still involved in agriculture, with 48.2 percent of that number raising poultry.[9] World War II, however, brought sweeping changes to the village of Freckleton. After the war, agriculture greatly diminished as an important sector of the village's economy.

Since the end of the 18th century, industry has coexisted with traditional family farming as an important segment of Freckleton's economy. In the early 1800s, the small port of Freckleton was busy building ships and was an important center for the distribution of coal throughout the region. In 1814, George Rigby and Robert Rawstone started the Freckleton shipyard. In 1871, the shipyard built its first ocean-going vessel, the schooner *Isabella*. The shipyard built vessels other than schooners such as trawlers, sharking boats, flat-bottom barges, and yachts. The yard also repaired and maintained watercraft including most of the lifeboats employed along the waters of northwest England. Industries ancillary to shipbuilding also developed around Freckleton. Sailcloth, weaving, rope making, and steam-engine maintenance provided steady work for the local inhabitants.[10]

Freckleton was a port since the time of the Romans. As mentioned earlier, the Romans brought supplies into Freckleton to support their troops stationed at Kirkham. In the 17th and 18th centuries, ships from Liverpool, Wales, Ireland and the Isle of Man unloaded their cargos at the brick quay located just below Naze Point (where the mouth of the River Ribble, River Douglas and River Dow meet together). With the advent of the industrial revolution, coal and slack became major commodities shipped through Freckleton. Flat-bottom barges brought coal and slack from the Wigan coalfields down the River Douglas to Freckleton. Workers unloaded the coal and deposited it behind a public house named the Ship Inn. The locals called this area "coal hill." Merchants, such as Harry Hall, sold the coal and slack throughout the entire Fylde region.[11] Ships sailing from Freckleton also took coal to Liverpool where it was used locally or shipped further down the coast. This rather circuitous route of shipping coal from Wigan to Liverpool remained the only option until the construction and opening of the Leeds and Liverpool Canal in 1820. The Leeds and Liverpool Canal gradually reduced the importance of Freckleton as a transit point for coal destined to the homes and factories of Liverpool.

The textile industry also provided employment for many Freckletonians. William Sowerbutts opened the Balderstone Mill in December 1880. The mill employed more than 100 workers. At the height of its operation, Balderstone Mill used more than 320 looms for the weaving of twills that were later bleached and dyed.[12] The firm then sold the finished cotton products on the Manchester Cotton Exchange. The Sowerbutts family eventually sold the company to John Bibby. The Bibbys sold the firm to its final owner, Mr. Birtwistle. Birtwistle closed the mill in December 1980, exactly 100 years after it had opened. At the time of its closing, Balderstone Mill employed fewer than 50 people and could no longer compete with textile mills operating in developing countries. A land developer demolished the mill and built houses on the land. Today, the only vestige of Balderstone Mill's existence is a remainder of the mill's outer wall that runs parallel to Memory Close. The village also named a new street Balderstone Road after the defunct mill.

By the beginning of World War II, the economic development of Freckleton was severely constricted by the lack of a bridge across the River Ribble and no direct access to a railroad in the village. The onset of World War II tabled any plans by the Regional Planning Committee to bridge the River Ribble and the railroad never got any closer than Kirkham, which is three miles away from Freckleton.

Religious historians are not sure when and how Christianity arrived in Freckleton. Definite facts only emerge after the Norman Conquest and the composition of the *Domesday Book*. In the 1100s, Freckleton was part of Kirkham parish and in the archdiocese of York. At one time or another, the village has been home to no fewer than seven Christian denominations: Anglicans, Congregationalists, Wesleyan Methodists, Primitive Methodists, Plymouth Brethren, Quakers, and Roman Catholics.[13] The Anglicans, Quakers, and Methodists have had the strongest influence on the spiritual and social development of the community.

The Anglican Church split from the Roman Catholic Church in the mid–16th century when King Henry VIII challenged the authority of the Holy See to govern English Catholics. During this time period, Freckleton remained part of the now Anglican parish of Kirkham. The Kirkham parish was part of the newly created diocese of Chester. From 1541 to the 1830s there was no Anglican church in Freckleton and worshippers had to travel by foot, horseback or carriage to attend services in Kirkham. The opening of an Anglican church in the adjacent village of Warton in 1725 considerably cut the travel time to services.[14]

In 1834, the Anglican Church erected a temporary chapel in Freckleton. Construction on a permanent edifice commenced on July 31, 1837, during the first year of the reign of Queen Victoria. John Latham was the architect and constructed the church in a Norman style of architecture. Construction of Holy Trinity Chapel was completed in 1838 and on June 13 of that year, Bishop John Bird Sumner of the diocese of Chester consecrated the church.[15] Holy Trinity Chapel remained without a resident curate until 1860 when Reverend G.H. Waterfall became the first person to hold that position. Finally on January 26, 1874, Holy Trinity became its own separate ecclesiastical parish in the diocese of Manchester. The chapel was now a church under its first vicar, Reverend W. Scott.

Holy Trinity Church fronts Lytham Road in the heart of Freckleton. The church is constructed of local brick with round arches over the windows. The tower at the west end of the church contains a bell that the vicar and churchwardens of St. Jude's Church in Preston presented to the parishioners of Holy Trinity Church in 1910. The church grounds contain the parish cemetery which serves as the final resting place for many of the village's most notable citizens.

At the start of World War II, the interior of the church consisted of a nave with a chancel recess at the east end.[16] The church contained seating capacity for about 250 worshippers. The ten windows in the church, eight of which are original to the structure, depict biblical scenes such as the crucifixion of Jesus, the adoration of the Magi, and Jesus blessing little children. The chancel is an arch flanked by two classic columns. The altar was made of solid oak and the altar rails were made of brass. The pulpit was the most eye-catching and extraordinary artifact in the church. Robert Weaver originally carved the Jacobean pulpit for the Kirkham Parish Church in 1633. In 1866, the parishioners of the Kirkham church gave the pulpit to Holy Trinity as a gift. Many of the detailed faces carved into the pulpit are no more than one inch in diameter.[17] Halfway along the gallery on the west wall sits a clock. Mr. J.S. Barlow donated the clock to the Church in 1944 in memory of his grandchildren, who died in the air disaster of that year, and his son-in-law, who died in action defending his country. In the 1990s, Boy Scouts irreparably damaged the clock when they dislodged it from the wall with their flag poles while recessing out the main aisle of the Church. Clifford and Sheila Gardner (née Barlow) replaced the clock and it remains on the gallery wall of the

Church as a memorial to the horrific losses suffered by the people of Freckleton during World War II.[18]

The Religious Society of Friends, better known as Quakers, established a meeting house in Freckleton in 1689 at Lawrence Coulborne's house. George Fox founded the Religious Society of Friends in 1647. The Quaker moniker developed because members of the society believed that they "trembled in the way of the Lord." To most 17th-century English persons, Quakers and their beliefs were Christianity gone insane. In a religious world filled with ornate churches, intricate liturgies and a hierarchy of clergy, Quakers met in houses, had no set liturgy and eschewed a vertical ecclesiastical structure. They believed that everyone was capable of salvation by following their "inner light" and doing God's will. Authority and salvation rested on the spoken word of God to each individual soul. Quakers believed in equality, supported the abolition of slavery and were pacifists. The English government and many Christian sects persecuted the Quakers because of their radical departure from traditional Christian beliefs and practices. Many Quakers escaped persecution in England by migrating to William Penn's "holy experiment" in North America, the colony of Pennsylvania.

In Freckleton in the 1720s, the Quakers held their weekly meeting at the Marsh Farm. In 1725, John Brown gave the "Twill Furlong," located on Lower Lane, to the Religious Society of Friends. The Quaker Burial Ground, known as "Quaker's Wood," is located here and is the final resting place for about 35 Quakers. In the Quaker tradition of humility and equality, the Quakers planted trees to memorialize their loved ones rather than engraved headstones. There is, however, one solitary gravestone in the burial ground. A servant of Joseph Jesper, a prominent Quaker leader in Freckleton in the 1870s and 1880s, erected the stone marker in 1890 to memorialize the lives of his employers, Mr. and Mrs. Jesper.[19]

In 1796, the Quakers established a "penny school" at Brades Farm. The school provided a low-cost educational opportunity for the youth of the Freckleton area. The school remained in operation until 1885 and served generations of young Freckletonians. In the early 1800s, the number of Quakers declined in Freckleton and they joined with a smaller band of Quakers in Newtown-with-Scales and held meetings at High Gate Hall. The Quakers, however, did not completely abandon Freckleton. In 1835, the Quakers erected a meeting house on the old Foldside Farm. They continued their penny school and their charitable activities. During the cotton famine of 1861–1863, caused by the southern cotton embargo during the American Civil War, the Quakers distributed groceries every week to the poor and needy of Freckleton who were unemployed because of the shortage of cotton.[20]

In 1868, Joseph Jesper, a hatter who lived in nearby Preston, moved his family to Freckleton and attempted to revive the Quaker movement. In 1870, Jesper tore down the old meeting house and built a new meeting facility on School Lane where the Quakers held their weekly meetings. In 1871, John Satterwaite of Preston registered the new building as a place of worship. William Segar Hodgson purchased the building in 1904 and donated it, along with 26 acres of land, to the village with the stipulation that the property be used for educational and recreational purposes. The building originally used as a Quaker meeting house now became known as the Hodgson Institute. In accordance with Hodgson's wishes, the Institute did not allow alcohol to be used or consumed on the premises. In the early 1900s, the Hodgson Institute became a sportsmen's mecca and housed the Women's Institute. As World War II approached, the Fylde Rural Council held its meetings in the building. The Hodgson Institute building was demolished in 1974.[21]

When Joseph Jesper died in 1890, the Quaker movement seemed to pass with him. By 1900, all that remained of the Religious Society of Friends in Freckleton was their burial ground at Quaker's Wood and a legacy of good works that had seen the village through many hard times.

The Methodist Church traces its roots back to the teachings of John Wesley. While studying at Oxford, John, his brother Charles, and several other students formed a group to study the Bible, pray, and help the underprivileged of society. Their fellow students labeled the group members "Methodists" because of the group's emphasis on rule and method in conducting religious affairs. The beginning of Methodism as a popular movement occurred in 1738 when the Wesley brothers, inspired by the Great Awakening in the American colonies, undertook evangelistic preaching that emphasized holiness and conversion. The Church of England barred the Wesley brothers, who were ordained ministers of the Anglican Church, from their pulpits because of their evangelical style of preaching. The brothers continued preaching in homes, barns, and open fields. In 1744, John Wesley held his first conference and the Methodists officially split from the Anglican Church.

Wesley and the Methodists rejected the Calvinist belief in predestination and taught that all people can be saved through the free grace of God. The Methodists believe that good works as well as faith are essential to Christian living. Wesley encouraged Methodists to improve the lives of others by caring for the poor, the prisoner, the widow and the orphan. Methodists sought systemic reforms to remedy social injustices such as slavery and debtor prisons. In the 19th century, Methodism identified itself with the temperance movement because drunkenness exacerbated many of the social ills that plagued society.

Methodists began worship in Freckleton in 1807 when George Richardson conducted the first Methodist Sunday school at the Park Nook farm on Bunker Street. There, three teachers instructed ten students in Bible study, prayers, and the basic tenets of Methodism.[22] From 1816 to 1884, Methodist services moved from place to place because the congregation lacked a permanent house of worship. Houses, barns, the Hodgson Institute building and an old sail cloth mill served as churches and Sunday schools. The Methodists finally erected a permanent church on Kirkham Road in 1884. The handsome brick structure has a seating capacity for 250 worshippers and is still the home of a robust and active congregation.

Primitive Methodists were a major offshoot of mainstream Methodism. In the early 19th century, many Methodists felt their congregations had moved away from the teachings of John Wesley. Under the leadership of Hugh Bourne, these disgruntled Methodists broke away from mainstream Methodism and formed Primitive Methodist congregations. They called themselves "primitive" because they saw themselves as the true guardians of the original, or primitive, form of Methodism. The Primitives focused attention on the role of the lay people, stressed simplicity in their churches and liturgy, and concentrated their mission on the rural poor.[23]

The primitive revival movement arrived in Freckleton in 1827. The Primitives held services at Nicolas Brown's cottage on Lower Lane. The congregation soon moved its services to the upstairs offices in the tan-yard building on Preston Old Road. In 1862, the congregation built their own house of worship on Preston Old Road. In 1910, the Primitives erected a new Gothic-style church adjacent to the old chapel and used the old structure as a Sunday school. Rapprochement between the two schools of Methodism began to occur in the 1930s when believers realized their theology and missions were more alike than different. In 1974, the Primitive Methodists amalgamated with the Kirkham Road Methodists. The Primitive Methodist church buildings on Preston Old Road were eventually demolished to make room for the County Library.[24] The teachings of the Anglicans, Quakers, and Methodists, combined with the religious fervor of the villagers, served to reinforce the strong sense of community and social justice possessed by the people of Freckleton.

Man does not live by bread alone! He needs drink to compliment the bread and sustain the soul. Water and juices were not the only beverages dispensed in the village. At one time or another before World War II, Freckleton, a village of about 1,000 inhabitants, had seven public houses to serve the community. Freckleton's maritime commerce and culture probably accounts for the plethora of pubs. Sailors on shore leave are often known to indulge in adult beverages until the sea beckons them to return. This probably accounts for why the earliest pubs in the village were located closer to the water and quay than the center of the village.

The oldest pub in Freckleton, and possibly the entire Fylde region, is the Ship Inn. The inn is located on Bunker Street and the Freckleton Marsh. The inn's elevated position commands an exceptional view of the River Ribble and Hesketh Bank on the way to Southport. The current owners of the inn claim that its origin dates back to the 14th century. Local historians, like Richard Spencer, place the origin around 1630.[25] The government first licensed the establishment in 1677. The Ship Inn's first clients were sailors whose ships brought goods to Freckleton from the west coast of England as well as from Ireland and the Isle of Man. Bargeman from the coal fields of Wigan frequented the establishment after they unloaded their coal and slack below the inn. Smugglers also cut deals within the friendly confines of the public house. The Ship Inn continued to provide a comfortable refuge away from base for American and British servicemen during World War II. The inn is still in operation today and is a cornerstone of social life in the village as well as a respite for weary sojourners ambling along the Coastal Walk between Freckleton and Lytham/St. Annes.

The Mariners Inn was located just below the Ship Inn about 200 yards toward the Naze. The location and name of the inn suggest that its main trade came from seagoing folk passing through Freckleton's port and bargemen lodged on Bunker Street. The Mariners Inn received its license in 1790 and served libations to its customers until its owners shuttered its doors in 1843. The movement of commerce away from the port to the center of town no doubt hastened the demise of the inn.

The Bush Inn opened in 1803. The inn had two beds, could feed 70 people and had a stable for two horses. The establishment was well known for its ales, porters and hearty pies. The inn attracted patrons from as far away as Preston and Blackpool. The Bush Inn closed in 1910 and the Mason and Sudell families farmed the property until after World War II. In 1974, British Aircraft Corporation purchased the property and demolished the last vestiges of the inn.[26]

In 1810, William Carter opened the Lamaleach Inn on Lytham Road.

The public house remained in operation until 1868 when competition from two new pubs brought about its demise.

The 1860s witnessed the movement of the pub trade away from the water toward the center of the village. In 1860, the Coach and Horses received its license to operate as a public house. The establishment had only one bed but could stable three horses and fed 60 people. Situated on Preston Old Road, the inn became a popular respite for travelers making the journey between Preston and Blackpool. The Plough Hotel on Lytham Road opened its doors in 1862. The Plough contained two beds, fed 40 people and could stable two horses. These two establishments weathered two world wars, the Great Depression, and the decline of the British Empire. They have watched Freckleton grow from a sleepy hamlet of 1,000 inhabitants in the 1930s to a vibrant village of more than 6,000 persons today. For the past 150 years, the doors of the Plough and the Coach and Horses have remained open, providing hospitality and cheer to tens of thousands of patrons.

In this time period, two more public houses opened in Freckleton. Neither of them achieved the long-term success of the Plough Hotel or the Coach and Horses. In 1869, the Stanley Arms opened its doors on Preston Old Road. Fifty-three years later, the establishment closed its doors forever. In 1871, the Cyclist Arms opened on Lytham Road. The pub remained in operation through 1938. The building that housed the Cyclist Arms did not survive World War II. On the morning of August 23, 1944, the former Cyclist Arms was one of the buildings destroyed when a B-24 Liberator crashed through the village.[27] During World War II, three public houses remained in operation: the Ship Inn, the Plough, and Coach and Horses.

Even though at one time or another Freckleton was the home of seven public houses, ironically the village was also the home of a strong temperance movement. The Methodists, especially the Primitives, had a reputation for temperance. Freckleton was one of the few villages in the Fylde to have a "Band of Hope." Anne Jane Carlile, a 72-year-old Irish Presbyterian, along with a young Baptist minister, Jabez Tunnicliffe, founded the Band of Hope in Leeds, England, in 1847. Carlile believed that children suffered abuse from adults because of the ready availability and the evil of strong drink. Tunnicliffe had administered to a dying alcoholic, who in his death throes, clutched Tunnicliffe and made the Baptist minister promise to warn children about the dangers of alcohol. Together, Carlile and Tunnicliffe formed the Band of Hope, a temperance organization for working-class children. All members of the organization took a pledge of total abstinence from alcohol and the Band of Hope taught children about the evils of drink. Members enrolled at the age of six and met once a week to listen to lectures and participate in activities. The members participated in marches, rallies and demonstrations to oppose the evils of hard liquor and to close establishments that dispensed demon rum to the public.[28]

By the outbreak of war in 1939, the Band of Hope had over three million members throughout the United Kingdom.[29] The temperance movement waned in Freckleton with the arrival of the war and the influx of R.A.F. (Royal Air Force) and American servicemen into the area. The movement also lost momentum when Methodism allowed the consumption of alcohol to be a personal choice of its members. The Band of Hope still exists in the United Kingdom as a charitable organization known as Hope UK. Its mission is to fight alcohol and drug abuse among the youth of the country.

Freckleton has a rich history of social clubs and communal activity based on its deep religious roots and strong sense of community. Club Day is one of the oldest traditions in the village and is still one of the most popular events on the social calendar. Club Day started in the 1880s when the Friendly Societies held their annual procession through the village to demonstrate their strength. Church congregations and Sunday schools soon joined in the march through the village. By World War I, the first Monday in August became the annual date for the procession (the event is now held on the third Saturday in June and extends into Sunday). Eventually, all of the churches participating in Club Day elected queens to lead their congregations through the streets of Freckleton. Around Club Day, traveling fairs set up on the Village Green to entertain the villagers. Jugglers, clowns, street actors, and trapeze artists performed for free but were compensated for their efforts by a free will collection passed through the audience. Children and adults alike waited in anxious anticipation for Club Day to arrive each year.

Today, Freckleton claims it is the "village of flower and music." The village's musical tradition centers on the nationally acclaimed Freckleton Brass Band. The band's origin dates back to 1886. Original band members Robert Rawstrone and James Hawthornwaite date the band's beginning to a social gathering at a cottage on Kirkham Road.[30] At the conclave, one of the individuals present suggested the formation of a band. The group raised £50 and bought a set of secondhand instruments. Group members then wandered through the village pushing the instruments in a cart and asked villagers if they could play any of the instruments. If they replied in the affirmative, the enthusiastic organizers asked them to join the band.

Once formed, the band practiced on Bunker Street. Their earliest known performance was at the laying of the memorial stone of the new Primitive Methodist Church chapel in August 1891.[31] There is also a record of a concert performed on December 10, 1892, in the village schoolroom. As the band became more established, it moved its practice facility to the stable block in the rear of the Coach and Horses Inn. Throughout the 1900s, the Freckleton Brass Band competed in regional and national competitions as well as being a mainstay in local parades and processions. The band still plays and competes in music festivals throughout England and maintains its headquarters in a new band room behind the Coach and Horses. The band remains a great source of pride to Freckletonians.

After World War I until the onset of World War II, Freckleton hosted a number of agricultural and horticultural shows as well as brass band competitions. In 1920, William Harrison formed a poultry society that held competitions in the barn on Preston Old Road. The competitions sparked great interest and heated rivalries because of the large number of poultry farms in the Freckleton area.

In the 1930s, the Methodist Church in Freckleton sponsored a chrysanthemum show that flowered into an annual event featuring a brass band competition, a queen pageant, a floral fete as well as a flower and produce show. The 1938 event featured 2,000 flower entries, 29 competing bands and 24 lovely queens from all over the British Isles.[32] In 1939, the outbreak of war with Germany cancelled the shows and competitions. In 1940, the village started the Freckleton Music Festival. The first festival featured 41 entries competing for prizes over three Saturday evenings. The musical festival provided some needed consolation and relief from the bad news coming from the battlefields of France and North Africa. The Freckleton Music Festival survived World War II and throughout the years grew both in size and stature. Today, thousands of contestants from around the globe participate in the largest rural music festival in the United Kingdom. The festival is now held each year in November/December and the choral rose bowl competition attracts choirs of international repute to the village of Freckleton.

World War I started in 1914 and ended in 1918. The human cost of the war touched every city and village in the British Isles. Nearly 887,000 British soldiers died in the war. Freckleton, a village of fewer than 1,000 persons in 1918, lost 21 of its sons in this conflict. The percentage of Freckletonians killed in World War I, 2.3 percent, was slightly higher than the national average of 2.1 percent. In November 1921, the village organized a committee to erect a memorial for the men of Freckleton who lost their lives in the Great

War. The committee raised money for the memorial through public subscription. Teams of two, comprised of one veteran of the war and one civilian, canvassed the village door to door for donations. The committee also held a fundraiser to supplement the block collections. One farmer, Mr. Alsup, sold one of his cows for £19 and donated the money to the memorial fund.[33]

Originally the committee only wanted to place the names of soldiers who died before the November 11, 1918, armistice agreement on the monument. After much heated debate and discussion, the committee decided to include on the monument the names of any Freckleton soldier who died of wounds from service in the war up to the time of the actual erection of the monument.[34]

Cookson's of Blackpool erected the obelisk-shaped monument on the Village Green at the cost of £255.[35] The monument was constructed of Glencoe granite and on one side contains the inscription "In grateful memory of the men of Freckleton who fought and fell in the Great War 1914–1918." The other side of the monument contains the phrase "Lest we forget." The names of the fallen Freckleton soldiers adorn the panels below the main shaft of the obelisk. The village dedicated the monument on November 11, 1924, the sixth anniversary of the armistice that ended the Great War. The Freckleton Brass Band provided the music as veterans, the Parish Council, the Memorial Committee and orphans of the deceased soldiers processed to the memorial site on the Village Green. Colonel Berthon unveiled the monument after the procession through the village. In August 1925, the Council erected railings around the Village Green. The council also laid out memorial gardens at the site and officially dedicated the gardens on Remembrance Sunday, November 14, 1926. The village still holds services at the memorial on every Remembrance Sunday in November, "Lest we forget."

In the late summer of 1939, just on the eve of World War II, Freckleton was a quiet, picturesque, rural English village of fewer than 1,000 inhabitants. The village's rich history dated back to Roman times and included a fierce battle in 1644 between the Royalist army and Parliamentary troops on the marshes of the River Ribble estuary during the English Civil War. In 1939, most of the village's inhabitants were blue-collar workers who earned their livelihood as farmers, mill hands, carpenters, bricklayers, shipwrights, and warehouse men. The village possessed a strong and deep religious tradition that emphasized social justice and community involvement. The various religious organizations lived in relative harmony with each other and a strong sense of ecumenical cooperation developed as witnessed in the annual Club Day processions. The pubs in the village provided a needed respite from the stresses and strains of daily life and became a focal point of social life in the community. At the beginning of the war in 1939, there were three pubs licensed and in operation in the village. Village fairs, flower shows, Club Day processions, brass band concerts and festivals as well as sports like rugby, football, snooker, and badminton provided recreational opportunities for Freckletonians.

Wars had touched Freckleton before 1939. The English Civil War had brought death and destruction to front door of the village in the 1640s. The dark days of the Great War claimed the lives of nearly two dozen Freckleton lads between 1914 and 1918. World War One also brought economic hardship to the village along with an outbreak of influenza. The village honored its slain heroes of the Great War with a monument on the Village Green that the hardworking citizens of Freckleton had paid for through their generous donations to the Memorial Committee. Not a Remembrance Day passed without Freckletonians recalling the high costs of war. Children in the village annually participated in peace celebrations that embraced the hope that the Great War would be "the war to end all wars."

In September 1939, war broke out between the United Kingdom and Nazi Germany. From their past experiences, the people of Freckleton knew that all wars had a cost. What they were unaware of was the extremely high price the village itself would have to pay in this conflict.

2

Base Air Depot 2

"It Can Be Done"—BAD2 motto

Throughout the 1930s, the winds of war blew across Europe and Asia with an ever increasing frequency and velocity. In 1931, the Japanese military invaded Manchuria and placed the Chinese province under its influence. Japanese militarists soon seized control of the Japanese government and developed plans for further incursions into Chinese territory. The Japanese wanted to eventually establish a "sphere of co-prosperity" throughout Asia and the Pacific Rim that would provide Japanese manufacturing with needed resources and markets. The sphere would also reduce Japanese dependence on American raw materials such as petroleum products, iron, and coal. The establishment of this "sphere of co-prosperity" required that the Japanese place European and American possessions such as India, Indo-China, the Philippines, and Indonesia under its hegemony.

In 1933, a former German corporal in the German Army rose to power in the Weimar Republic. Adolf Hitler immediately began to throw off the shackles of the Treaty of Versailles and injected the German people with a virulent strain of jingoistic nationalism. Hitler snuffed out the last vestiges of democracy in Germany and established a fascist regime that suppressed individual freedom while creating a cult of leadership around *Der Fuhrer*. Hitler sought to unite all German people at home and abroad as a "master race" that would control the destiny of Europe. By 1935, Hitler had renounced the Treaty of Versailles and Germany began an intensive program of rearmament. In March 1936, Hitler ordered the revitalized German Army to occupy the Rhineland in violation of the Versailles and Locarno treaties. The British and French passively withdrew from the region. After securing the Rhineland, Hitler assured world leaders that he wanted nothing else, a disingenuous claim he would repeat after every new conquest.

Fascism arrived in Italy in 1922 with Benito Mussolini's ascension to power. Mussolini established a police state in Italy that deified the state at the expense of human rights. Mussolini envisioned an Italian empire that would embrace both southern Europe and northern Africa. In the fall of 1936, Hitler and Mussolini concluded a treaty creating the Berlin-Rome Axis. At the same time, Germany, Italy, and fellow aggressor Japan concluded the Anti-Comintern Pact, a military alliance directed primarily against the Soviet Union. The forces propelling the world toward war were now beginning to act in concert.

In 1938, the Japanese tightened their grip on China. In the same year, Hitler's troops invaded Austria and annexed it to Germany. In March, Hitler threatened to invade and seize the Sudetenland, a German-speaking region in Czechoslovakia. In September, at a meeting in Munich, the United Kingdom and France allowed Germany to annex the Sudetenland to prevent armed conflict over the issue of German expansion. British Prime Minister Neville Chamberlain on his return to England from the Munich conference triumphantly exclaimed about the Munich Pact: "It is peace in our time."[1] The irony of these words came back to haunt Chamberlain and the British people in the spring and summer of 1939 when German forces took all of Czechoslovakia and later invaded Poland.

Hitler—bolstered by British and French appeasement and non-action in the Rhineland, Austria, and Czechoslovakia—now turned his attention toward Poland. Hitler demanded the return of the small corridor of land that allowed Poland access to the Baltic Sea. This small parcel of real estate separated East and West Prussia. The victors in World War I had sliced off this piece of territory from Germany and gave it to Poland so the country would not be landlocked. Hitler considered it degrading that the Germans needed Polish permission to establish and maintain transportation links between two areas of sovereign German territory. This time the United Kingdom and France stood fast against Hitler's demands and refused to cede Polish territory to Nazi Germany. The British and French also promised to protect Polish sovereignty in case of a German invasion. Despite British and French threats of imminent war, Hitler launched his attack on Poland on September 1, 1939. On September 3, the United Kingdom and France declared war on Germany. World War II had begun!

The German Army, employing the concept of *blitzkrieg*, smashed through the Polish defenses in a matter of weeks. Poland capitulated to Germany before the end of September without receiving any direct military support from either the United Kingdom or France.

During the winter of 1939–1940, Germany steadfastly stood behind the newly created Siegfried Line built to protect Germany from a French attack. Hitler refrained from attacking British or French forces because he held out hope that with Poland securely in his hands he could negotiate a settlement with the two countries that would prevent the further effusion of blood. Not fully prepared for war, British and French troops remained silent along the western front. U.S. Senator William Edgar Borah of Idaho called this period of inactivity "the phony war," while Winston Churchill termed it "the winter of illusions."[2]

In the spring of 1940, "the phony war" came to a violent end when Germany suddenly invaded Belgium and the Netherlands in order to flank French defenses anchored to the Maginot Line. The Germans conquered the Netherlands in five days and their forces pushed toward the English Channel. On May 21, the Germans reached the Channel and cut off the British expeditionary force that had rushed to the aid of Belgium and France. The German troops trapped British forces on the beaches of Dunkirk, France. British Foreign Minister, Lord Gort, ordered the evacuation of British troops back to Great Britain. The desperate evacuation from this precarious position commenced on May 26 and continued until June 4. Over the ten days, British naval vessels and hundreds of small civilian craft plucked more than 338,000 soldiers from the shores of France and ferried them to the safety of England. In many ways, the civilian population of the United Kingdom had saved the British Army. On June 22, France and Germany signed an armistice ending hostilities. The United Kingdom now stood alone against the Nazi onslaught.

With France defeated and the British confined to their island fortress, Hitler contemplated an invasion of Great Britain. The last successful invasion of England was in 1066 when William the Conqueror and his Norman forces accomplished the feat. History and geography were not on Hitler's side. Hitler also lacked the landing craft and equipment to launch an amphibious assault on such a massive scale. Hitler decided to follow the advice of his *Luftwaffe* commander Marshal Hermann Goering and launched a massive air attack on Great Britain. Goering intended the air assault to cripple British defenses and industry. Once brought to its knees by air attacks, Great Britain would be ripe for invasion by the German Army. If the damage caused by the air assault was severe enough, the British might sue for peace before an amphibious assault was necessary.

In the summer and fall of 1940, German airplanes rained terror down on British cities. The air assault, known as "the blitz," targeted cities like London, Coventry, and Birmingham. The destruction caused by the almost nightly raids was immense and the civilian casualties ran into the tens of thousands. By October, however, the gallant British fighter pilots flying their Spitfire and Hurricane aircraft, aided by a chain of radar posts located in southern and eastern England, had begun to turn the tide in the Battle of Britain.

The fight in the air over Britain required not only planes, pilots, and radar but also airfields and maintenance/repair facilities. The British Air Ministry began to reassess sites for air fields that had been previously rejected prior to the war. One of the sites the Air Ministry rejected was the Grange Farm located in the Freckleton Marsh area. In 1936, the Air Ministry was interested in building an aircraft factory and airfield on the site. The local council backed the project because it would provide employment for Freckletonians who were hard hit by the Great Depression. In November 1938, Air Minister Sir Kingsley Wood informed the council that the Air Ministry was no longer considering the Grange Farm location because surveys revealed that the ground at the site was too unstable for building a factory or an airfield.[3]

In 1940, with war a reality, the British Air Ministry once again reviewed the Freckleton location. The ministry made the decision to move the proposed Grange Farm airfield a half-mile along the coast toward the village of Warton. Surveys showed that the marshland here was more stable and could support an airfield as well as adjacent facilities. The council again welcomed the building of an air facility for both economic and patriotic reasons. The sole objection came from some of the local poultry farmers because their farms would be lost in the construction of the airfield.[4]

The chickens eventually lost out to the airplanes when the Air Ministry began construction on the Warton facility in 1940. The newly constructed airfield was to serve as a satellite facility for the Royal Air Force (R.A.F.) base already in operation in nearby Squires Gate. The Squires Gate Air Base housed fighter and bomber units. The United States' entry into World War II changed the mission of the Warton base and ultimately the fate of the village of Freckleton itself.

Despite its self-proclaimed neutrality in the mid–1930s and its penchant for isolationism, the United States was gradually inching toward war by the end of the decade. President Franklin Roosevelt tried to nudge Americans away from isolationism toward a realization of the evils and dangers of fascist totalitarianism in his famous Quarantine Speech in 1937. Americans turned a deaf ear toward Roosevelt's warnings and wanted their government to steer a path clear of the shoals of war.

With the outbreak of war in Europe in 1939, the Americans remained neutral in name only. Americans could not side with the forces of fascism and oppression. President Roosevelt and others realized that the best chance the United States had of not becoming embroiled in another European war was to rearm and resupply the United Kingdom so it could effectively wage war against Germany and Italy. The United States amended its neutrality laws and sold weapons and ammunition to the British on a cash-and-carry basis. As the British cash flow waned, and the need to protect British convoys headed home increased, the United States traded 50 mothballed destroyers to the United Kingdom in exchange for the use of British naval bases overseas. In 1941, Congress passed the Lend-Lease Act. This act circumvented previous neutrality laws by authorizing the president to sell, transfer, exchange, lease or lend any military supplies to the government of any country the president deemed vital to the defense of the United States.

To alleviate stress on British military assets and to insure that lend-lease material safely reached its destination, President Roosevelt authorized naval patrols in the western Atlantic Ocean and U.S. troops replaced British soldiers protecting the sovereignty of Iceland. By December 1941, the United States was engaged in an undeclared naval war with Germany as the Americans attempted to protect lend-lease aid headed to the United Kingdom and the newest victim of German aggression, the Soviet Union. It was events in the Pacific Rim, however, and not the naval confrontation in the Atlantic that eventually dragged the United States into World War II.

American diplomatic relations with Japan deteriorated when the Japanese invaded Manchuria in 1931. By 1937, the Japanese had overrun much of northern China. Japan had also withdrawn from the League of Nations and began to strengthen as well as modernize its navy. Japanese planes sank the American gunboat *Panay* on patrol on the Yangtze River in China. This incident might have sparked a war between the two countries if not for a quick apology from the Japanese government and reparations for the American lives lost in the attack. The United States continued to supply Chinese forces with aid to resist Japanese conquest while the Americans still sold resources to Japanese industry.

The United States' relations with Japan worsened with the outbreak of World War II on the European continent. With the United Kingdom and France engaged in a war against fascism, the Americans feared that Japan would add European colonies in Asia to its growing empire. To deter further Japanese conquest in Asia, President Roosevelt ordered the transfer of the United States Pacific Fleet's base from San Diego, California, to Pearl Harbor in Hawaii in May 1940. The United States also withheld aviation fuel from the Japanese. The Japanese responded to these American moves by taking over French Indo-China. After the Japanese takeover of Indo-China, the Americans embargoed iron, steel, and scrap metal going to Japan. In response to the American embargo, Japan signed the Tripartite Pact with Germany and Italy. This agreement created the Axis powers. Under the pact, Germany, Italy, and Japan pledged to establish a new order to promote mutual prosperity and welfare. Each country also promised to protect each other if attacked by another country not already involved in the war. Japan now had the allies it needed to conduct a war against the United States.

In 1941, The American government froze all Japanese assets in the United States and President Roosevelt warned the Japanese not to expand their control over any more territory or the United States would take all steps necessary to safeguard its interests. The Japanese responded to these American actions by freezing all American assets in Japan and expanding its influence in China. In the fall of 1941, war looked imminent between the United States and Japan. Both countries made one last-ditch effort to diplomatically resolve their differences. By the end of November, diplomatic talks were at an impasse as neither country would compromise their position.

As diplomatic discussions proceeded in Washington, D.C., the Japanese government, led by General Hideki Tojo, planned a surprise attack on American forces in the Pacific if diplomatic talks broke down in the American capital. The Japanese plan called for the destruction of the American Pacific Fleet anchored at Pearl Harbor coupled with simultaneous attacks on European and American possessions throughout the Pacific Rim. Japanese leadership believed that it would take the United States two full years to mobilize and rebuild its forces in the Pacific. During that time, Japan would build an impregnable line of island defenses throughout the Pacific. The Japanese could then negotiate a settlement with the Americans from a position of strength rather than weakness.

When the diplomatic talks broke down in Washington, D.C., the Japanese military put their plan into motion. On the morning of December 7, 1941, Japanese airplanes, launched from aircraft carriers, attacked the United States naval facility at Pearl Harbor. In two waves of attacks, Japanese planes sank or severely damaged most of the ships anchored in the harbor. The Japanese also damaged or destroyed most of the American aircraft on the ground before they could get airborne to defend themselves. When the assault on Pearl Harbor was over, 2,400 Americans were dead and another 1,200 lay wounded in medical facilities.[5]

The next day, December 8, Congress declared war on Japan. On December 11, Japan's Axis allies, Germany and Italy, declared war on the United States. Congress immediately returned the favor and declared war on Germany and Italy. The United States was now a full participant in World War II, allied with the United Kingdom and the Soviet Union against the Axis powers.

The Allies made Germany public enemy #1. It was clear to the Allies that Germany was the strongest link in the Axis chain. If the Allies could remove this link, the chain would be rendered useless. To achieve this goal, the United States and the United Kingdom had to achieve air and sea supremacy over the Germans. Once the Americans and British had established air and sea supremacy, they could successfully move against the Germans on land. The Americans would need air bases in the British Isles for the Allies to gain air supremacy. Here begins the American interest in the Royal Air Force field in Warton.

American interest in the Warton site began in October 1941, two months before the United States entered World War II. Sensing that war with Germany was inevitable, high-ranking officers of the United States Army Air Forces (U.S.A.A.F.) visited the United Kingdom and met with officials from the British Air Ministry to discuss suitable sites for American air depots. The U.S.A.A.F. was going to use air depots to maintain, repair, and overhaul U.S. aircraft stationed in the U.K. After discussion and investigation, the British and Americans finally proposed four sites for air depots including the Warton airfield. In January 1942, the British and Americans finalized plans to use Warton as an air depot. At the time, the R.A.F. was in the process of constructing two runways but little work had commenced on the support buildings.[6]

In June 1942, construction at Warton picked up in intensity. Sir Alfred McAlpine and Son Limited served as the main contractor for the facility. The firm specialized in civil engineering and had its headquarters in Hooton. McAlpine's company built over 10 percent of Britain's motorways and was well-equipped to handle the Warton project. The U.S.A.A.F. planned on having 1,000 planes operating out of British bases by August 1942 and planned to increase that number to 3,500 aircraft by the summer of 1943. To meet these optimistic goals, the U.S.A.A.F. needed its air depot system to be in operation. The building of air depots required more than the construction of runways. Air depots required the erection of large hangars, repair facilities, warehouses for parts, a hospital and barracks to billet servicemen. Despite some early delays, the Warton air depot was almost complete at the end of 1942.[7] At the height of its operation in 1944, the Warton facility had three

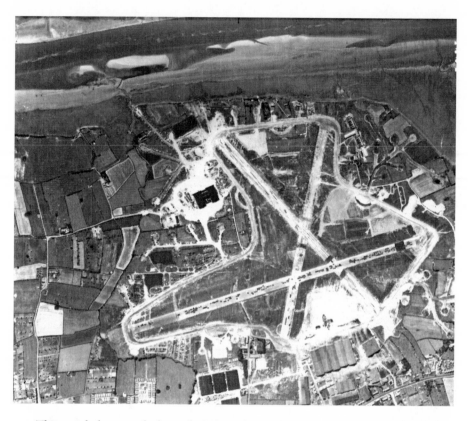

This aerial photograph shows the U.S. air base at Warton on August 10, 1945. The U.S.A.A.F. established the base on September 5, 1942. The facility had three runways, nine main hangar buildings, and ten living sites with a capacity of 15,902. During the war, the facility processed more 10,000 aircraft. The U.S.A.A.F. deactivated Warton on September 3, 1945. BAe Systems now operates an assembly and testing facility on the site of BAD2 (courtesy of BAe Systems Heritage Division).

concrete runways, with the longest 5,631 feet in length. The base had nine hangars and more than 623,000 square feet of repair shop area. There were ten living sites capable of housing 15,902 persons. The depot also contained about 137,400 square feet of storage space.[8]

The Americans destined to operate the Warton base were members of the Eighth Air Force known as the "Mighty Eighth." The U.S.A.A.F. activated the Mighty Eighth on January 28, 1942, at the Chatham Armory in Savannah, Georgia. General Henry H. "Hap" Arnold, commander of the U.S.A.A.F., appointed General Charles Spaatz head of the Mighty Eighth and General Ira Eaker to command its bomber force. General Eaker took command of the Mighty Eighth in December 1942 when General Dwight Eisenhower appointed General Spaatz head of air force operations in the Mediterranean.

The 8th Air Force was organized into four commands: Air Service Command, Ground-Air Support Command, Fighter Command, and Bomber Command. All four commands reported to General Eaker. The base air depot in Warton came under the supervision of Air Service Command.

The 8th Air Force bomber, fighter and ground crews were comprised of Americans from every walk of life. Cowboys, miners, clerks, construction workers, college graduates and lawyers all joined the Mighty Eighth. Hollywood even contributed two of its brightest stars, Jimmy Stewart and Clark Gable, to the bomber squadrons of the 8th Air Force. During the war, approximately 350,000 officers and enlisted men served in the Mighty Eighth. The 8th Air Force suffered more than 26,000 fatalities by the end of the war. This number exceeded the death toll for the entire United States Marine Corps during World War II.[9]

The first American servicemen stationed at Warton arrived on August 18, 1942. The contingent consisted of 92 enlisted men and four officers from the 8th Air Force. The following day, the original group was reinforced by 38 officers and 643 enlisted men.[10] Major John Shuttles commanded this initial group of Americans though the Warton base itself remained in the hands of the R.A.F. On September 5, an order issued by the 8th Air Force Service Command officially established the Warton Air Depot and Colonel Ira A. Rader became Warton's first commanding officer on October 9.[11]

The main purpose of the Warton Air Depot was to overhaul, modify or repair American aircraft that flew in the European Theater of Operation. With the air depot now operating, planes soon began arriving at Warton in the fall of 1942. The servicemen modified new planes to meet battle conditions over the skies of Europe. They repaired and refurbished combat-damaged aircraft and returned them to service. The men cannibalized aircraft that could not be repaired for every salvageable part that could be used on other planes. At the same time, the men continued to organize the new base to make its operation more efficient.

The Warton Air Depot suffered its first accident, and unfortunately not its last, on November 26, 1942. A P-38 Lightning radioed a distress call to Warton and made an emergency landing. The fighter touched down on the runway but skidded off the concrete surface into the grass. When the P-38 went into the grass, it tore off its undercarriage and ended up on its belly. The ambulance and fire crews arrived in time to see the pilot exit safely from the aircraft.[12] For the servicemen of Warton, the romance of flight had just been jarred by the reality of war.

The R.A.F. officially turned the Warton Air Depot over to the United

States on July 17, 1943. Lieutenant General Henry J.F. Miller of the 8th Army Air Force accepted the hand-over of the base from Air Vice Marshal R.D. Robertson of the R.A.F. The ceremony included a parade and review of the troops with an R.A.F. band providing the music.[13] On October 25, the Warton Air Depot became known as Base Air Depot 2 (BAD2) and was integrated into the newly created Base Air Depot Area Command. Colonel John G. Moore assumed command of BAD2 and through his leadership he inspired the men to greater productivity. Colonel Moore's personal mantra, "it can be done" soon became BAD2's motto.[14]

The servicemen of BAD2 performed a variety of different tasks. The aircraft section modified planes with armor plating, bulletproof glass, long-range fuel tanks, and wing shackles. This section repaired planes wounded in combat and new planes damaged in transit. The men performed engine repair that ranged from fixing a small part to a complete overhaul. They modified and repaired guns, bombing equipment, bomb sights, and gun turrets. Technicians completely overhauled and rebuilt cameras, gyros, pumps and hydraulic instruments. Radio technicians repaired, modified and installed transmitters as well as receivers. Some servicemen checked, cleaned and repaired parachutes. Others repaired electrically heated flying suits, life vests, and life rafts.

Another important function was the salvaging of parts from aircraft that could not be repaired. Salvaged parts not only saved money, they kept aircraft up in the air. Spare parts manufactured in the United States had a long and arduous voyage to bases in the United Kingdom. A large supply of salvaged parts meant that mechanics did not encounter a shortage of parts when repairing an aircraft. Constant inspection of modifications and repairs insured the quality of the work done on the base and the safety as well as the reliability of aircraft sent back to bomber and fighter groups. Finally, test pilots flew the aircraft before it was released for combat. Planes that did not pass inspection or test flight were returned to the service hangars to remedy the deficiency.[15]

The men worked on a great variety of aircraft. Records show that more than 20 different types of airplanes were assembled, modified or repaired at BAD2. B-17s, B-24s, P-47 Thunderbolts and P-51 Mustangs were among the most common aircraft to pass through Warton. Test pilots had to be familiar with a wide variety of planes and often flew over 100 flights in a month. From August to December 1943, BAD2 processed and released 335 planes.[16] Of the 335 planes, 217 were B-17 bombers known as "Flying Fortresses." The B-17 was one of the workhorses of the Mighty Eighth bombing campaign against Nazi-occupied Europe. At BAD2, technicians installed external life raft switches, modified radio and intercom equipment and enlarged ammunition boxes on the "Flying Fortresses." As 1943 progressed, so did the workload at BAD2. In August, the base processed just three planes. In December, the number had risen to 170 aircraft.

In 1944, the 8th Air Force intensified its bombing campaign against German targets. More planes, men, ammunition, and supplies poured into the airfields in the United Kingdom. Daytime bombing runs took a high toll on aircraft, pilots and crews. Base air depots found themselves flooded with new planes that needed to be processed and old aircraft in need of repair and modifications. As a result of the increased workload, the 8th Air Force Base Air Depot Administration reorganized the depot system to effectively and efficiently meet the needs of bomber command. To increase productivity, the Base Air Depot Administration (BADA) headquarters assigned specific bomber and fighter types to each air depot. BADA allocated the responsibility of P-51 Mustangs and B-24 Liberators to Warton. Later in the year, servicemen at Warton also worked on the A-20 Havoc, the A-26 Invader and C-47 transports.[17]

The reorganization quickly cleared up the backlog of work at Warton. In April 1944, teams had become so efficient in their jobs that they were beginning to run out of work. Part of the problem was that the 8th Air Force command limited the number of heavy bombers at Warton to no more than 25 at a time. Colonel Moore, base commander at Warton, produced a work-efficiency study that demonstrated that Warton could handle at least 15 bombers a day.[18] Once bomber command received and reviewed the Warton study, they removed the artificial restrictions and allowed Warton to operate at peak efficiency.

In the late winter and early spring of 1944, the men overhauled and repaired B-24s and P-51s. In one modification, crews fitted larger fuel tanks into the B-24's fuselage. This allowed the bomber to have a greater range to attack targets on the continent. They converted some B-24s for "carpetbagger" operations. Operation Carpetbagger was the code name used for aerial resupply of weapons and other materials to resistance fighters in France, Italy, Belgium and the Netherlands. The Warton servicemen modified B-24 bombers for these clandestine operations by removing the ball turret, nose guns, and other equipment unnecessary for the mission. By removing the unnecessary equipment, the aircraft became lighter and faster and had more room for cargo. The rear guns were kept as protection against night fighters. The men painted the planes glossy black to evade enemy searchlights.

Weapons, supplies and men were dropped through a cargo hatch that replaced the ball turret and parachuted to the surface below. In its 17 months of operation, the carpetbaggers flew more than 1,860 missions and delivered more than 32,000 containers of vital supplies to the resistance movements in Nazi-occupied Europe.[19]

In March 1944, there were 10,408 men stationed at BAD2. The number of GIs housed at BAD2 was ten times larger than the population of Warton and Freckleton. Locals soon referred to the area as "Little America." The servicemen not only worked hard, they also played hard. BAD2 Special Services created three sections for recreational activity: athletics, entertainment, and education. Servicemen kept themselves in shape playing baseball, football, and boxing. Warton had a base theater and screened newly released films on a daily basis. Musically inclined individuals solicited donations and formed a base orchestra. The BAD2 orchestra's first concert raised over £400, which the musicians contributed to the British Army, Navy and Air Force Relief Fund.[20] The men also enjoyed the ales and porters of the local pubs as well as the delights and amusements of nearby Blackpool. At Christmas, the local children were invited to the base for a holiday party. The GIs, who could not be home to celebrate Christmas with their own families, entertained the children and provided them with plenty of food, candy, and toys.

In April 1944, BAD2's commander, Colonel Moore, announced that the base would conduct a war bond drive. The goal of the drive was to raise enough money ($114,000) to purchase two P-51 fighters. When the drive ended, the patriotic and generous servicemen of BAD 2 had oversubscribed their goal and had contributed enough money to purchase three Mustangs. The first P-51 was named *Too Bad* in honor of the base personnel. Two enlisted men, who had their names pulled from a lottery by Colonel Moore, named the remaining two planes. The first winner, Private Sam Silverman, named one P-51 *Pride of the Yanks* and the other winner, Private Stanley Ruggles, called his aircraft *Mazie R* in honor of his mother.[21] How American! One plane was named for a baseball legend, Lou Gehrig, the other after a serviceman's mom. All that was missing was an apple pie.

On May 16, 1944, Lieutenant General James H. Doolittle visited BAD2. General Doolittle was an iconic American legend and was the new commanding officer of the Eighth Air Force. Doolittle's fascination with flying began when he enlisted as a flying cadet in the Army Signal Corps. He spent World War I as a flying instructor in the United States. After the war, he received his doctorate in aeronautical engineering from MIT in 1925. He was a skilled pilot and flew on the air race circuit during the 1920s and 1930s. He was the first person to fly across the United States in a single day. When he left the military service in the 1930s, he became a manager for Shell Petroleum. In this position he pushed the development of high-octane aviation fuels that led to the development of high-performance piston engines in aircraft.

With war looming on the horizon, Doolittle returned to active duty in the Army Air Corps in 1940. After the devastating attack on Pearl Harbor, the American government wanted to launch a retaliatory strike on the Japanese homeland. An attack on the island of Japan would provide a measure of revenge for the attack on Hawaii and would give a needed boost to sagging American morale. Doolittle volunteered to lead a bomber raid on several Japanese cities including Tokyo. The top secret attack commenced on April 18, 1942, when Doolittle led 16 B-25 bombers off of the deck of the aircraft carrier *Hornet* toward Japan. All the planes reached their targets and bombed the Japanese homeland. Doolittle flew his B-25 to China where he and his crew bailed out of the aircraft when it ran out of fuel. Doolittle eventually reached safety with the help of Chinese forces who helped him work his way through Japanese-held territory. When word of the raid was broadcast to the American people, Doolittle instantly became a national hero. For his leadership of the raid and his conspicuous bravery in carrying out the mission, President Roosevelt presented Doolittle with the Medal of Honor at a White House ceremony.

U.S.A.A.F. command sent Doolittle to Europe to command the 12th Air Force during the invasion of North Africa (1942–1943). In 1943, Doolittle took command of the 15th Air Force during the Mediterranean campaign of 1943. In January 1944, with an invasion of France planned for May or June of that year, Doolittle replaced General Eaker as commander of the "Mighty Eighth." General Doolittle commanded a force that had 26 heavy bombardment groups (1,300 bombers) and 16 fighter groups (1,200 fighters).[22] As commander of the 8th Air Force, Doolittle completely reversed the air war over Western Europe. Instead of keeping fighter escorts close to bomber formations until enemy planes attacked, Doolittle wanted his fighter pilots to be proactive and intercept enemy aircraft before they reached the bombers. He also wanted his fighters to strafe enemy airfields and destroy aircraft on the ground. Doolittle's fighter strategy altered the air war in the skies over Europe and gave the Allies air superiority as the invasion of France began in June. Adolph Galland, German fighter commander, stated the day the 8th Air Force's fighters "went on the offensive was the day Germany lost the air war."[23]

The servicemen of BAD2 greeted General Doolittle with genuine warmth and enthusiasm. The visit was a once-in-a-lifetime chance to meet and talk to an authentic American hero. Doolittle did not plan the trip as an official inspection of the base but rather as a public relations *tour de force*. He wanted to congratulate the men on their outstanding record of productivity and raise base morale. Doolittle took the opportunity to meet as many BAD2 personnel as he could during the allotted time. His magnetic personality, his legendary achievements and his "can do" style of leadership left a lasting and inspiring memory of his visit on the servicemen who met him on his short stay at the Warton facility.

The Allies planned an amphibious invasion of Normandy, France, for June 1944. President Roosevelt and Prime Minister Churchill appointed General Dwight D. Eisenhower to command all invasion forces. Eisenhower dubbed the invasion Operation Overlord. In preparation for the attack, Allied bombers attacked rail networks in Belgium and France to cut off the main supply and transportation routes of the German Army. Allied fighters attacked almost any moving target on French roads and railways. Allied planes dropped 71,000 tons of bombs on the French rail system alone.[24] After the war, German Field Marshal William Keitel, head of German Armed Forces High Command, told Allied interrogators, "Nobody can ever prove to me that we could not have repelled the invasion had not the superiority of the enemy air force in bombers and fighters made it impossible to throw reserve divisions into the fight."[25]

Before the invasion, BAD2 was in operation day and night to insure the air superiority necessary for Allied success in France. BAD2 saw a steady increase in the number of planes that went through the facility. The base also assembled gliders used in the initial stages of the invasion. Sergeant Ralph Scott remembers that in "early 1944, we went to two shifts. No one told us that we were gearing up for an invasion of Europe but we were getting more than the usual number of planes to work on."[26] Sergeant Thomas Miller echoed Scott's observation. Miller states that "during the summer of 1944, we had to work very hard, 12-hour days, 7 days a week. The war was in full swing and so were we."[27] Another harbinger of the upcoming invasion was the removal of the anti-aircraft guns that ringed the base. Since BAD2 had not come under attack from the *Luftwaffe*, the guns were moved to southern England and eventually crossed the English Channel into France as part of the D-day invasion.

The increased need for planes to support the invasion of France put an additional stress not only on the mechanics but also on the test pilots, alert crew, and air traffic control of BAD2. The ten pilots stationed at the airfield needed to test-fly more than 800 planes a month. In one day, the pilots might test as many as 50 aircraft. Some aircraft needed to be test-flown two or three times before BAD2 inspectors would release the plane to a combat unit.[28] Since there was a shortage of test pilots, crew chiefs and mechanics often served as co-pilots to keep the delivery of planes on schedule. These men had little or no official flight training. Sergeant Scott, a radio technician serving at BAD2 with no training as a pilot, served as a co-pilot on several test runs. Scott states that "there weren't enough officers who could qualify as test pilots, so the co-pilot was almost always a sergeant. I went along on test flights when I didn't have other duties."[29]

The alert crew had the responsibility for dispersing aircraft around the field and maintaining all cleared aircraft in a ready state to be sent back to their units. As the number of aircraft arriving at the field increased, this became an enormously complex task. With almost 800 planes on the airfield, parking was at a premium. The crew had to skillfully maneuver planes around the base without damaging parked aircraft. They also had to maintain on a daily basis about 300 aircraft scheduled to return to combat.[30] This thankless job of moving, parking, and maintaining planes was an essential task necessary for the effective and efficient operation of BAD2.

Air traffic control performed an important function during these hectic days at BAD2. The air traffic control tower at BAD2, whose call signal was Farum, managed approximately 100 planes a day. The controllers managed traffic that included test flights, planes arriving to be processed, aircraft returning to their units, visitors coming into the base on transports and even the occasional arrivals of cross-country training flights as well as emergency landings. The air traffic controllers of Warton maintained order in the sometimes hectic skies above Warton and Freckleton.

On June 6, 1944, Allied troops invaded France. Prior to the assault, the Allies had assembled a force of nearly 2.9 million men and 2.5 million tons of supplies in the United Kingdom. On D-day, 160,000 troops stormed five beaches along 50 miles of Normandy coastline. Over 5,000 ships and 11,000 aircraft supported the invasion forces. In the struggle to establish beachheads in France, the Allies suffered more than 9,000 casualties. By June 12, the Allies controlled a continuous beachhead 70 miles long and from five to 15 miles in depth. Over one million Allied troops occupied the area. The battle for Normandy ended on July 24 with the British capture of Caen and the Americans in control of Saint-Lo. The war in Western Europe had turned in favor of the Allies and the race to liberate Paris was now underway.

The men at BAD2 had worked long, hectic hours to insure Allied air supremacy prior to the Normandy invasion. After the successful invasion, base personnel continued to endure arduous schedules to provide the aircraft necessary for total victory over the Germans in Europe. To boost the morale of the servicemen, the 8th Air Force command sent sports figures and famous entertainers to visit the troops stationed at BAD2. On July 6, 1944, two famous boxers visited the base. Joe Louis was probably the most famous fighter in the United States. The African American pugilist was the reigning heavyweight champion of the world. Two of Louis' most memorable fights were against the German boxer Max Schmeling. On June 19, 1936, at a crowded Yankee Stadium, Schmeling ended Louis' consecutive win streak at 27 bouts with a twelfth-round knockout of the Brown Bomber. Louis' defeat left the American boxing community stunned and Adolf Hitler elated. Schmeling's defeat of a black man reinforced Hitler's theories of a superior Aryan race. Louis eventually captured the heavyweight title when he defeated James Braddock in 1937.

Louis felt that he would never truly be the champion until he avenged his defeat to Schmeling. Promoters scheduled a rematch for June 22, 1938, at Yankee Stadium. Louis had trained incessantly for the fight, believing the only way to regain his pride and reputation was to defeat Schmeling. On the night of the fight, 70,043 fans crammed themselves into every nook and cranny of "the house that Ruth built." The fight lasted a total of two minutes and four seconds. In that short amount of time, Louis knocked Schmeling to the canvas three times. After the third knockdown, Schmeling's trainer threw in the towel and the referee stopped the fight. Louis' victory made him a national hero and dealt a crushing blow to Nazi beliefs in racial supremacy.

When World War II broke out, Joe Louis volunteered for the service and enlisted in the army. The army placed him in the Special Services Division and used him to raise the morale of the troops rather than kill Germans. During the war, the Brown Bomber travelled 21,000 miles and staged more than 96 boxing exhibitions before an estimated two million soldiers.[31]

Accompanying Louis to BAD2 that day was another American boxing icon, Billy Conn. The Brown Bomber and Conn had met three years before under less amicable conditions at the Polo Grounds in New York City. Conn was an excellent boxer who began his career as a welterweight and fought his way to the heavyweight division. By the age of 21, Conn had defeated nine present or former world champions. In 1939, Conn became the light heavyweight champion of the world when he defeated Mellio Bettina. Not content with this title, Conn abdicated the light heavyweight championship to fight in the heavyweight division.[32]

On June 18, 1941, Conn was in the ring challenging Joe Louis for the heavyweight crown. The heavily favored Louis outweighed Conn by 30 pounds. For 12 rounds Conn out-boxed and out-slugged the champ. At the end of the twelfth round, Conn almost sent the staggering Brown Bomber to the canvas. Ahead on points, the overconfident Conn decided to go for a knockout win in the thirteenth round. Caught in the moment, Conn abandoned his boxing skill and carelessly slugged it out toe to toe with Louis. The bigger, stronger Louis now sent numerous crushing blows to the torso and head of Conn, knocking him out with only two seconds left in the round. Many boxing pundits and historians still refer to the Conn/Louis bout as the greatest fight of all time. A hand injury to Conn and American entry into World War II postponed the rematch scheduled for 1942.

Conn, like Louis, joined the army and went into the Special Services

B.A.D.2 Warton 6 July 1944
Joe Louis With Billy Conn

On July 6, 1944, two of America's best known boxers visited the servicemen stationed at BAD2. Joe Louis and Billy Conn had lunch with the men of the 829th Engineers and spoke to a large gathering of GIs assembled in front of the base's instrument shop. Conn returned to Warton in September and sparred with base personnel (photograph courtesy of BAe Systems Heritage Division).

B.A.D.2 Warton
Mitzie Mayfair

All types of celebrities entertained the troops at Warton, including Trent Jones, Bing Crosby, Glenn Miller and Mitzie Mayfair. Mayfair, a famous Broadway tap dancer, appeared in shows such as *Take a Chance* and *The Show Is On*. In 1944, she performed for the GIs at BAD2 on a stage erected in front of Hangar #4 (photograph courtesy of BAe Systems Heritage Division).

Division. The two adversaries turned patriots toured bases together and delighted admiring GIs wherever they went. At BAD2, the pair had lunch with the men of the 829th Engineers. Afterward, they spoke to a gathering of servicemen in front of the instrument shop. Before leaving, Conn and Louis promised to return to BAD2 and put on a boxing exhibition. Conn kept his part of the promise and returned to Warton in September to spar with base personnel.[33]

On August 6, Lt. Colonel Robert Trent Jones played an exhibition match at nearby Royal Lytham–St. Anne's Golf Course against the club pro, Tom Fernie. The legendary golfer Bobby Jones, winner of 13 major titles, delighted the BAD2 personnel fortunate enough to see him with a dazzling display of his golf skills. Jones won his first of three British Opens at Royal Lytham–St. Anne's in 1926. After that victory, Jones returned to the United

States and New York City greeted him with his first of two ticker tape parades.[34]

On August 13, 1944, Captain Glenn Miller and his famous orchestra arrived at BAD2 aboard two C-47 transports. Glenn Miller formed his first band in 1937 and critics immediately acclaimed his arrangement of "I Got Rhythm." Miller disbanded his original orchestra in 1938 and formed a new one. It is with this ensemble that Miller developed his trademark sound of a clarinet playing melody doubled by a tenor saxophone playing an octave lower and other saxes in harmonic support.[35] Miller's new orchestra played ballrooms and casinos throughout the east coast and they had a radio show that aired three times a week. The band recorded records and also soundtracks for movies. Miller's first million-selling record was his own composition "Moonlight Serenade." Miller's orchestra grew to be America's most popular big band and produced such hits as "In the Mood," "Tuxedo Junction," and "Perfidia."

Miller stunned the big band scene when he disbanded his orchestra and enlisted in the army in 1941. He spent from October 1942 to December 1944 leading the all-star Army Air Force Band. The band was a 42-piece orchestra with a 19-piece swing band at its core.[36] The band not only entertained troops in the field, it also raised millions of dollars for the war effort. Miller informed the army the he "wanted to put a little more spring into the feet of our marching men and a little more joy in their hearts."[37]

Miller and his Army Air Force Band spent two nights at BAD2. On the first night Captain Miller received word that he had been promoted to major. While Miller rested at the base, some band members motored to Blackpool. There they were joined by the BAD2 band, The Yankee Clippers, who were playing a gig in the resort's Spanish Hall. On August 14, Miller's band performed a concert for more than 10,000 servicemen from a platform erected in front of Hangar #4.[38] The base came to a virtual standstill from 4:00 p.m. to 5:05 p.m. as the band performed popular favorites. For 65 minutes the war was on hold and everyone could reminisce about what had been and what would be. Glenn Miller's life tragically ended on December 15, 1944, when the plane he was flying in from London to Paris mysteriously disappeared on route.

Also on August 13, the BAD2 baseball team beat the SHAEF Yanks at Kingstom by a score of 4 to 2. The BAD2 nine, coached by Lt. Colonel William H. Britton, ended the Yanks' hopes of an undefeated season by handing the Yanks their first loss of the campaign. The personnel of Warton, already celebrating the arrival of Glenn Miller, became ecstatic when news of the upset victory reached base.[39]

By mid–August 1944, BAD2 had been in operation almost two years and was one of the most productive air base depots in the European theater. Its more than 10,000 servicemen had processed, repaired, and overhauled a wide variety of aircraft. Under the command of Colonel Moore, BAD2 hummed like a well-oiled machine. In concert with the personnel of other commands of the Mighty Eighth, the servicemen of BAD2 had done their part in giving the Allies air superiority in the skies over Western Europe. The question was no longer if the Allies would win the war, but when. Until the morning of August 23, 1944, the personnel at BAD2 had faced nothing but success and triumph.

3

Ground Pounders, Fly Boys and Their Amazing Machines

"They also serve who only stand and wait" —John Milton,
On His Blindness

The servicemen stationed at BAD2 were ordinary Americans. They came from every occupation and economic class. The men hailed from every corner of the United States. There were servicemen from the bayous of Louisiana, the rural farmlands of the Great Plains, the crowded cities of the east and the mountainous forests of the northwest. All of them had been children of the Great Depression, an experience that honed their survival skills and taught them the necessity of hard work. They had all been socialized by parents, schools, churches, and peers to value the principles of democracy and representative government. The United States now called these ordinary men to become citizen soldiers and perform the extraordinary task of defeating Nazi Germany and the other Axis powers.

At the outset of the war, the fledgling United States Army Air Forces needed hundreds of thousands of men to fly planes and maintain its aircraft. To train pilots, crews, technicians, mechanics and air traffic controllers, the U.S.A.A.F. became one of the largest educational organizations in existence.

The largest contingent in the U.S.A.A.F. was the ground pounders. These men were not pilots or crew members. They stayed on the ground and performed invaluable tasks such as repair, maintenance, armament, radio communication, radar operation, and air traffic control. Without ground pounders, the great American birds of prey could never leave their nest. The U.S.A.A.F. established the Army Air Technical Training Command to orient, classify and train enlisted men in the skills necessary to keep American planes in the air. By October 1942, the A.A.F. Technical Training Command had

15 of its own technical schools as well as 34 civilian contract mechanics schools, five universities, seven basic training centers, and 50 factory training institutes providing training for ground pounders. Tens of thousands of young enlisted men passed through U.S.A.A.F. technical schools each year. The training the servicemen received allowed them to keep American planes in the air and allowed the Allies to establish air superiority in the European theater of operations. Servicemen also used their training and experience to obtain jobs at the conclusion of the war.

Two servicemen stationed at BAD2 in August 1944 were typical examples of the experience and training received by ground pounders stationed at Warton. Thomas Miller was born in Olden, Texas, on April 6, 1923, to Thomas and Rose Miller. Miller's father was in the oil business in Texas when the Great Depression robbed the elder Miller of his livelihood and the Millers moved back to the family farm in Perryville, Louisiana. Tom was just seven at the time. For the next 12 years, Tom and his mother Rose farmed the land while Tom's father worked the oil fields of Louisiana.

Miller had just finished Spencer Business College and was working in the office of the Louisiana Creamery when the United States entered World War II. The 19-year-old Miller realized he was likely to be drafted and did not want to go into the infantry. He always liked airplanes and built models of them as a youth. On June 30, 1942, Miller made his decision and enlisted in the U.S.A.A.F. The Army Air Force sent Miller to Randolph Field in San Antonio, Texas, for basic training. Miller remembers that basic training "was comprised mostly of marching and physical calisthenics. We didn't have guns to carry. We were sent there mainly to get into good physical condition."[1]

Miller remained at Randolph Field for six weeks. He was then sent to Sheppard Field in Wichita Falls, Texas. Sheppard Field was a training facility the U.S.A.A.F. used mainly for the maintenance of airplanes. At Sheppard, technicians trained Miller on the operation and maintenance of B-25 and B-26 bombers. In late November, Miller was transferred to the Glen Martin plant in Baltimore, Maryland. Glen Martin built B-26s. In Baltimore, Miller studied B-26s in class and witnessed their production on the assembly line. After six weeks in Baltimore, Miller was shipped to Omaha, Nebraska, where he again observed and studied the building of B-26s.

Miller left Omaha in a B-26 headed for MacDill Field in Tampa, Florida. From Tampa, his unit was destined for North Africa. When Miller's plane made a stopover in Memphis, Tennessee, the crew noticed a hydraulic leak in the landing gear during a routine check. It was ten days before the repaired aircraft could get airborne again. By the time Miller reached Tampa, his unit had already left for North Africa. The U.S.A.A.F. assigned Miller to the 4th Replacement Depot and he was sure that he would be shipped to England as a gunner replacement on a bomber crew.

In early 1943, Miller boarded the *Orion* and set sail for Glasgow, Scotland, in a convoy with 20 other ships. The convoy safely negotiated its way through packs of German submarines in the north Atlantic and landed in Glasgow two weeks after departing New York City. In Scotland, Miller received his assignment. He would not be a gunner replacement. He was assigned as a mechanic to BAD1 in Burtonwood, England. After a short stay at Burtonwood, the U.S.A.A.F. reassigned Miller to BAD2 in Warton. At that time, Miller did not know that his reassignment to BAD2 would change his life forever.

Ralph Scott was another typical ground pounder at BAD2. Scott was born in Scranton, Pennsylvania, on May 28, 1916. Scott's father, William, worked as a maintenance electrician at the headquarters building of the Delaware, Lackawanna and Western Railroad. Scott's mother died when he was ten years old and his father married Hannah Waldmann two years later. During the Great Depression, Scott's father lost his job. William Scott started his own business as an electrical contractor. Ralph helped his father wire houses when he was not attending school. As the Great Depression worsened, new housing starts plummeted and people did not have the discretionary funds to rewire their old houses. Scott's father's business failed and the family lost their home in a sheriff's sale.

Scott's father went to Delaware to look for work. He sent his wife Hannah and Ralph to live with Hannah's family. William Scott eventually found work with a Wilmington, Delaware, newspaper as a maintenance electrician and the family moved into a bungalow in the suburbs of Wilmington. Scott graduated from high school in 1934 and took a part-time job with the Associated Press as an attendant in the telegraph room. In 1935, he took a full-time position as the office boy in the advertising department of the News Journal Company in Wilmington.

In July 1941, the United States Army drafted Scott for one year of service. While at basic training at Fort Dix in New Jersey, Scott enlisted in the army for a term of three years. After advanced training in Savannah, the army assigned Scott to the 43rd Bomber Group at Langley Field, Virginia. Following a brief stop in Bangor, Maine, the U.S.A.A.F. sent Scott to radio school at Scott Field in Illinois. Upon his return to Bangor, Scott briefly served as a drill instructor showing recruits how to use their gas masks in the tear gas tent, led them through exercises and physical training, and instructed them in the proper care and use of their rifles.

Through most of 1942 and early 1943, Scott bounced from base to base and continued to rise in rank. He was in charge of the radio section at Langley Field. He was then transferred to bases in South Carolina, Louisiana, and Michigan. During this time, he ran a radio section, installed switchboards and continued to train troops. He rose from the rank of corporal to tech/sergeant with five stripes. While stationed at Selfridge Field in Michigan, there was a race riot in Detroit.

The riot started on June 20, 1943, when a fist fight broke out between a black man and a white man at Belle Isle Amusement Park. The brawl eventually grew into a confrontation between groups of blacks and whites and spilled into the city of Detroit. Rioters looted stores and burned buildings in the predominately African American neighborhood of Paradise Valley. On June 21, President Roosevelt ordered 6,000 federal troops into Detroit to restore order.

Scott's unit was among the troops the army sent into Detroit to establish law and order. The troops lived in tents in Grand Circus Park in downtown Detroit. Scott and others patrolled the streets in pairs armed with carbines, machine guns, and tear gas. Scott wore a steel helmet and carried a Thompson sub-machine gun while on patrol. During his service in Detroit, Scott's commanding officer ordered Scott to provide protection for a local business. As Scott recalls, "I was ordered to accompany the cashier of a nearby restaurant so she could deposit their receipts for the past week. We took a cab to the bank and I escorted her into the bank. As far as I have heard, I am the only member of our family who was ever in a bank carrying a machine gun."[2] Before federal troops restored order, 34 people, including 25 African Americans, died in the riot. Detroit also suffered an estimated two million dollars in property damage.[3]

In August 1943, Scott's squadron moved to Camp Shanks, New York. From there the men boarded the *Atholone Castle*, a pre-war British cargo vessel, and sailed from New York harbor to the Mersey River, Liverpool, England. In England, the U.S.A.A.F. assigned Scott to the radio section of BAD2. Scott said of his first year at Warton that "most of my job there involved intercom systems on B-17s and B-24s. I went along on a few test flights, checked the radios and enjoyed the few minutes of sunshine when we were above the clouds and fog."[4] Scott lived on Site #10 and was billeted in a Nissan hut. He described the hut as "having curved sides that became the roof, with a door and windows at each end. There were usually 12 men to a hut. We had a short metal stove in the middle of the room for heat."[5] Scott, like Miller, had no idea how the events of August 23, 1944, would shape his life.

Even before the Wright brothers' plane took flight on December 17, 1903, in Kitty Hawk, North Carolina, American youth had been fascinated with the idea of soaring into the wild blue yonder. Flying touched the American imagination because it contains so many elements of the American national character. Courage, intelligence, pragmatism, and fantasy all worked in synergy to lift humans and their machines off the ground. By World War II, planes were larger and faster than their World War I predecessors and pilots needed more than daring and intestinal fortitude to fly them. Pilots in World War II needed intelligence, physical strength, superb eye/hand coordination, and the leadership ability to keep their crews motivated and alive.

Individuals who wanted to be pilots in the U.S.A.A.F. had to be 18 years old. Prior to January 1942, candidates had to be 20 years old and needed to have two years of college. The U.S.A.A.F. dropped or lowered these qualifications to increase the candidate pool. The candidates had to pass rigorous physical, psychological and written tests to be admitted into flight school. At this stage, nearly 50 percent of the candidates failed to qualify for flight school.[6]

After passing their physical, psychological, and written examinations, candidates became air cadets and attended basic training for six to eight weeks. After completing basic training, cadets went through three flight schools. In primary flying school, cadets received 60 hours of flight training over a nine-week period. The cadets generally flew a two-seat biplane, the Stearman PT-13D "Kaydet."[7] In the classroom, the cadets learned Morse code, navigation, meteorology as well as maintenance and repair of aircraft.

Cadets then moved on to basic flying school after successful completion of primary flying school. In basic flying school, cadets spent approximately 70 hours in the air during a nine-week period. At this stage of their training, the cadets flew planes of greater weight, speed, and horsepower. They also learned how to fly at night and by instruments. After completion of basic flying school, instructors would decide whether the cadet would go to single-engine or twin-engine advanced flying school.[8]

In advanced flying school, cadets flew either single- or multi-engine planes. The decision of what type of plane a pilot would fly was usually based on two factors, the current need for fighter or bomber pilots and the physical strength necessary to handle the heavy controls of bombers. Single-engine cadets learned aerial gunnery, combat maneuver and flying in formation. The multi-engine school emphasized mastering the handling of a larger, heavier aircraft as well as instrument and night flying. Cadets generally logged over 70 hours of flight time during the nine weeks of advanced flying school. After successfully completing all three schools, the cadet received his wings and a commission as a second lieutenant. Nearly 40 percent of the cadets who entered the program washed out or were killed in training accidents.[9]

The pilots who successfully completed flight school went on to transition training. In transition training, pilots flew the specific aircraft that they would fly in combat. Transition training lasted approximately two months. Upon completion, pilots were shipped overseas to combat units. The training American pilots went through was arduous, thorough and stringent. By the time an American pilot saw combat, he had accumulated almost 360 hours of flying time. This was more than three times the flying experience logged by German, Italian, and Japanese pilots during their training periods.[10]

Most American pilots were assigned to combat units. Some pilots saw duty in ferrying squadrons that moved planes from one base to another. Other pilots served as instructors in the various levels of flight schools. A handful of flyers served as test pilots in the United States and overseas at base air depots. Though test pilots did not have to face flak and enemy fighters, their job was still very dangerous. Test pilots had to be familiar with and able to fly a wide variety of single- and multi-engine aircraft in different stages of modification and repair. They needed to possess an in-depth knowledge of each aircraft and know how it operated under many different conditions. They needed an excellent feel for each type and model of aircraft and a keen ability to sense how the plane behaved in flight. Tests pilots had to cope with things going astray during a flight and be quickly able to solve problems. These fly boys were above-average pilots who had the physical endurance to test fly 35 to 40 planes a week.

Among the test pilots stationed at BAD2 in August 1944 was John Bloemendal. Bloemendal was born on June 1, 1917, to Hendrick and Grace Bloemendal in St. Paul, Minnesota. He was the oldest of three children. His sister Bessie was the middle child and his brother Ernest was the baby of the family. John's father was a woodsman from northern Minnesota who moved to the St. Paul area to take a position with a local transit company as a motorman. Hendrick Bloemendal, like over 16 million other workers, lost his job at the start of the Great Depression. He eventually found work with Johnson's Construction Company as a carpenter's helper. He, along with his wife Grace, instilled the values of hard work, discipline, and love of family in their children.

John attended Washington High School where he was an outstanding athlete starring in both baseball and hockey. He was a serious student who enjoyed all subjects but especially math. Bloemendal graduated number one in his high school class in 1935 and was the valedictorian speaker at the commencement exercises. In 1936, he matriculated at the University of Minnesota and majored in engineering. While at college, John held a part-time job to pay for school and help support his family. In 1937, Bloemendal left the University of Minnesota to provide financial support for his parents, who had fallen on hard economic times. He worked full time at the local Montgomery Ward store where he managed the camera department. Shortly before the war, John married his sweetheart Margaret Loftus. They had no children.

The 6'1", 163-pound Bloemendal enlisted in the U.S.A.A.F. on March 25, 1942. His brother Ernest said that John "enlisted out of patriotic duty and because he wanted to choose the branch of service that he was in."[11] Bloemendal enlisted for the duration of the war and decided to become a pilot even though he had no specific interest or fascination in flying as a youth. The star athlete and former valedictorian had no problem passing the physical or intelligence exams for flight school. After completing basic training and the compulsory three flight schools, he won his wings in April 1943. His brother Ernie followed in John's footsteps and enlisted in the U.S.A.A.F. in November 1942. The younger Bloemendal, however, washed out of flight school and became a ground pounder.

After winning his wings, Second Lieutenant Bloemendal was assigned to BAD2 as a test pilot. His athletic build, keen mind, and prowess as a pilot made him a perfect choice for the position. His brother Ernie was also stationed at BAD2. The two brothers worked together for several months and Ernie sometimes flew with John as his co-pilot on test flights. Ernie returned to the United States on New Year's Eve 1943 and once again tried to become a pilot. Unfortunately, Ernie washed out a second time.[12]

On the morning of August 23, 1944, First Lieutenant John Bloemendal was the Officer of the Day and also scheduled to test a B-24, the *Classy Chassis II*. John was also waiting official word on his rumored promotion to captain. At BAD2, Bloemendal had flown and tested all kinds of bombers, fighters and transports with confidence and skill. With promotion waiting in the wings and a routine test flight to complete, John looked forward to another normal day on the base.

Most of the men stationed at BAD2, like the majority of American GIs, had never traveled abroad. Millions of American servicemen passed through the British Isles on their way to North Africa and Europe. Some individuals, like most of the personnel at BAD2, remained on British soil for the duration of the war. The United States War Department published and distributed in 1942 a pamphlet entitled *Instructions for American Servicemen in Britain 1942.* The purpose of this seven-page pamphlet was to prepare American soldiers for a different culture and to prevent conflict between the Allies. American leadership, both civilian and military, believed that the military alliance depended on cordial relations between the Americans and their British hosts. The introduction contained in the pamphlet states that the "major duty Hitler has given his propaganda chiefs is to separate Britain and America and spread distrust between them. If he could do that, his chance of winning might return."[13] General Carl Spaatz, commander of Strategic Air Forces in the European theater of operations, echoed this sentiment when he said there were "three crimes a member of the Air Force can commit: murder, rape and interference with Anglo-American relations. The first two might conceivably be pardoned, but the third one, never."[14]

The pamphlet itself provided the reader with a quick overview of war-ravaged Britain and portrayed the British people as stoically handling the problems brought on by years of war. The pamphlet also provided American servicemen with helpful hints on how to behave in public places such as pubs and public transportation. The instructional manual included a list of things to do and not to do such as "don't make fun of British speech or accents and avoid comments on the British government or politics." The manual instructed Americans to "BE FRIENDLY—but don't intrude anywhere it seems you are not wanted." At times the pamphlet could be quite blunt yet sarcastically amusing. In a segment warning GIs to keep out of arguments, the publication states, "The British don't know how to make a good cup of coffee. You don't know how to make a good cup of tea. It's an even swap."[15]

American military commanders harbored concerns that American servicemen in the United Kingdom would be boastful show-offs and compete with English men for the local women. The instructional pamphlet warned GIs "not to be a show-off. The British dislike bragging and showing off. They won't think any better of you for throwing money around."[16] The pamphlet cautioned American soldiers not "to swipe" a British soldier's girlfriend or wife. Human nature, however, won out. Americans lonely and far from home soon found solace in the arms of equally as lonely British women who had witnessed most of the eligible bachelor pool go off to war. Tom Miller, stationed at BAD2, explains, "We would go into Blackpool just about every chance we had. We would normally go into Blackpool in a 6 × 6 army truck. Sometimes we would take a cab. We had to go to see our English girlfriends."[17]

By the war's end, nearly 50,000 GIs stationed in the United Kingdom had married English women.

What did the British think of the American invasion of their homeland? The British army printed its own guide to transatlantic harmony, *Meet the Americans*.[18] Like its American cousin, the pages of *Meet the Americans* were filled with worn-out clichés and stale stereotypes about the Yanks. Mass-Observation, the British equivalent of the Gallup Poll, provided some insight into how the British people felt about American servicemen stationed in the UK. In 1942, Mass-Observation polled 1,500 people about their impressions of American GIs. About 47 percent of the people surveyed said they had a favorable impression about the Yanks. In 1943, only 34 percent of the respondents had a favorable impression. When asked what they disliked about Americans, respondents cited boastfulness, immaturity, and materialism.[19] The Mass-Observation poll gave credence to a phrase popularized by English comedian Tommy Trinder that American soldiers were "overpaid, over-fed, oversexed and over here." The traits that the British people admired most in Americans were their "open-handed generosity, their vigor and impulsiveness, their friendliness, and their lack of inhibitions."[20]

It took time and frequent interaction to wear down the stereotypes that British and Americans had of each other. Where stereotypes died quickest were in the small towns and villages like Freckleton and Warton. At facilities like BAD2, there were thousands of ground pounders stationed for the duration of the war. Ground pounders, unlike the less permanent fly boys and infantry, developed more stable relationships with the local inhabitants. It was in villages like Freckleton that American GIs learned that not every British family had a butler and the British realized not every American had the swagger of Clark Gable or John Wayne. These favorable relations and interactions between ground pounders and villagers drew community and base closer together.

The men of BAD2 worked on and flew more than 20 different types of airplanes. These amazing machines helped to provide the firepower that liberated Europe from the clutches and oppression of fascism. The Allies never would have been able to establish air superiority in the European theater without the selfless contribution of ground pounders and test pilots at facilities like BAD2. In many ways they were the unsung heroes of the war. While the fly boys received the much deserved admiration of the American public, it was the personnel at bases like BAD2 that kept the fighting machines up in the air. The symbiotic relationship between ground pounders and flight crew made the U.S.A.A.F. a force to be reckoned with in the skies over Europe.

From late 1942 until August 1944, the personnel at BAD2 predominately processed four types of aircraft: The P-47 Thunderbolt, the P-51 Mustang, the B-17 Flying Fortress and the B-24 Liberator. Republic built the P-47 fighter and the 8th Air Force operationalized the plane in the United Kingdom on April 8, 1943. The plane was over 36 feet long and had a wing span of 40'9". Empty, it weighed 9,950 pounds and had a maximum speed of 433 mph. The aircraft contained eight 12.7mm wing-mounted machine guns and could carry up to 2,500 pounds of ordnance.[21] The P-47 was almost twice as heavy as any German fighter plane. The aircraft's main deficiencies were its poor rate of climb, cumbersome maneuverability and short range. Republic modified the P-47 in 1943 by adding external fuel tanks to increase range and lengthening the fuselage for increased maneuverability. The main assets of the P-47 were its sturdiness, its firepower, and its ability to outdive any German bomber. Robert Johnson, a P-47 pilot attached to the 56th Fighter Group, shot down 27 German aircraft over Europe. Johnson said of the P-47, "Unless we plunged nose first into the ground, we couldn't hurt the Thunderbolt."[22] As a testament to its survivability, only 0.7 percent of P-47s were lost in aerial combat with the enemy.[23] During the duration of the war, the Thunderbolt logged almost two million flight hours and destroyed nearly 7,000 aircraft in the European theater.

The P-51 Mustang was probably the best plane in the American fighter arsenal. The North American Aviation Company first built the plane for the R.A.F. The British used the aircraft as a low-level tactical fighter because its underpowered engine made it unsuitable for high-altitude flying. Lt. Colonel Thomas Hitchcock, serving as an American air attaché in London, suggested that the Mustang be turned into a high-altitude fighter by replacing the current P-51 engine with a Rolls Royce Merlin 61 engine.[24] The addition of drop tanks increased the range of the Mustang to 2350 miles. The P-51, which was 32 feet long and had a wing span of 37 feet, could now fly at 41,000 feet at a speed of 440 mph. The Mustang was faster, lighter, and nimbler than anything the *Luftwaffe* had in its arsenal, until the introduction of jet aircraft, and could escort Allied bombers round trip to their targets. The P-51 was a well-armed airplane with six .50-caliber machine guns and an external bomb load of 2,000 pounds.

The Mustang proved to be a very effective fighter. In their first three months of operation, Mustang pilots shot down three times the number of planes their Thunderbolt counterparts did.[25] Robert Goebel flew Mustangs with the 31st Fighter Group based at San Serio, Italy. Goebel said that "we soon found out that the P-51 Mustang was indeed a different breed of air-

plane. It was fast, for one thing. It was pretty good in the climbing department, too, and accelerated very fast in the dive. But the thing that really set
the Mustang apart from any fighter, friend or foe, was its range."[26] By the fall
of 1944, P-51s provided fighter escort for Allied bombers while P-47s
attacked bridges, airfields and railways in France. At the war's end, Mustangs
had destroyed 4,950 enemy aircraft in Europe.[27]

The personnel at BAD2 were responsible for making modifications and
repairing P-47s and P-51s. The men placed needed wing brackets and installed
water injection systems in P-47s. They also prepared and modified the Thunderbolt for its bombing and ground support missions after the invasion of
France. Crews worked on P-51s, adding an additional 85-gallon fuel tank in
the fuselage. Personnel also fitted the Mustang with drop tanks and added
adaptors to the G-suit used by the planes' pilots.[28] After two deadly test flights
of P-51s in June 1944, BAD2 engineers solved a problem that no doubt saved
many Mustang pilots' lives. In a weight-saving measure, North American Aviation had removed the uplocks from the undercarriage of the D model of the
P-51. The absence of the uplocks allowed the wheels of the plane to bounce
around in the wells, which in turn could cause the wheel doors to open in
flight, extending the wheels. The excessive bouncing and the extension of the
wheels led to structural failure that could cause the wings of the aircraft to
rip off at flight speed. The engineers quickly reported their findings to the
U.S.A.F. and North American Aviation.[29] The diligent investigative work
of the BAD2 engineers led to North American Aviation refitting the P-51Ds
with uplocks and adding this part to all Mustangs in production.

The two heavy bombers used by the 8th Air Force were the B-17 Flying
Fortress and the B-24 Liberator. Both planes were designed for long-range,
high-altitude bombing strikes. Both planes carried a ten man crew. The pilot
and co-pilot flew the bomber from the cockpit while the navigator and bom-
bardier sat below them in the nose of the aircraft. The flight engineer, who
was also the top turret gunner, was behind the pilot. In a separate compartment was the radio operator who also operated the top side machine gun.
The crew also contained two waist gunners, a ball turret gunner and a rear
gunner. Seventy-seven percent of the men who served in bomber crews before
D-day ended up as casualties.[30] Long-range fighter escorts and the near extinc-
tion of the *Luftwaffe* greatly reduced these figures in the last year of the war.

Boeing built the first prototype B-17 in 1925. In September 1939, the
United States had only 30 B-17s in its air corps. The production of B-17s
rapidly increased after the Japanese attack on Pearl Harbor. In the summer
of 1942, the Eighth Air Force used B-17s in its bombing raid on the railway

yards of Rouen, France, and the Flying Fortress remained one of the most potent weapons in the Mighty Eighth's arsenal. Throughout the war, the B-17 went through many production models and modifications. The B-17G, introduced in 1943, had a length of 74'4" and a wing span of 103'9". Four 1,200-horsepower engines powered the aircraft. The Flying Fortress averaged about 200 mph at 25,000 feet when carrying a normal bomb load of 6,000 pounds. The 36,135-pound behemoth was protected by thirteen .50-caliber machine guns. There were more than 12,000 B-17s built during World War II. Flying Fortresses dropped over 500,000 tons of bombs and fired 99 million rounds of ammunition. Of the 250,000 crew members who flew B-17s, 46,000 were either killed or wounded in the air war.

The other heavy bomber employed by the 8th Air Force was the B-24 Liberator. Consolidated Aircraft built the B-24 in 1939 after the U.S. Army Air Corps initiated a request for a new heavy bomber that exceeded the performance of the B-17. Though the B-17 was seven feet longer than the B-24, the Liberator had a larger wing span of 110 feet. The B-24's four 1,200-horsepower, turbo-charged radial piston engines allowed the plane to fly faster than the B-17. The Liberator also had a greater range and more bomb capacity than the Flying Fortress. The B-24 had two bomb bays, each of which could match the B-17's one bay for capacity. The Liberator's original design allowed it to carry an 8,000-pound payload. Production modifications eventually allowed the payload to rise to 12,500 pounds by the end of the war. Ten .50-caliber machine guns protected the B-24 from fighter attack. Two guns each were located in the nose, tail, top and bottom turret with one located on each side of the waist of the plane.[31]

The B-17 was an easier plane to take off, fly and land than the B-24. The B-24 was a difficult plane to maneuver and it took great physical strength to operate the yoke. Most pilots agreed that it was the most difficult plane to fly in the entire air force. B-24 pilot Guyon Phillips said he "never knew a pilot who asked to fly a Lib [Liberator] as a choice. There were so many other planes that were preferable to fly."[32] Another pilot noted that the B-24 "took its own good time to do whatever it was going to do."[33] The crew had a difficult time entering and exiting the plane. Once inside, quarters were extremely cramped and uncomfortable. Consolidated Aircraft designed the plane to deliver a maximum payload on distant targets. The engineers sacrificed creature comforts to achieve their goal. Despite its difficult handling, the B-24 became a workhorse of the 8th Air Force. Over 18,000 B-24s were produced during the war and it was the most prolific bomber in the U.S.A.A.F.'s arsenal.

BAD2 personnel processed over 325 B-17s and B-24s during the war, with Liberators comprising 90 percent of that number. BAD2 personnel installed external life raft switches, modified radio and intercom equipment, and enlarged the ammunition boxes on B-17s. The ground crews overhauled, modified and repaired B-24s, including the preparation of Liberators for Operation Carpetbagger. Of the nearly 10,000 aircraft processed at BAD2 from August 1943 to the conclusion of the war, 32 percent were heavy bombers.[34]

Most of the crews of the Mighty Eighth decorated their aircraft with nose art, the painting of an image on the skin of a plane. Nose art began when crew members pasted pages from *Esquire*, *Men Only*, and *Look* magazines onto the nose, fuselage, and tail of their plane. The decoration of aircraft allowed the crew members to personalize the plane they would fly for the duration of their tour of duty. The practice evolved into an art form when crews began to paint the image onto the plane. The practice survived because the U.S.A.A.F. had no regulations against it and unofficially approved it as a morale booster. As the number of aircraft increased in the European Theater, so did the demand for artists. By 1944, a top-notch artist could command up to $15 per plane.[35]

There were many reasons why nose art thrived among American airmen. The art bolstered morale and allowed each crew to feel that their plane and painting were special and unique. In dangerous times in a deadly occupation, many airmen believed their painting would bring them luck and a safe return from the hostile skies over Europe. Some of the images were patriotic and helped reinforce the positive attitude that the airmen were fighting a just war against the barbarian Hun. Others, like Captain Robert Morgan of the famous *Memphis Belle*, saw nose art as "a way of holding onto individuality, or sense of humor, in a war overwhelmingly vast, mechanized and brutal."[36]

Nose art derived from several cultural sources including comic books, Hollywood movies, Disney Studio characters, and pin-up girls. Though Mickey Mouse, Dog Patch, and the Dragon Lady appeared on their fair share of planes, it was the voluptuous temptress in seductive pin-up poses that dominated the genre. Nose artists duplicated the works of famous pin-up artists such as Alberto Vargas, George Petty and others. The crews often named their aircraft after the scantily clad women who adorned their plane. In naming the airplane, double entendre was the order of the day. Robert Morgan remarked after the war that "to the German fighter pilots honing in on our American bombers, it must have looked sometimes as though they were being attacked by a wave of flying underwear catalogues."[37]

Today this type of nose art would be considered politically incorrect and derogatory to women. In the 1940s, it provided young men with a sense of pride and enthusiasm that comes with individual expression. The artist created an idealized American woman who fit the youthful dash of homesick, sexually undernourished airmen. In a world turned upside down by the incongruities of war, the pin-up represented life in a universe filled with death. Josephine Howard, a member of the American Red Cross Aero Club in England and a female nose artist during the war, challenged contemporary criticisms of World War II nose art as degrading to women when she stated: "The art may have been frivolous at times, but it was never anti-social."[38] In the fall of 1944, nose art began to disappear from American planes. With new aircraft arriving from the United States on a regular basis and two crews for every bomber, fliers no longer baptized their aircraft with names and art. The need for luck generated by nose art also diminished due to the virtual disappearance of German fighters in the European skies. Nose art continues to be an American military tradition; however, art today must be gender neutral and woman cannot be portrayed on aircraft.

During its operation, thousands of planes passed through BAD2 and most of them were not memorable. There were two aircraft, however, that the men stationed at Warton would never forget. One was a P-51 Mustang, *Spare Parts*, the other a B-24 Liberator, *Classy Chassis II*. The two planes, for completely different reasons, would forever etch their memory into the hearts and souls of the servicemen of BAD2. Both aircraft would meet tragic ends, one covered in a shroud of mystery, the other in a fireball that changed the village of Freckleton forever.

The story of *Spare Parts* began on the docks of Liverpool on the morning of February 20, 1944. Stevedores began unloading 12 P-51s from a ship christened the *Spica* that had arrived the night before from the United States. As the dockworkers lowered the P-51s from the *Spica* to trailers waiting below, one of the Mustangs slipped from its sling and crashed to the ground. U.S.A.A.F. inspectors arrived on the scene and investigated the wreckage. The inspectors deemed the P-51 permanently damaged and unflyable. They ordered the P-51 sent to BAD2 to be salvaged for parts.[39]

On March 1, 1944, the damaged aircraft arrived at BAD2. The plane sat in Hangar #5 for weeks because spare parts were plentiful and the men were preparing aircraft to be used in the June invasion of France. Some of the engineers at Warton believed that the damaged P-51 could be rebuilt and be used in combat. The engineers asked Colonel Moore, BAD2 commander, for permission to rebuild the Mustang on their own time. Moore granted the men permission and believed the project would bolster morale on the base.[40]

The men stripped down the P-51 and rebuilt or replaced the damaged parts. Personnel from all sections of the base contributed their time, knowledge, and skill to the project. After the men installed the overhauled Merlin 61 engine in the aircraft, the Mustang was ready for inspection. Inspectors found no problems with the aircraft and cleared the P-51 for flight. Colonel Moore decided that the plane should not be shipped to a fighter group but should remain at BAD2. The men had their own, personal Mustang and now decided to customize the P-51 for their needs. They removed the oxygen system and relocated the command radio in order to install a second seat behind the pilot. Base personnel named the P-51 *Spare Parts* because sections of five other aircraft went into the rebuilding of the Mustang. Sergeant Bob Vroman painted the name of the aircraft on the nose with a scantily clad pin-up hyphenating the words *spare* and *parts*.[41]

In early July, test pilot First Lieutenant Jack Knight took *Spare Parts* up for its maiden voyage. He was accompanied by radio specialist Sergeant Lee Maudlin. Maudlin had won the back seat assignment in a lottery containing the names of all the men who worked on the rebuilding project. The plane performed well and stayed aloft for about 25 minutes. Knight put the Mustang through its paces and provided the men below on the airfield with an acrobatic air show that included 19 rolls. The personnel of BAD 2 gave *Spare Parts* and its pilot a rousing cheer when the plane safely landed on the runway.[42] Sergeant Maudlin allegedly ran to the nearest latrine.

Spare Parts performed many functions in its time at Warton. The plane served as a VIP transport, a shuttle for spare parts to combat units and as a trainer for ground crews learning how to taxi and park an aircraft. Perhaps *Spare Parts* most vital mission was as a whiskey transport. Several times a month, pilots would fly *Spare Parts* to Renfew, Scotland, where pilots would purchase scotch whiskey from a local distillery. The plane would return home with cases of scotch strapped in the rear seat and bottles stowed in the wing gun compartment.[43] The bootleggers of the prohibition era would have been proud of the servicemen of BAD2.

Spare Parts met its demise in late 1944 when it crashed after catastrophic engine failure. The exact location of the crash remains a mystery because the U.S.A.A.F. had already declared the plane officially lost on February 20, 1944, when it was damaged beyond repair on the docks at Liverpool. Since the P-51 was already officially off the books, the subsequent crash months later does not appear in the official records of the U.S.A.A.F. The crash of *Spare Parts* is rumored to have occurred over the Irish Sea or in the south of England.[44] The plane was lost, but the memories it created never were.

Classy Chassis II, a B-24H Liberator, arrived at BAD 2 on August 6, 1944. Consolidated Aircraft built the B-24H in the spring of 1944 in Fort Worth, Texas. The B-24H model featured changes in the nose turret and tail turret. The added weight in the nose caused a change in the center of gravity of the aircraft as the previous B-24 models were somewhat tail heavy. The U.S.A.A.F. assigned the B-24, serial number 42–50291, to the 490th Bomber Group in Suffolk, England. The bomber began its journey to England on April 12, 1944. From Fort Worth, the B-24 went to Florida. It then leap-frogged to Trinidad, Brazil, Dakar, Marrakech, and finally made its way to the United Kingdom. Once in the U.K., the U.S.A.A.F. reassigned the bomber to the 486th Bomber Group, 832nd Bomber Squadron in Sudbury. While attached to the 486th, the B-24 made bombing runs on German defenses and airfields in France.[45]

Pilot Lieutenant Borman, and the crew of B-24–42–50291, named their plane the *Classy Chassis II* while stationed at Sudbury. This aircraft should not to be confused with the original *Classy Chassy*. The original *Classy Chassy* was a B-24 stationed with the 487th Bomber Group. *The Classy Chassy* had a well-endowed red-haired pin-up painted on its nose. The vixen was barely attired in a red bra, red panties, nylon stockings, and red stiletto heels. She had a welcoming smile on her face as she reposed on her back with a smoking cigarette in her left hand. The word *chassis* (*chassy*) is misspelled on the plane. This could have been a simple mistake made by nose artist Davne Bryers or a deliberate attempt at rhyme.

The pin-up on the *Classy Chassis II* was inspired by the work of Peruvian artist Alberto Vargas who worked for *Esquire*. The *Classy Chassis II* temptress was seated on a cloud looking backwards. The brunette was clad in a two piece white swim suit and appears to be undoing her top. The pin-up's facial expression suggests that someone behind her is watching her disrobe. The pin-ups on the *Classy Chassy* and the *Classy Chassis II* are classic examples of World War II nose art and distinguish the two non-descript B-24s from each other.

General Doolittle, commander of the 8th Air Force, decided to convert the 3rd Combat Division (to which the 486th and the *Classy Chassis II* were attached) to an all-B-17 unit. Doolittle sent the B-24s from the 3rd Combat Division to BAD2 to be completely refurbished. Once the project was completed, Doolittle assigned the B-24s to the 2nd Combat Division. Once at Warton, the *Classy Chassis II* and the other B-24s had their flak wounds covered with permanent patches. Base personnel thoroughly repaired and inspected the planes. The servicemen armed the B-24s with the latest guns and made the required modifications.

Base personnel completed work on the *Classy Chassis II* on August 22. Corporal Roy Lewis, the crew chief responsible for the *Classy Chassis II*, reviewed the plane's work completed forms. With its paperwork in order, Lewis fired up engines two and three on the *Classy Chassis II*. He also performed daily and pre-flight inspections on the B-24. Lewis checked to see if the *Classy Chassis II*'s fuel tanks were filled to capacity, 2793 gallons. After completing all of the inspections and paperwork, Lewis posted notice in the engineering office that B-24, serial number 50291, was cleared for a test flight the next day, Wednesday, August 23.[46] Like *Spare Parts*, *Classy Chassis II* was destined for a tragic end.

4

Accidents

On the occasion of every accident that befalls you, remember to turn
to yourself and inquire what power you have for turning it to use.
— Epictetus, *The Enchiridion*

Airfields are intrinsically dangerous places. Add war to the equation and
the risk increases exponentially. At U.S. airfields alone from 1941 to 1945,
the U.S.A.A.F. reported 6,351 fatal accidents that led to more than 15,000
fatalities and the loss of 7,100 planes.[1] BAD2 was no stranger to mishaps. In
the first eight months of 1944, a series of accidents brought death and tragedy
to the personnel stationed at Warton. The growing number of aircraft processed at BAD2 increased the probability of accidents. There were more planes
taking off and landing at the airfield. The workload pushed test pilots to their
limits. Ground pounders worked 12-hour shifts seven days a week to keep up
with the influx of planes. Tired, exhausted men working with power tools,
flammable liquids, and heavy equipment became a recipe for mishaps. The
surprise was not that there were accidents at BAD2 but how few occurred
given the number and variety of planes processed at the facility.

The Americans at BAD2 had hardly finished ringing in the New Year
when tragedy struck the base. On January 4, 1944, First Lieutenant Lloyd
D. Bingham, Jr., took a P-51 up for a test flight. He and the plane never
returned to Warton. Witnesses in Blackpool reported seeing the Mustang
roll over and dive into the Irish Sea. The plane and pilot were never
recovered.[2] Less than two weeks later, an A-20 Havoc caught fire during an
engine test behind the main hangars. By the time the base fire crew arrived
on the scene, flames had completely consumed the plane. Fortunately, no
fatalities occurred as a result of the fireball.

The base recorded two mishaps in March. The first accident on March
3 was a near miss. An A-26 Marauder, coming to visit the base, had trouble
lowering its landing gear and made a belly landing on the main runway. The

The growing number of aircraft in 1944 increased the probability of accidents at the base. In this photograph, a GI, taxiing a P-51 to a repair hangar, crashed the aircraft into a parked P-51. Flaws in the construction of P-51Ds led to several fatal crashes around Warton during the summer of 1944 (photograph courtesy of BAe Systems Heritage Division).

pilot and aircraft both remained intact on impact. No serious injuries were reported as a result of the incident. On March 18, Flight Officer William Valee of the 310th Ferrying Squadron died when the P-38 he was flying from Warton to its fighter group crashed near Woodvale.[3]

In April, there were several noteworthy accidents that clustered around the middle of the month. On April 16, an electrician on the graveyard shift was working on a P-47 Thunderbolt named *Miss Georgia Peach*. The electrician accidently touched the gun button and the plane's eight guns fired multiple rounds into the hangar. The gunfire ripped a huge hole in the hangar's roof before the electrician was able to get the situation under control. The next day a similar accident occurred. This time the gunfire originated from the top turret of a B-24 and sprayed the hangar with .50-caliber machine gun fire. Through sheer luck, no one was wounded or killed in either incident.[4]

Another accident occurred on April 17, this time with a tragic ending. A P-51 Mustang taxiing from its parking space struck the rear of a truck. The plane's propellers tore apart and killed George Cooke, a civilian contractor who was riding on the back of the vehicle. The driver and two other passengers escaped injury. To cap the fatal day, a fire broke out in the Engine Test Block area. The fire crew eventually got the flames under control and reported no serious injuries resulting from the blaze.[5]

On May 27, personnel at BAD2 received distressing news. A Cessna VC-78, piloted by First Lieutenant Pliny R. Blodgett, was reported missing on its flight from Warton to Renfrew, Scotland. The U.S.A.A.F. later informed BAD2 that the plane had crashed into the hills just northwest of its destination. The pilot and two passengers perished in the mishap. Fire again struck the base on May 30. The blaze trapped three servicemen in cells five and six. Sergeant Terrence J. Miller, in complete disregard for his own safety, rescued the trapped men from the flaming inferno. All three men survived and Miller received the Soldier's Medal for his gallant behavior.[6]

The intensity of the workload accelerated and the number of flights at BAD2 increased in June because of the invasion of France. The probability of accidents increased in direct proportion to the increased number of flights into and out of Warton. On June 11, a technician was involved in the first of a series of accidents that plagued the base in June. The enlisted man narrowly escaped decapitation when a propeller struck him in the head. Fortunately he lived to tell the tale. On June 12, a crew chief taxied a newly processed B-17 across the main runway. The crew chief slammed on the brakes of the aircraft when he thought he saw another airplane about to land out of the corner of his eye. The force of the braking caused the plane to stand on its nose, which immediately crumpled back into the cockpit windshield. Fortunately, there was no plane coming in for a landing at the time, otherwise the situation could have been more serious. The crew chief probably saw a bird or some other object in his peripheral vision, mistook it for an aircraft and erred on the side of caution. Though the incident embarrassed the crew chief and was a source of great amusement at his expense, no one was hurt in the accident and the servicemen quickly repaired the damaged Flying Fortress.[7]

On the same day, Second Lieutenant Bill Clearwater was not as fortunate as the crew chief. Clearwater took a P-51D Mustang on a test flight above Warton. The pilot put the aircraft through its paces for about 20 minutes. When the P-51 passed over the airfield at about 3,000 feet, observers heard a change in the sound of the plane's Merlin 61 engine when Clearwater applied power to the aircraft. Witnesses then observed the plane diving vertically as the starboard wing detached from the Mustang. The P-51 nose-dived into the tidal flats of the River Ribble. Base personnel rushed to the scene of the crash and recovered the remains of Clearwater and most of the wreckage of the plane. Engineers assiduously examined the wreckage in search of the cause of the structural failure that allowed the P-51's wing to detach from the aircraft.[8] They found nothing.

The next morning, test pilots Jack Knight and John Bloemendal each took off from Warton in P-51Ds. Each pilot carefully looked at the other's aircraft to see if they could observe any structural flaws occurring during flight. They tempted fate by putting their Mustangs through a series of rolls. Neither pilot observed any unusual behavior from their aircraft or could see any structural flaws in the P-51s. Both pilots safely landed their planes at Warton after about 30 minutes in the air.

On June 27, a second P-51D, flown by Lieutenant Burtie Orth, plummeted from the skies near Fulwood, a small, unparished area of the city of Preston about two miles north of the city center. Orth, born on June 11, 1920, in Richfield Kansas, was one of thirteen children of Charles and Elizabeth Orth. Orth's father was a rancher and his mother operated a boardinghouse in Richfield. His mother, Elizabeth, also wrote and published poetry and prose about her native Kansas and her family. Through hard work and self-discipline, Orth's parents were able to provide their family with economic security throughout the years of the Great Depression and Dust Bowl. Burtie attended school in Richfield and played baseball and basketball. After the school day was over, Orth and his brothers worked with their father on the ranch and then they all went into town to have dinner with their mother at the boardinghouse. After graduating from high school, Burtie moved to Pasadena, California, to live with his sister Mildred. He attended Pasadena Junior College and when World War II began he enlisted in the U.S.A.A.F. and successfully completed flight school. Burtie's brother, James, was also a pilot and flew 50 missions out of Italy in a B-24 bomber.[9]

Lieutenant Burtie Orth was a victim of fate. The morning's flight schedule called for Orth to test fly a P-47 Thunderbolt that day. The crew chief of the P-47 informed Orth that the plane's engine power did not meet standards and the plane was not ready for a test flight. Orth then decided to fly a P-51D that was cleared for flight. Early morning showers had left a 70 percent cloud cover over Warton so Orth headed toward the clearer skies over Preston. Orth climbed to about 7,000 feet and leveled off. As the plane flew above Fulwood, the plane's engine made the same sound as Clearwater's doomed aircraft. Immediately after the engine noise, the right wing detached from the Mustang and fluttered to the ground. On the ground below, children and teachers at the morning assembly at the Fulwood and Cadley schools heard the plane's engines run out and saw the wing detach from the plane.[10] The children watched in horror as the P-51 descended downward.

Orth was flying over a populated area. Instead of bailing out, he stayed in the cockpit and struggled to keep the plane from hitting the houses and school below. He managed to steer the P-51 clear of the houses and school and the plane crashed into the surrounding farmland. Police and fireman recovered his body in the wreckage. Burtie left behind his British wife of three months, Freda Jones of Blackpool. Freda had informed Burtie on the morning of the crash that she was pregnant with their first child.[11]

Orth's selfless heroics prevented a tragedy of epic proportions. His last thoughts must have been about his pregnant wife and the innocent school children below him. He chose to surrender everything dear to him so that others might live. The children of Fulwood never forgot Orth's sacrifice. Today Orth's gallant action is memorialized on a plaque that hangs in the Fulwood and Cadley County Primary School. The inscription reads: "He stopped the crippled aircraft clear of this school and nearby houses. His courageous act is remembered by the school community past and present."

It was from the wreckage of the two Mustangs that BAD2 engineers solved the mystery of the two P-51 crashes. As was mentioned in the previous chapter, BAD2 engineers discovered that North American Aviation's removal of uplocks in the undercarriage of the P-51D model allowed the wheels of the aircraft to bounce around in the wells. The bouncing led to possible structural failure that could cause the wing of the aircraft to detach at flight speed. North American Aviation solved the problem by refitting the P-51s with uplocks. BAD2 pilots flew the retrofitted Mustangs without further incident.

Danger at BAD2 could come from a variety of sources. The Aircraft Salvage Department's role was to cannibalized unflyable aircraft for spare parts. One salvage crew received a scare while stripping a war-weary B-24 of its top turret. The men noticed a large hole in the turret but no exit opening. Further observation revealed a high-explosive cannon shell lodged in the turret with its detonator still in place. The salvage crew scurried from the B-24 and notified the Ordnance Department of their situation. The Ordnance Department sent an expert who defused the shell without incident. In another instance, a salvage crew in the process of scrapping a tired and worn-out C-47 transport found German land mines and rifles in the cargo bay of the aircraft. Once again, the men of the Ordnance Department rode to the rescue of the salvage crew.[12]

Compared to previous months in 1944, August had been relatively free of accidents and mishaps. The only major accident happened off base on the night of August 19. Private First Class Franklin Bailey was driving a taxi truck from Kirkham to BAD2 when he struck a cyclist and fatally injured him.[13] The workload at the base was beginning to lighten up and as each day passed, personnel stationed at BAD2 became more confident and proficient in their roles and work. Engineers had solved the riddle of the P-51D's structural deficiencies and the plane became safe for pilots to fly. Air traffic control effectively managed the planes coming into and leaving the Warton airfield. The U.S. Army's Engineering Aviation Battalion resurfaced the perimeter track around the airfield that had deteriorated under the immense girth of the Liberators and Flying Fortresses. By the middle of August, BAD2 was running like a finely tuned Swiss watch.

On the night of August 22, 1944, the *Classy Chassis II* patiently awaited its test flight in the morning. If all went well, the battle tested war bird would move on to its new assignment with the Second Combat Division. August had been a productive month for the Allies on the battlefield as British and American forces roared through France on their way to Paris. It had also been a productive and safe month at BAD2. Accidents at Warton were part of the job description. The servicemen at BAD2 had to shrug off the death and sadness caused by accidents if they wanted to continue to do their assigned tasks in an efficient and effective manner. The men also learned from their mistakes. If the P-51 crashes had taught the personnel of BAD2 any lesson it was that redemption and positive achievements could rise from the ashes of catastrophe. The deaths of two of their test pilots may have saved dozens of other pilots' lives. There was, however, nothing in the previous experiences at BAD2 that could prepare the servicemen for the events about to unfold in Freckleton the next morning.

5

The Crash: Wednesday, August 23, 1944

We could see the fire at Freckleton, and regardless of what the tower told us, we knew what had happened.
—Sergeant Dick Pew, co-pilot of B-24 #1353

On the morning of August 23, 1944, B-24H-20, serial number 42–50291, awaited its test flight in Area 1. Roy Lewis had completed the final inspection of the *Classy Chassis II* the day before. At 7:00 a.m., the flight test crews finished breakfast in the mess hall and headed for their assignments. The local weather forecast called for "some early sunshine and light clouds followed by rain showers later in the morning," but base personnel described the early morning weather as "dull, overcast, and misty."[1] Sergeant James (Jimmie) Parr, a 5'11", 140-pound former sales clerk from Duval, Florida, was the line chief. In this role, he assigned crew members to perform final inspections on aircraft before their test flights. Parr selected 26-year-old Corporal Gordon Kinney to inspect the *Classy Chassis II*. Gordon, a 5'7", 173-pound automobile serviceman from Tillman, Oklahoma, repeated the inspection from the day before and informed Parr at 8:00 a.m. that the *Classy Chassis II* was fit for flight.[2]

First Lieutenant John Bloemendal had double duty this day. The experienced, athletic and handsome pilot from Minnesota served as both a test pilot and Officer of the Day. After finishing his breakfast, Bloemendal drove down to the Operation Shack for Test Flight. He selected several aircraft parked at Area 1 for test flight and assigned himself to the *Classy Chassis II*. Since his arrival at BAD2, Bloemendal had flown over 744 hours as a test pilot, 253 of those hours in the cockpits of B-24s. Bloemendal was aware of the eccentricities of the B-24H model, especially the shift of gravity from the tail to the nose of the plane. By August 23, Bloemendal had logged almost 108 hours in B-24Hs. In August, Bloemendal averaged about 4.5 hours of flight time each day.[3] Bloemendal had the experience, the knowledge and the physical strength necessary to fly a B-24.

Crew chiefs and other flight test crew members also doubled as co-pilots and plane crew because of the shortage of test pilots, as well as the intense workload at the base. Bloemendal selected crew chief Jimmie Parr to serve as his co-pilot and Gordon Kinney to act as his flight engineer aboard the *Classy Chassis II*. Parr, as co-pilot, read the pre-flight checklist and assisted Bloemendal when the plane was in flight. Kinney had the landing responsibilities of turning on the auxiliary landing pump and visually checking the landing gear. Bloemendal and his makeshift crew picked up their para-

The U.S.A.A.F. assigned the B-24H Liberator, serial #42–50291, to the 490th Bombardment Group, 849th Bombardment Squadron. The "Mighty 8th" transferred the aircraft to the 486th BG, 832nd BS, where it made bombing runs against airfields and coastal defenses in France. The U.S.A.A.F. then sent the Liberator to BAD2 for refurbishment and repair. Lt. Borman and his crew (seen in picture) named their aircraft the *Classy Chassis II*. On August 23, 1944, John Bloemendal took the *Classy Chassis II* on a test flight over Warton. The plane was caught in a severe thunderstorm and the Liberator crashed into the village of Freckleton, killing Bloemendal, his two crew members and 58 other people. Members of the crew in the back row from left to right: Charles E. Middleton, John E. Palcich, Robert J. Moore, Edward Healy, Fred Borman, Jr., Stanley R. Bond. In the front row from left to right: Donald N. Holbrook, Leonard O. Payne, Harvey H. Shepherd and Clarence Gill, Jr. (photograph courtesy of the National Archives).

chutes and headed for the *Classy Chassis II*. The plane was scheduled for an 8:30 a.m. takeoff. Just before the crew boarded the B-24, the Area 1 phone rang. The call was for Bloemendal. He was needed immediately at another part of the base in his capacity as Officer of the Day.[4] Fate had cruelly intervened and the test flight was scrubbed until later in the morning.

In the village of Freckleton, everything seemed normal on the morning of August 23. Patrons at the Sad Sack Café sipped their coffee and enjoyed their breakfast while 176 students and their teachers at Holy Trinity School on Lytham Road prepared for the second day of class after the summer recess. Ruby Whittle (now Currell), a five-year-old enrolled in the Holy Trinity Infants' School remembers the start of the day as a "lovely, bright and sunny morning."[5] She also recalls not wanting to go to school that morning: "It was very unusual for me to not want to go to school. I wasn't ill; I didn't know what was wrong with me. But my dad was having none of it. He sat me on his bicycle crossbar and rode me to school."[6] Ruby's father never forgave himself for that decision.

Twenty-one-year-old Freckleton native Jennie Hall prepared herself for her second day as a teacher at Holy Trinity Infants' School. Miss Hall had lived in the village her entire life and had attended Holy Trinity School. After Holy Trinity, she went to Queen Mary School and from there attended a training college for teachers in Bangor. Her first teaching assignment was in Manchester and she had just started the position at Holy Trinity on August 22. She personally knew many of the children in the infants' school, including Georgina Lonsdale and Georgina's cousin, Judy Garner.[7]

Harry Latham was a nine-year-old evacuee from Salford. Latham was one of 14 children relocated to Freckleton to escape German aerial attacks. Some of the children arrived in Freckleton as part of Operation Pied Piper in 1939–1940. During this operation, approximately 500,000 children left British cities enduring the blitz for the safety of the countryside. A few of the children came from London as part of Operation Rivulet. In June 1944, Hitler launched V-1 rocket attacks against London. The German rocket attacks were meant to avenge the Allied bombardment of German cities and to terrorize the British people. Operation Rivulet evacuated about 1,000,000 women, children and elderly people from the London area. Nine-year-old Ellen Cavalier and seven-year-old Patricia Grafton were two evacuees who came to Freckleton as part of Operation Rivulet.

Latham remembers going to school in the rain and the sky darkening as the morning progressed. He recalled, "I never saw the sky so dark. It looked weird and felt as though something was going to happen."[8] The early morning drizzle had ominously deteriorated into a more severe weather pattern.

David Madden was a five-year-old transplant from Brighton, England. August 23 was his first day of school. His father was an instructor based at the R.A.F. airfield in Kirkham. Tired of the stress and strain of trying to visit his wife and son in Brighton each weekend, Corporal Madden moved his small family to the village of Freckleton. Madden rented an upstairs room for his wife and son from Mr. Battersby, a foreman at Balderstone Mill. The five-year-old Madden recalled that his first day of school "was all very new and strange. I was miles from home and the friends I had known. I had yet to make friends at the school."[9]

Madden recalled that the morning of August 23 "started well enough. It was dry, not very warm and a bit gloomy."[10] Madden's teacher was Jennie Hall. Madden stated that "even to my young eyes I could see that although she was obviously a grown-up, she was very young and pretty. Miss Hall, however, was stern and serious."[11] As the morning progressed, Madden noticed that "the gloomy weather had gotten darker and darker."[12] Miss Hall had to turn the lights on in the classroom for the students to do their work.

Alice Culter, age seven, accompanied her four-year-old cousin, Annie Herrington, to school on the morning of August 23. During the war, Annie had moved to Freckleton from nearby Kirkham because her parents believed it was safer in Freckleton. Kirkham had an R.A.F. airfield that the Herringtons thought might be subject to German air assault. Alice remembers hanging her cousin's school bag on the peg in the cloakroom and then waved goodbye to Annie as she headed for her classroom. Alice, who had just moved into the junior classroom at the end of summer recess, said that as the morning progressed it grew darker and then "there was terrible thunder and lightning."[13]

Joan Singleton (now Richardson) was seven years old and had moved from the infants' school to the junior class at the beginning of the new term. Her mother had made her a new dress and jacket to celebrate her advancement to the next level. She remembers that she "carefully hung up the jacket and had gone into the classroom. Mrs. Owens, our new teacher, had given each one of us a new pencil and we knew we just dare not lose them. The rain was very heavy but I don't remember being concerned even though it was really a thunderstorm."[14]

Barbara Banks' (now Hall) seventh birthday was just four days away. She, like Joan Singleton, had just moved out of the infants' school into Mrs. Owens' class. The classroom was at the back of the school dividing the girls' and boys' playgrounds. Two older girls from the top class had just finished distributing milk to the children in Mrs. Owens' class. Barbara recalls that "Mrs. Owens was telling us not to be frightened as it had grown very dark outside and we could hear the thunder and see flashes of lightning. Mrs. Owens began to read a story to keep the children calm."[15]

Warrant Officer William G. Bone and some other R.A.F. airmen stationed at the nearby R.A.F. camp were in Freckleton on the morning of August 23. Bone was born on September 24, 1923. He was the last of five children. His father deserted the family when Bone was a one year old. His mother's aunt took in the family and helped raise the children in her two-story terrace type house in Downham, near London. At the outbreak of World War II, Bone worked for a small company that made alternators for anti-submarine detection. On the weekends, Bone attended South East London Technical College.[16]

On his 18th birthday, the 5'7" Bone enlisted in the R.A.F. and was accepted into the pilot training program. Bone washed out of pilot training and went to Number 1 Wireless School in Cranwell where he learned to become a wireless operator. It was at the wireless school that Bone befriended Ray Brooke, Douglas Baston and Robert Bell. After wireless school, the four friends then sailed to Hamilton, Ontario, for navigation training. After returning to England from Canada, the R.A.F. assigned the four men to the No. 22 Aircrew Holding Unit at Kirkham.[17]

On the morning of August 23, the four R.A.F. friends, Bone, Brooke, Baston, and Bell, decided to walk into Freckleton. The Sad Sack Café in Freckleton, owned and operated by Alan and Rachel Whittle, was a well-known snack bar to both the R.A.F. airmen and the personnel of BAD2. It became a gathering place for servicemen who wanted a tasty breakfast and a decent cup of tea. The R.A.F. airmen departed on their journey in a misty rain. According to Bone, about 10:40 a.m. "it started to rain heavily with heavy, heavy clouds. We ducked into the Sad Sack and closed into the bar for tea."[18] Ray Brooke, who accompanied Bone and the others into Freckleton, echoes Bone's recollection: "I was off duty with three mates when a tremendous storm blew up. We made a run for the Sad Sack snack bar and ordered some tea."[19] The four friends never got to enjoy their tea and in seconds their lives changed forever.

Shortly after 10:00 a.m., John Bloemendal returned to the Operations Shack. He had finished his administrative duties and was ready to take the *Classy Chassis II* up for a test flight. The weather conditions at 10:00 a.m. were 100 percent cloud cover at 700 feet with 2,500 yards visibility and continuous light rain.[20] Bloemendal gathered his crew of Parr and Kinney and they headed for the aircraft to perform pre-flight inspection. First Lieutenant Peter Manassero, an experienced test pilot from San Mateo, California, commanded a second B-24 scheduled for a test flight at the same time. His crew of Dick Pew and Lawrence Smith, both crew chiefs, had already completed pre-flight inspections on the second Liberator. By 10:25 a.m., both B-24s were ready for takeoff.

By 10:30 a.m., weather conditions had temporarily improved. Captain Zdrubek, the station weather officer, reported a ceiling of 1,200 to 1,500 feet and two miles of visibility. The light rain had become intermittent.[21] The two B-24s taxied out to the intersection of the perimeter track and runway 08, the longest of the three runways at BAD2 and the one used by heavy bombers. Runway 08 ran in an east-to-west direction with landing usually from west to east. Bloemendal, in *Classy Chassis II*, was first in line for takeoff, followed by Manassero's B-24.

At approximately 10:30 a.m., Bloemendal asked the control tower at Warton, code named Farum, for clearance to take off. The tower granted him clearance and the Liberator lifted off the ground into the Lancashire sky. The control tower then cleared Manassero's aircraft and the other B-24 became airborne about a minute later.

After takeoff, the two B-24s headed northward, flying at an altitude of approximately 1,500 feet. Both pilots were standing by on VHF radio when Bloemendal called Manassero's attention to the cloud formation toward the south, southeast. Manassero later described the formation as "a very impressive sight and looked like a thunderhead."[22] At approximately the same time, General Isaac Ott, commander of BAD1 at Burtonwood, telephoned BAD2 Headquarters. Ott informed Lt. Colonel William Britton, Base Executive Officer, that a violent storm was approaching Warton from the Warrington area.[23] This was the same storm that Bloemendal and Manassero observed from their aircraft. General Ott also ordered Britton to recall "any of Warton's airborne craft to the ground at once."[24] Britton immediately called the control tower and told them to recall the two B-24s back to the base.

Weather conditions at BAD2 had already seriously deteriorated by the time of General Ott's call. Captain Zdrubek reported that by 10:40 a.m. "the sky was suddenly darkened from the south, and long streaks of lightning were observed. Heavy rain began, lowering the ceiling to 400 feet and visibility to 300 yards. The wind shifted from NE at 18 MPH to SW at 35 MPH and then back to NE at 20 MPH within ten minutes."[25] First Lieutenant James Harper, the flying control officer, stated that "at approximately 10 40 hours some low dark clouds were observed moving in toward this field from the southeast. The Control Tower was instructed to recall the local aircraft, but the cloudburst moved in so quickly that they did not have time to land."[26]

At the base hospital, Army Nurse Jane Chestnutwood was recovering from influenza. The crash of thunder and the howling of the wind caught her attention. She arose from her bed and walked into the hallway. There she observed the storm from a window. The driving rain and lightning bolts were interesting but what truly fascinated her was the absolute lack of visibility as she looked east toward Freckleton.[27]

In Freckleton, the rain came down with torrential intensity. Sergeant Ray Cox was in the village headed to Preston to celebrate his birthday. As the storm raged around him, Cox took refuge in a glass-enclosed bus stop on Lytham Road across from the Sad Sack Café. Cox later recalled that "the rain hit and it was so heavy that I couldn't see across the road."[28] The Hutton Meteorological Station reported wind gusts of up to 60 mph, water spouts on the River Ribble estuary, and flash flooding in Southport as well as Black-pool. The wind gusts uprooted trees and overturned chicken coops in the Freckleton area.

At Holy Trinity School, teachers and students saw the darkness descend on the village. The pounding rain was overshadowed by the gusting winds, the roar of thunder and lightning bolts briefly illuminating the sky. Ruby Whittle remembers that "it went very, very dark. There was thunder and lightning, and all sorts of crashes and bangs overhead. I remember the teacher putting the classroom light on and she began reading to us."[29] David Madden has similar memories of the storm. He recalls that one of the teachers switched the lights on when "it became very noisy. There was a loud noise close by. I think the teachers thought the building had been struck by lightning. It was very dark outside. We stopped what we were doing and both classes were encouraged to sing a nursery rhyme."[30]

In the junior class, Alice Cutler remembered the gloom and noise. She said that "because we could hardly see anything, our teachers told us to fold our arms and put our heads on the desk until the storm passed."[31] Seven-year-old Val Preston (now Whittle) was in the junior class and her brother George was in the infants' school. Val remembers "writing in my exercise book when it turned very dark during a severe thunderstorm."[32] Thunderstorms of this ferocity were unusual meteorological occurrences in northwest England and were a frightening experience for the children. Harry Latham, nine years old at the time, later recalled that "it was a thunderstorm that has not to my knowledge been seen since. The sky went black and it rained like I have never seen it rain. Everybody was quite frightened."[33]

At approximately 10:41 a.m., the BAD2 control tower radioed Lt. Colonel Britton's order to land the two B-24s to Bloemendal. The following is a transcript of the conversation between the Warton control tower, Farum, and Lieutenant Bloemendal:

> CONTROL TOWER: Hello, Gorgeous John and Gorgeous Peter. This is Farum control. Are you receiving? Over.
> BLOEMENDAL: Hello, Farum control. This is Gorgeous John. Over.
> CONTROL TOWER: Hello, Gorgeous John. This is Farum control. You are to land immediately. Over.
> BLOEMENDAL: Hello, Farum control. This is Gorgeous John. Can you give the reason? Is it weather?
> CONTROL TOWER: Roger, Gorgeous John, that is correct. Ceiling and visibility decreasing rapidly. You are clear and No. 1 to land on runway 08.
> BLOEMENDAL: Gorgeous John, Roger, Farum control. End.[34]

This was the last communication that the Warton control tower received from Bloemendal and the *Classy Chassis II*.

After receiving the message to return to Warton from the BAD2 control tower, the two B-24s turned toward the base. Lieutenant Manassero flew about 100 yards off Bloemendal's right wing. As the two B-24s approached the airfield, Manassero moved further to the right to be in position to land his aircraft after Bloemendal touched down in the *Classy Chassis II*. The two planes were now about four miles northwest of the airfield and had dropped down to about 500 feet. At this point, the pilots encountered heavy rain and extremely low visibility as they made their approach to runway 08. On the base leg turn into the Warton airfield both pilots lowered their landing gear.[35]

On the approach to the airfield, visibility began to erode toward zero. Manassero lost visual contact with the *Classy Chassis II*. Manassero's aircraft, now over Lytham, turned left and began its approach toward runway 08. Manassero later told investigators: "At this time I heard Lieutenant Bloemendal notify Farum that he was pulling up his wheels and going around." Manassero then radioed Bloemendal and told him "we had better head north and get out of the storm. He answered 'OK.' I then told him I would take a heading of 330 degrees. He said 'Roger.'"[36] That was the last time the two pilots communicated with each other.

Manassero was able to retract his plane's landing gear and gained altitude. He flew on a heading of 330 degrees and was clear of the storm in about four to five minutes. Sergeant Richard Pew, the crew chief serving as Manassero's co-pilot, later recalled their escape from the storm's forceful grip. Pew stated that "the turbulence was extreme, but not being a pilot at the time, I did not appreciate how skilled and cool Pete was."[37] Once clear of the storm, Manassero radioed Bloemendal and asked if he was okay. Manassero received no reply from Bloemendal so he then called the control tower at BAD2 and asked them to contact Bloemendal. Farum also could not make radio contact with Bloemendal.

As Bloemendal and his small crew tried to retract the landing gear and pull the aircraft out of its approach to runway 08, disaster struck the *Classy Chassis II*. Trying to pull out of his approach, Bloemendal tightly gripped the controls and ordered Jimmie Parr, the co-pilot, to give him maximum speed to gain altitude. As Bloemendal banked the plane to the right, the violent turbulence that accompanied the thunderstorm grabbed hold of the air-

On August 23, 1944, the *Classy Chassis II* crashed into the village of Freckleton. Fuel from its ruptured tanks engulfed the Holy Trinity School in flames. The fireball completely destroyed the infants' wing of the school (shown above). Thirty-eight children and their two teachers died in the inferno (photograph courtesy of BAe Systems Heritage Division).

craft. On the ground, Flight Test Engineer Robert Lewis was preparing another B-24 for a test flight. Lewis picked up intercom transmission emanating from inside the cockpit of the *Classy Chassis II*. Lewis heard what might have been John Bloemendal's last words: "My altimeter and air speed have gone crazy! I can't tell if I am right side up or inverted! My compasses are spinning! I don't know my heading! I have no control at all!"[38]

Out of control with its wings nearly vertical, the 25-ton aircraft with more than 2,700 gallons of fuel on board went careening into the village of Freckleton. *The Classy Chassis II* first clipped a tree and then cartwheeled down Lytham Road. The B-24 partially damaged three houses and demolished the Sad Sack Café. The plane's momentum slid it across the road into the infants' wing of Holy Trinity School. The whole area erupted into a fireball when the 2700 gallons of 100-octane aviation fuel ignited and burst into flame. The impact of the crash immediately killed John Bloemendal, Jimmie Parr, and Gordon Kinney. The time of the crash was approximately 10:47 a.m.

The Warton control tower was still trying to contact the *Classy Chassis II* when the air traffic controllers received their first inkling of the plane's and crew's fate. A C-47 transport, parked in Area 6 on the northeast corner of the field, reported seeing a column of dark smoke in the vicinity of Freckleton. Tech Sergeant Doyle Shaw of Control Tower Operation said he "verified the message and checked it visually. We notified flying control and informed them that we had lost contact with Lieutenant Bloemendal. We attempted to contact Lieutenant Bloemendal without any results."[39] The fate of *Classy Chassis II* was no longer a mystery. Why and how the accident occurred still is today.

The crash of the *Classy Chassis II* is still shrouded in mystery and controversy because the exact flight pattern of the plane and the actual cause of the accident are still matters of speculation. There are many reasons for this speculation. In 1944, planes did not carry "black boxes." To determine the cause(s) of an accident you needed survivors, reliable eyewitnesses, salvageable wreckage, or any combination of the three. All the crew members of the *Classy Chassis II* perished in the crash. The only evidence of what went on in the cockpit was the alleged last anguished words of Bloemendal as interpreted years later by Bob Lewis. There was no official communication between Bloemendal and the control tower or Lieutenant Manassero after Bloemendal's decision not to land the aircraft. Visibility was near zero so the trained eyes of the servicemen stationed at BAD2 did not see the crash. The eyewitnesses who saw the incident were not aviation experts and had their vision impaired by the storm. The ensuing fireball destroyed most of the aircraft, hindering a careful and thorough examination of the wreckage. To complete the litany of problems, the U.S.A.A.F. investigation of the crash was shallow and perfunctory in its scope.

What did eyewitnesses see on the morning of August 23 at or about 10:45 a.m.? Eric Greenwood, an eight-year-old boy visiting the Browns' home on 21 Kirkham Road, said that about 10:45 a.m. he was standing at the window on the ground floor of the house looking at a field. He then "saw a Liberator and heard its roar right over the house. It was flying very low and I saw the right wing go down as the left came up. It seemed to be swaying in the air."[40] He claimed not to see any flames coming from the plane and moments afterward he heard the plane crash.

Charlotte Allsup from Clitheroes Lane in Freckleton was in her backyard hurriedly trying to get her chickens out of the pelting rain. She told investigators that when she looked to the north "the storm was at its fiercest, rain was teeming down. I saw a ball of fire in the sky flash and then hit the plane. The plane spun around and hit the earth. I could not tell the direction of the plane. The ball of fire was lightning."[41]

Mrs. S.J. Rockey was in the electrical showroom of the St. Anne's Corporation on the opposite side of Lytham Road from Holy Trinity School at the time of the storm. She heard a plane flying low but attached no particular significance to it since she lived near the Warton airbase. Mrs. Rockey believed the plane was flying in an easterly direction. Suddenly there was a large noise that she thought was a clap of thunder. She opened the front door of the store and looked out. She told investigators that "the street was aflame. I could see the Sad Sack aflame. I couldn't see the school because of the fire but I could hear the children screaming."[42]

William Banks was in the post office in Freckleton at the time of the crash. He was watching the storm through a window with a westward exposure when he observed a vivid flash of lightning. He then saw the tail of the *Classy Chassis II* in the center of the road in front of the school. He said the plane "looked like a lorry. As I was looking, almost instantaneously the school, highway and plane burst into flame."[43]

At home that morning was Mrs. Vera Cartmell. She was watching the storm through a window in her home at 30 Kirkham Road when she spotted a B-24 Liberator flying extremely low to the ground. She noted that the aircraft was "in a banking position—that is, the wings were straight up and down. It was flying so low I felt it would crash. I tried to follow it but I couldn't see it anymore. I heard the crash and then saw the flames."[44] She also recalled that the plane was not on fire when she saw it pass her home.

Sergeant Ray Cox, crouched in the glass-enclosed bus stop across from the Sad Sack Café, remembered hearing the "roar of engines as if the plane were in power drive. I looked for the source and thought for sure that it was coming right for me. I was frozen with fear, and then I saw the flash as it hit the snack bar."[45] The Sad Sack Café instantaneously disappeared from Cox's view and exploded into a ball of flames.

Nurse Jane Chestnutwood remained at the hospital window to watch the thunderstorm. She remembers seeing the *Classy Chassis II* appear from the clouds on a northerly heading at an altitude of about 600 feet. The nurse claimed that she then saw a bolt of lightning streak from the clouds and strike the B-24 at the juncture of the wing and fuselage. She alleged that the lightning strike split the Liberator into two pieces that helplessly plummeted to the village below.[46]

Dick Pew, aboard Manassero's B-24, said Manassero tried to keep in contact with the *Classy Chassis II* throughout the storm but to no avail. When Pew radioed the control tower at BAD2 that they had lost contact with the other Liberator, air traffic control assured Manassero's crew that there was no problem with Bloemendal's aircraft. Pew recalled that as Manassero's B-24 approached the Warton airfield, "we could see the fire at Freckleton and regardless of what the tower told us, we knew what had happened."[47]

The eyewitness testimony is both confusing and contradictory. Witnesses have the plane flying in different directions at the time of the crash. Some individuals saw the plane being hit by lightning, while others suggested that the plane was hit by severe turbulence while it attempted to bank and fly to safety. For now, the direction of the plane and the cause of the crash are irrelevant. The relevant factors are that the B-24 had crashed into Freckleton, immediately killing three American airmen, and the village was now engulfed in a raging inferno. The crash had been tragic; the ensuing fireball was a holocaust.

6

The Inferno

"There's no tragedy in life like the death of a child. Things never get back to the way they were."
—General Dwight D. Eisenhower

The *Classy Chassis II* violently smashed into the village of Freckleton just as the worst of the vicious thunderstorm began to abate. The time was approximately 10:47 a.m. As the B-24 crashed to earth, it ripped off the top of a tree and lost its right wingtip as it clipped the corner of a building. The aircraft damaged three houses on Lytham Road and its tail turret, as well as the main wheel, slammed through the Sad Sack Café. The momentum of the B-24 carried it across Lytham Road toward the Holy Trinity School. The main landing gear broke loose on the sidewalk beside the school while the engines broke free of the disintegrating bomber and slid into the schoolyard. The nose turret of the *Classy Chassis II* ground to a halt in the classroom building.[1] The 2,793 gallons of 100-octane aviation fuel spewed from the ruptured tanks of the B-24 and instantaneously the entire area erupted into flames, engulfing several buildings including the infants' wing of Holy Trinity School and the Sad Sack Café.

There were 176 students in attendance at Holy Trinity School on the morning of August 23, including 14 evacuees who had come to the safe haven of Freckleton to escape the wrath of German bombs elsewhere in England. The day before, August 22, Headmaster F.A. Billington had welcomed the students back to school from the summer recess and encouraged them to be diligent in their studies during the new term. For many of the 41 students and two teachers in the infants' wing (four- to six year-old students attended class here), this was their first week of school. Holy Trinity School was located on Lytham Road. The infants' classroom was in the eastern wing of the building. The older children's classrooms were on the northern and southern flanks of the infants' wing. The school playground

A wheel from the *Classy Chassis II* looms ominously in the foreground as GIs from BAD2 search the rubble of the crash site for possible survivors. The fire still rages in the background (photograph courtesy of BAe Systems Heritage Division).

was at the southern end of the school adjacent to the junior children's wing. Holy Trinity Church, a separate structure, was situated just west of the school building.

The eastern portion of Holy Trinity School, the infants' classroom, endured the brunt of the B-24 crash into the school building. The plane's nose turret slammed into the room and the bomber's flaming fuel enveloped the 41 students and their two teachers, Jennie Hall and Louisa Hulme, in a sea of flames. Ironically, Miss Hall was just in her second day of teaching at the school. She had replaced Doris Catlow, who left only a few days before to take another position. In another ironic twist, Miss Hulme was scheduled to retire the following week.

In a matter of minutes, Freckleton lost a generation of children. Thirty-four of the students immediately died in the inferno. Rescuers were able to pull seven children and their two teachers from the burning rubble. Four of the children and both teachers later died in the base hospital from the injuries they sustained in the fire. Of the 43 people in the infants' wing at the time of the crash, only three survived the fireball. The three children who survived their

American GIs, medics and MPs, as well as British first responders, sift through the rubble of the infants' wing for survivors. Only three of the 41 children from this section of Holy Trinity School lived through the carnage. The three survivors, Ruby Whittle, George Carey and David Madden, were badly burned and endured years of painful surgeries to repair their bodies (courtesy of BAe Systems Heritage Division).

terrible burns were Ruby Whittle (now Currell), David Madden and George Carey.

David Madden was a five-year-old transplant from Brighton, England. His father was in the R.A.F. and stationed at Kirkham. Earlier in the year, Madden's father had moved his small family to Freckleton in order to be closer to them. Madden was in his first week of school at Holy Trinity and assigned to the infants' room. He sat four desks from the front of the classroom in the sixth row, just one row from the door on the left hand side of the room. Jennie Hall, his teacher, sat in the front of the room at her desk facing the students. Miss Hall turned on the lights as the classroom grew dark because of the approaching storm. The noises generated by the thunderstorm grew closer and more intense. To ease the tension of the young students, Miss Hall and Miss Hulme ceased normal instruction and led the children in the singing of nursery rhymes.[2]

The noises from the storm continued to get closer and more vociferous until an extremely loud sound caused concern among the teachers and students. Madden looked over his shoulder and could see flames outside. The roof also appeared to be on fire. Smoke drifted down from the ceiling and began to fill the classroom. Hall and Hulme decided to evacuate the room and told the children to stand by their desks. Madden recalls that this process was "taking a long time. I wanted to go at once but dare not disobey."[3] The teachers told the first row of students to file out but no one moved. The classroom had quickly filled up with smoke from the roof and a piece of burning debris plummeted to the classroom floor igniting it on fire. Madden continued to wait for the order to leave the room. It never came. As Madden stared at Miss Hall sitting at her desk he saw her faint, no doubt from smoke inhalation. Madden recalled that Miss Hall "very slowly bent forwards and laid her head on the table with her face to the side."[4]

When Miss Hall slumped to her desk, Madden no longer felt constrained by adult authority and bolted to his left toward the exit door. He then passed through a small room to the outside door. When he came to the outside door he found a small group of children hesitating to go through the opening because the door frame was a ring of fire. Madden did not hesitate. He decided to run through the dark area in the middle of the flames. That quick, critical decision saved the five-year-old's life.

Severely burned from his thighs to his shins, Madden ran out into the yard behind the school. Madden could not get to the front of the school and the road because there "was a huge mass of flames with no dark holes in the middle."[5] Madden decided to go into the back lane and through the yard of the adjacent car repair shop. This way he could reach the road and avoid the wall of flames. While fleeing to safety, a rescue worker spotted Madden and placed him in a U.S.A.A.F. ambulance with several other burned children and raced them to the BAD2 hospital for treatment.[6]

Ruby Whittle, the five-year-old girl who did not want to attend school that morning, must have had a subconscious premonition about the accident. She remembers the darkness of the storm and the loud noises associated with the lightning and thunder. She then recalls an "almighty bang and saw a teacher and a girl fall to the floor so I dived under my desk."[7] She looked toward the door and saw a pile of debris blocking it. Flaming rubble continued to fall from the roof above Ruby but her desk sheltered her from a direct hit from the falling material. The terrified, trapped five-year-old could see little from underneath her desk but could hear the panicked screams of her classmates and smell the engulfing smoke as well as the overpowering fumes from the aviation fuel.

The frightened Ruby again glanced at the door. She saw it begin to move. She could make out the faces of two men through what had once been a glass panel in the door. The men, Headmaster Billington and Sergeant Edward Stinger from BAD2, shoved the door open and worked their way through the debris toward Whittle. Billington had heard a "great crack and saw the flames spread rapidly everywhere."[8] Billington immediately attempted to evacuate the school and played a prominent role in the rescue work. He had pulled several children out of the wreckage and had severely burned his hands in the process. Eddie Stinger, a military policeman stationed at BAD2, responded to the sound of the crash by rushing into Freckleton. He was one of the first American servicemen at Holy Trinity School and was involved in the search for survivors. Together, the two men had found Ruby huddled under her desk.

The two men tried to coax Ruby to come from under the safety of her desk. Frightened, severely burned, and probably suffering from shock, the five-year-old refused to budge. Stinger then walked over to the desk and picked Ruby up in his arms. Stinger carried Ruby out of the charred building and took her to an American ambulance, probably the same one that contained David Madden. Ruby suffered burns over most of her body. When she arrived at the BAD2 hospital, a nurse gave her a shot to put her to sleep so she would not have to endure the excruciating pain caused by her burns. When she awoke, Eddie Stinger was by her side. Stinger continued to maintain his vigil until Whittle was transferred to a hospital in Manchester.[9] Ruby Whittle's father spent the rest of his life regretting sending his daughter to school on that late August morning.[10]

Thirteen-year-old Jacky Nichol provided another account of the devastation in the infants' wing. When the thunderstorm hit Freckleton, Mr. Billington assigned Nichol the task of going into each classroom's cloakroom to check and see if the windows were closed in each closet. When Nichol entered the infants' room, he heard an explosion and saw a blinding orange flash. The window in the room blew in and a fireball crossed the room around the ceiling. The flames from the ceiling then ignited the walls. Nichol threw himself to the floor and remembers seeing "Miss Hulme engulfed in flames."[11] He also felt the air being sucked out of his lungs as the fire rapidly consumed the available oxygen.

Realizing that remaining in the room was not an option, the 13-year-old stood up and ran for the door leading to the playground. The storm had flooded the playground and Nichol, acting on reflex, decided not to get his feet wet. What Nichol identified as water was most likely aviation fuel that had spilled out from the ruptured fuel tanks of the *Classy Chassis II*. He scurried back through the wreckage into the classroom and then out another door. In the schoolyard, he joined other terrified and injured students. He saw the badly burned body of Miss Hulme wrapped in a blanket awaiting evacuation to the BAD2 hospital.[12] American servicemen eventually led Nichol to safety away from the burned-out school. Miss Hulme, who came to Freckleton in 1940 as an evacuee from Salford, died of her injuries in the base hospital on August 25, 1944.

Jack Nichol came out of the fire without a physical scratch on his body but admits that the disaster "mentally scratched me forever."[13] Whenever Jack thinks or dreams of the tragedy, he has trouble breathing. He is still racked by survivor's guilt and vividly recalls the "sickly smell of fuel and burning flesh." Nichol deeply regrets that he did not do more to help Miss Hulme and the children in the infants' room. The cruel reality is that there was nothing a 13-year-old boy in a state of shock could do to stem the tide of the raging inferno he witnessed that late August morning. Unfortunately for Jack Nichol, the sights, sounds and smells of the disaster still trigger flashbacks and painful memories of the school fire 68 years later.

The devastation in the infants' school was lethal and complete. Thirty-eight of the 41 children perished in the tragedy. Both teachers succumbed to their injuries. Thirty-four of the children died immediately while four more died in the BAD2 hospital. Seven of the victims were either first or second cousins to each other. Three of the young scholars were evacuees from the London area. Only two children from Freckleton, Ruby Whittle and George Carey, escaped the infants' room holocaust. For years to come, the local school was missing an entire grade level.

The older children in the rooms north and south of the infants' room fared much better than the younger children. There were no deaths among the older students, though many escaped a fiery demise through almost miraculous intervention. Throughout the thunderstorm, the teachers distracted the older students from the sights and sounds of the storm by reviewing time's tables and reading poetry as well as prose. Though they were older than the students in the infants' room, the older boys and girls were still uneasy about the noise and darkness of this unusual summer storm.

Barbara Banks (now Hall) remembers her teacher, Mrs. Owens, telling the class not to be frightened by the storm. Suddenly, there was a loud noise and the students started to shout. Mrs. Owens, who was reading at the time, told the children to run out of the school. Barbara fled through the boy's cloakroom and turned left onto the playground. Classmate Jackie Cole was in front of Barbara and once on the playground they both ran off to the right. They saw flames in front of them and turned back and then ran out an open gate from the playground into the school yard. Jackie and Barbara were now trapped because the iron gate was locked and the wall surrounding the school yard was too high to scale.[14]

Fortunately for the girls, American servicemen from BAD2 had raced to the crash site and had climbed over the school yard wall. The men began to toss the children over the wall to servicemen who caught them on the other side. On the other side of the wall, Elsie Snape, the Banks' milk delivery person, held Barbara's hand until her grandmother arrived and took the almost seven-year-old to her house on School Lane. There she was reunited with her cousin Doreen who had also survived the fire. Barbara's grandfather wrapped the two wet, shivering children in towels and blankets while their grandmother went in search of her other three grandchildren. She was able to find two more but one her granddaughters, Sylvia Bickerstaffe, perished in the infants' room fire. Later that day, Barbara's mother took her home to 22 Bush Lane. The smell of burnt fuel, buildings, and flesh lingered in the summer air. Even today, six decades later, Barbara says, "I will never forget the smell in the air" on the walk home.[15] She has also never forgotten the two cousins she lost in the fire, Dorothy Sudell and Sylvia Bickerstaffe, and is thankful for her six cousins who survived the inferno.

Val Preston (now Whittle) was seven and half years old. Her mother had died five years before and her father and grandmother were raising Val and her younger brother George. Her brother was in the infants' school and Val was in the class above him. She remembers that there was "a loud crash and a brilliant flash of light and then the flames were visible across the school-yard."[16] She ran into an adjacent cloakroom on the opposite side of the class and escaped through a window. She recalls "jumping down into water which appeared to have lovely colors floating on the surface."[17] Later, Val realized that what she identified as water was really aviation fuel from the decimated Liberator. She then ran onto the field at the back of the school.

When she was safely in the school yard, Val recalls turning around to look at the infants' room where her brother George was in class and she saw "the gable and wall come crashing down. I remember also being upset because my coat was in the cloakroom there and I was going to have to leave it to burn."[18] Like Barbara Banks, Val was trapped in the school yard because of the high wall surrounding it. American servicemen hoisted Val over the wall and a local woman walked her to her house. In the comfort and warmth of her home, Val's grandmother told her the tragic news that her brother George would not be coming home. Val was less than eight years old and had already lost her mother and her baby brother.

Seven-year-old Joan Singleton (now Richardson) was in Mrs. Owens' class. The students had just received new pencils from her when there was a loud noise and a flash of light. Joan remembers that "suddenly there was chaos. We ran from the classroom into the boys' playground. I was unaware of what was exactly happening. In fact, I vividly recall one boy on his hands and knees picking up the dropped pencils."[19] Once on the playground, Joan followed the other children through the open gate onto the school field. Like others before her, the GIs from BAD2 lifted her over the six-foot wall into the waiting arms of safety on the other side of the barrier.

Once over the wall, Joan ran home. The wet, frightened child found no one in her house. Her neighbor, Mrs. Coulton, spotted Joan and brought her into her home. Mrs. Coulton dried off Joan and wrapped her in a blanket to keep her warm. Joan and her mother were quickly reunited and the comfort of her mother's arms brought a calm feeling to the panic-stricken child. That night, Joan thought she "was so fortunate to have been a seven-year-old and not a five-year-old."[20] It is a sentiment that continues to reverberate through her being every day of her life.

Alice Cutler had walked her younger cousin Annie Herrington to school that morning. After getting Annie situated in the infants' room, Alice waved goodbye to her cousin and went into the junior classroom. Alice had no way of knowing that this was the last time she would see little Annie. As the storm approached, Alice's teacher told the class to put their heads on their desks until the harsh weather passed by them. Alice remembers that "there was a terrific crash and I looked around to see flames shooting all over the place. I remember running through the cloakroom and could see what I believed were bodies lying on the floor and then got out of the school."[21] Like the students before her, she ran from the playground to the school yard where American personnel from BAD2 lifted her over the wall to safety. Alice's cousin Annie and another cousin, Georgina Lonsdale, perished in the infants' school inferno.

Margaret Mason was seven at the time of the crash. She remembers the moments before the demise of the *Classy Chassis II* as being "pitch black outside because of the storm."[22] She then recalls that "suddenly there was a big flash and everything went orange. We all tried to get out of the building and there were bits of fire dropping through [the roof] onto the floor in front of us."[23] Margaret finally reached the school yard where the Americans helped her over the wall. She ran to her aunt's house where she was eventually reunited with her father. For decades after the crash, she suffered from reoccurring nightmares about the catastrophic event. Like so many of the children who survived the tragedy, she "still shudders when there's a very bad storm and torrential rain."[24]

Seven-year-old Nellie Sudell (now Hankinson) walked to school with her five-year-old sister Dorothy. Nellie left Dorothy at the infants' room and proceeded to join her class. During the storm, she heard an explosion and could see flames outside. She recalls that she eventually left the school and "my father found me. He must have realized that there was no hope as far as my sister was concerned. He was crying, of course. I had never seen a man cry before. It broke my mother's heart; there was nothing else you could say."[25]

Ellen Cavalier, age 9, and Patricia Grafton, age 7, were evacuees from London. Ellen was in a classroom adjoining the infants' room when the B-24 crashed and ignited the school on fire. She recalled that "there was a crash and bricks fell all over and fire burst out very quickly. I dashed along the corridor out of the back door of the school and over the fields to home. Fire seemed to be all over."[26] Patricia Grafton raced out the rear entrance of the school. As she made her sprint to safety, a burning beam fell around her while bricks from the collapsing chimney, narrowly missed her slight frame. Grafton, like Cavalier, ran to her home near the school. Both young girls had left London to escape the bombs and rockets of the German war machine. Quiet, friendly Freckleton provided them with an oasis of peace in the desert of war. When they went to school on the morning of August 23, Ellen and Patricia could hardly imagine that the war would come to Freckleton and they would narrowly escape the clutches of death in a fiery inferno that once was their school.

Nine-year-old Harry Latham was an evacuee from Salford, England. He was in Mrs. Rawcliffe's class located at the end of the school. The storm frightened a number of students in the class so Mrs. Rawcliffe began to tell them a story. Though Mrs. Rawcliffe encouraged the students to remain calm through the storm, Latham remembers having a premonition that something was going to happen.[27] He recalled that "suddenly there was a huge flash, an orange flame and the crashing of glass with an explosion like a fireball. It seemed like everything was on fire."[28] Latham made his way through the classroom to the boys' cloakroom but found the doors to the playground bolted shut. With the help of other classmates, the students eventually forced the doors open only to find a sea of burning aviation fuel. Unsure of the cause of the fire, Latham and some of the students headed for the two air raid shelters located on the playing fields.[29]

After a short period of time, Latham and the other students emerged from the bomb shelters to find American servicemen helping children over the school yard wall to safety. He also saw fire brigades extinguishing the flames and desperately searching the rubble for survivors. Latham returned home and expected to be reprimanded for losing his coat in the fire. Instead, he found more than 60 children taking shelter there because their routes home had been blocked by the fire.[30] He recalls that "parents who had lost children were inquiring whether their boy or girl was there, that was very sad."[31] Latham's vague premonition became a vivid, tragic reality that continues to shape the ethos of Freckleton to the present day.

On the morning of August 23, Elsie Barlow (now Dollin) did not attend Holy Trinity School. That day her mother was taking her to Preston to enroll her in Smarts College to learn typing, bookkeeping, and shorthand. Her younger sister Renee, however, went off to school as usual. Elsie was helping her mother with chores when the thunderstorm arrived in Freckleton. At approximately 10:50 a.m., Elsie and her mother saw a neighborhood boy, Colin Clifton, running through the street shouting, "The school is on fire!"[32]

Elsie and her mother bolted from their house and ran to Holy Trinity School. They saw the school in flames and the wreckage from the B-24. The two frantically searched the area for Renee. After a half-hour of gut-wrenching anxiety, Elsie and her mother finally found Renee safe and in the company of Sergeant Frank Guercioni from BAD2. Renee and the rest of the Barlow family were well acquainted with Guercioni because his wife and infant son lived with them. Guercioni had run to the village when he received news of the crash and was one of the servicemen aiding in the rescue of students from the school yard. Unfortunately for Elsie, her two four-year-old cousins, Judith Garner and Georgina Lonsdale, did not escape the infants' room inferno.

The crash of the *Classy Chassis II* devastated Holy Trinity School and completely obliterated the infants' wing. Of the 61 people killed in the air disaster, 40 (65.5 percent) died in the school. Nearly 21.5 percent of the students present that morning perished in the catastrophe. All of the deaths at the school occurred in the infants' wing. Ninety-three percent of the students and teachers in the infants' rooms died as a result of the fire. Only 3 students (7 percent) survived the crash and they were all severely burned from the flames.

The B-24 also completely demolished the Sad Sack Café on the other side of Lytham Road from Holy Trinity School. The fireball that consumed the snack bar killed 18 people, including seven civilians, four R.A.F. airmen, and seven servicemen from BAD2. The 18 deaths in the café comprised 29.5 percent of the individuals killed in the air disaster. Ninety percent of the patrons in the Sad Sack were consumed in the flames while only two badly burned R.A.F. airmen escaped the deadly inferno.

Allan and Rachael Whittle owned the Sad Sack Café and they lived there with their 15-year-old daughter Pearl. The café was in a converted garage on Lytham Road. The snack bar was a popular respite for R.A.F. airmen stationed in Kirkham and the personnel of BAD2. The BAD2 GIs named the eatery after a popular American comic strip character called Sad Sack. Sergeant George Baker was the artist who created Sad Sack. Baker was born and raised in Lowell, Massachusetts. After graduating from high school, he worked as an artist in a commercial art house drawing advertisements for newspapers. In 1937, Baker went to Hollywood to work for Walt Disney. He

The landing gear of the *Classy Chassis II* ended up near the bus shelter at the junction of Preston and Kirkham roads. Crews from BAD2 used heavy equipment through the night to remove wreckage and debris from local roads (courtesy of BAe Systems Heritage Division).

helped to animate motion pictures such as *Pinocchio, Fantasia, Dumbo,* and *Bambi.* In June 1941, Baker was inducted into the army. He spent most of his evenings drawing cartoons of the army life he was experiencing as a soldier. The Sad Sack character represented the bewildered, confused, inept civilian trying to adjust to military life. *Yank,* an army newspaper, first published Baker's cartoons in 1942 and Sad Sack quickly became a popular character among America's citizen soldiers. Most of the men stationed at BAD2 could identify with the trials and tribulations of Sad Sack.

The Sad Sack Café was a home away from home for both American and British servicemen. It was a place one could go to get away from the everyday drudgery of base life and the less than tasty morsels served up at the mess hall. The café provided the opportunity for British and Americans to communicate with each other and break down mutual stereotypes. More than anything else, the Sad Sack Café provided the young men of BAD2 a place to just hang out.

There was only a small contingent of customers inside the Sad Sack at 10:45 a.m. on August 23. The rain kept many British and American servicemen from making the trek from their bases to the Freckleton eatery. The Whittles, and their small staff of three, were in the process of serving breakfast, coffee and tea to their ten patrons, including two R.A.F. airmen, one local, and seven GIs from Warton. One of the R.A.F. servicemen, Sergeant Walter Cannell, was a regular at the snack bar. The 20-year-old sergeant pilot had just written a letter to his parents stating that "there is this little café near here which sells lovely breakfasts. I often stay in bed and miss breakfast then get up and scrounge off after parade and go there."[33]

R.A.F. sergeant Bill Bone and his three service buddies, Ray Brooke, Robert Bell, and Douglas Batson, walked into Freckleton from their R.A.F. camp on Kirkham Road. When the rain grew torrential in nature, the four British airmen ducked into the Sad Sack Café for a cup of tea. Just as the men approached the counter for service, the *Classy Chassis II*'s main wheel and tail turret slammed into the building and the café immediately erupted into flames. Ray Cox, the BAD2 servicemen waiting for a bus to Preston across the street, heard the roar of the B-24's engines and saw a flash of orange as the bomber hit the snack bar.

Sergeant Bill Bone recalls that as he approached the counter for service "that was it. I found myself completely in the open, no building. The skin from my hands was hanging down from the nails. Ray and I progressed from the area by the grace of God."[34] Two American servicemen from BAD2 noticed Bone and loaded him into a truck that then sped off to the base hospital in Warton. Bone later stated that the "young man who found me must have been truly shocked but held on and he has been my hero ever since. I would not have made it otherwise."[35]

The young American who helped Bone probably was Morton T. Kitchen. Warrant Officer Gerald Andrews and Kitchen were headed for Freckleton in a truck at approximately 10:45 a.m. that morning. They had just passed through the gate at Site 10 when they saw a fire ahead on Lytham Road. Kitchen, the driver, parked the truck and the two men rushed to the blaze with fire extinguishers in hand. They saw a R.A.F. airmen trying to crawl away from the burning wreckage. Kitchen and Andrews pulled him to safety. Andrews went to a nearby phone booth and notified the operator about the crash. Kitchen flagged down another truck and the two men loaded the injured British airman into the vehicle. Kitchen held the British service-man in his arms to prevent any additional injury while the truck sped to the base hospital. Andrews remained at the scene of the crash and continued to fight the blaze as well as to help with the evacuation of the older children from the school yard.[36]

At the hospital, orderlies placed Bone on a stretcher. A chaplain administered last rights to him as he awaited treatment. Bone was not only severely burned on his face and hands; he also suffered a broken right arm and right leg in the explosion. The Americans also rescued Ray Brooke from the rubble of the café. Brooke had suffered severe burns to his face, arms and thighs.

For several days, the two men's grip on life was tenuous. Bone actually remembers "looking down a long black tunnel and seeing light at the end."[37] Both men survived their injuries. Over the next five years, Brooke endured almost 50 operations while Bone went through 15 surgeries on the road to recovery. Of the 20 individuals in the Sad Sack Café at the time of the crash, only Bone and Brooke survived to tell their stories.

The fireball at the Sad Sack claimed 18 lives in an instant. The fire killed Allan Whittle, his wife Rachael, and their 15-year-old daughter Pearl, who was home on a school holiday. Pearl was a student at the Queen Mary School in Lytham and was helping her parents at the snack bar the morning of the crash. Three staff members, Kathleen Forshaw, Gwendolyn Franken, and Evelyn Rhodes, along with a local customer, 15-year-old James Victor Silcock, also perished in the flames. Silcock was an employee at the Lytham–St. Anne's Electricity Depot that was adjacent to the snack bar. Four R.A.F airmen enjoying their breakfast never made it back to their camp on Kirkham Road. The dead airmen included Sergeant Walter Cannell, the young man who was a frequent patron of the café; Bone's and Brooke's two friends, Sergeants Douglas Baston and Robert Bell, both 20 years old; and Sergeant Eric Newton, 23, of South Norwood, Surrey.

Seven American servicemen stationed at BAD2 also died in the destruction of the Sad Sack Café. Private George Brown, 35, was from Pennsylvania. He worked as a truck driver before entering the service in January 1942. Brown was assigned to the maintenance division at Warton. Rescuers pulled Brown alive from the rubble of the café but he succumbed to his injuries a week later at the base hospital. Corporal Herbert Cross hailed from Bristol, Tennessee. He was a high school graduate and attended college for three years. Cross enlisted in February 1942 and worked in the maintenance division. Private Minas P. Glitis, 38, was born in Egypt. He moved to New York City in the 1930s and worked as a tailor. He was not a citizen of the United States when he enlisted in the army in November 1942. He was a man of slight build standing 5'1" and weighing 118 pounds. Glitis was a member of the station complement squadron at BAD2. Private Samuel Mezzacappa, 35, was from Staten Island, New York. His mother and father immigrated to the United States from Italy. Mezzacappa was the middle child and had six siblings. He was single and enlisted in the military in March 1941. Mezzacappa served in the station complement squadron with Private Glitas.

Sergeant Theodore Nelson, Corporal Arthur J. Rogney, and Sergeant Frank Zugel were also killed while eating at the snack bar. Nelson was from Seattle, Washington. He had attended college for a year and then dropped out to work as a statistical clerk for a Seattle company. He was married to his wife Dorothy and they had no children at the time of his death. He enlisted in the service in October 1942 and was assigned to the maintenance division. Rogney, 26, was from Kent, Michigan. His father was a foreman and his mother, who emigrated from Germany, was a nurse. Rogney was the oldest of two children and a high school graduate. He was single and enlisted in the military in January 1943. At BAD2, he worked in the maintenance division. Zugel, 28, was from Joliet Township, Illinois. He was the fifth child of Martin and Johanna Zugel. He attended one year of high school and enlisted in July 1942. Like most of the Americans killed at the snack bar, Zugel worked in the maintenance division.

Rescue operations commenced immediately after the *Classy Chassis II* slammed into the village. At first the operations were serendipity as villagers and BAD2 personnel rushed to the crash scene. Within ten minutes the rescue activities became more organized and systematic with the arrival of the National Fire Service and the BAD2 Fire Fighting Platoon. One of the first individuals on the scene was a local police officer, Robert Nelson. He was at his home in the police station at the time of the crash repairing a chair when the phone rang. On the line was a constable from the Kirkham police station. The constable instructed Nelson to "come down here right away, there's a plane on the school."[38] Nelson put on his uniform coat and rushed toward Holy Trinity School. As Nelson approached the school, he could see the flames from the wreckage cascading down Lytham Road. When he turned away from the fire, he saw his wife Doris who had followed him to the school. Nelson told his wife that it was too dangerous for her and to return home. Years later, Doris Nelson recalled her thoughts when she saw the plane wreckage and the school on fire: "They teach us about Heaven and Hell, this must be Hell."[39] The intense heat of that hell kept rescuers from getting too close to the devastated buildings.

Instead of going home, Doris Nelson went to the Methodist Church. Village authorities had previously designated the church as an emergency center if there was ever a catastrophe in Freckleton. When she reached the church, the door was locked and no one had the key. The small group that assembled at the church decided to force the door open. Once inside, Nelson and others began to turn the house of worship into a rescue shelter.

Robert Nelson joined Deputy Head Warden Durant, whose daughter was in the school, and Section Leader Hunt of the National Fire Service in coordinating rescue efforts. Hunt's main problem was that the debris from the B-24 and the demolished buildings blocked the main water supply necessary to fight the fire. In a herculean effort, 50 GIs from BAD2 lifted a trailer pump and carried it over the debris and down Lytham Road to the Balderstone Mill.[40] The men hooked the pump into the water supply at the mill and efforts to battle the flames commenced in earnest. The firefighters were then able to run hoses to the rear of the school and put the fire under control. Durant later found out that his daughter Pattie had escaped from the school unharmed.

Battling the flames that morning was a 21-year-old firewomen from Preston, Irene Woods (now Cottam). She had joined the National Fire Service in 1940 and the Service trained her in all aspects of firefighting. Her assignment was to drive the petrol (gasoline) truck and distribute the fuel to the firemen. The firefighters used the petrol to operate the fire engine pumps necessary to douse the flames with water. Woods' truck was an old furniture van filled with gasoline cans. Once at a fire, Woods would park the truck and schlep the gasoline cans to the various engine companies.

On the morning of the crash, Woods drove her truck to Freckleton and parked it opposite of the Plough Hotel on Kirkham Road. Throughout the late morning, she continued to carry gasoline cans from her truck to the engine pumps. Woods not only recalls the horror and devastation she witnessed on Lytham Road, she also saw the irony in her task. She claims to be "the only woman allowed to take petrol to a fire legally."[41]

Edna Lonsdale heard the sound of the crash and saw a flash when the B-24 ignited into a fireball. She alerted her husband, who was a member of the National Fire Service, and the couple ran up Lytham Road together. Along the way, the two were joined by Edna's sister, Anne Herrington. When they reached the news agent's shop, Joe Hoskins, a shoemaker, informed them that Holy Trinity School was on fire.[42] Mr. Lonsdale hustled to join the other members of the National Fire Service who had gathered at the scene of the crash. Edna and Anne worked their way to the rear of the school through the churchyard. At the rear of the school, Jane Garner joined her sisters, Edna

American servicemen continued to hose down the smoldering ruins throughout the afternoon and evening of August 23. The deadly crash eventually claimed 61 lives including the three crew members in the *Classy Chassis II*, 18 people in the Sad Sack Café, and 40 students and teachers at Holy Trinity School. The Freckleton air disaster was the largest accidental air catastrophe the Allies suffered during World War II (photograph courtesy of BAe Systems Heritage Division).

and Anne. All three sisters had daughters in the infants' school. As they stared at the fire-ravaged structure, they observed that the plane had completely demolished the infants' wing of the school. Their thoughts turned to deepest despair when they realized that their children lay trapped beneath the flaming rubble. In the afternoon, a policeman visited the Lonsdale home and confirmed the sisters' worst suspicions, all three girls, Georgina Lonsdale, Annie Herrington, and Judy Garner had died in the fire. The policemen brought scraps of material cut from Georgina's and Judy's dresses for the mothers to confirm the identities of their children.[43]

Once the fire was under control, the search for survivors buried in the rubble began. Hundreds of Americans and villagers sifted through the debris with their hands or rudimentary implements. Sergeant Dodson, stationed at BAD2, told his son James decades after the war had ended that he heard a "big roar overhead followed by an explosion. I was one of the first to reach the school. God, what a sight. Burning fuel was running down the street. I remember pulling away pieces of plane, bricks, and mortar and all those precious little kids inside, buried alive."[44] Sergeant Stinger, like Dodson, searched the smoldering debris and with the help of Headmaster Billington carried Ruby Whittle to safety.

Later in the day, the operation switched from search and rescue to recovery. The Americans brought in bulldozers, cranes, and other heavy equipment to remove the debris of the burned buildings and the wreckage of the plane. When darkness fell on Freckleton, American servicemen brought in searchlights so they could continue to work through the night. The men removed sections of the B-24 and transported them back to the salvage yard of BAD2. Some of the wreckage was still smoldering and when a crane attempted to lift a nacelle (a cover housing holding an engine or other equipment to an airplane) onto a flat-bed truck, flames erupted from it shooting a fiery funnel 20 feet into the air.[45] As August 23 slowly drifted into August 24, the rescue and salvage workers found no more survivors or bodies. By the morning of August 24, American and British workers had cleared a majority of the rubble from Lytham Road and traffic proceeded at an almost normal pace. Life in the village, however, did not.

After the crash, ambulances and jeeps removed the wounded from the accident scene to the hospital at BAD2. All off-duty personnel reported to the hospital and worked around the clock until the evening of August 24. The hospital staff moved all of the regular patients, many suffering with contagious diseases, to the newly constructed wards of the facility so that the newly arrived accident victims would not be exposed to them.[46] The most severely burned victims came from the infants' school (students Maureen Clarke, Beryl Hogarth, Alice Rayton, Joseph Threlfall, David Madden, Ruby Whittle and George Carey and as well as their two teachers, Jennie Hall and Louisa Hulme) and the Sad Sack Café (R.A.F. airmen Walter Cannell, Robert Bell, Bill Bone, Douglas Batson, and Ray Brooke as well as U.S. serviceman George Brown). Only five of the 15 most severely burned patients (Bone, Brooke, Carey, Madden and Whittle) survived their injuries. Alice Rayton, age 4, was the first to die shortly after admission to the hospital on August 23. Maureen Clarke was the last victim of the air disaster when she passed away on September 4.

The hospital staff turned some of the offices in the hospital building into temporary morgues. Badly burned and unidentified bodies laid on gurneys waiting to be claimed by grieving relatives. Orderlies brought the bodies of the crew of the *Classy Chassis II* (Jimmie Parr, John Bloemendal, and Gordon Kinney) into the offices to be identified by base personnel. Pilot John Bloemendal was identified by the remnants of his dog tags and by his wedding ring. Bloemendal was the only married member of the crew of the ill-fated B-24 bomber.[47]

The storage room at the Coach and Horses public house also served as a temporary morgue for many of the children killed at Holy Trinity School. The children were laid out under linen sheets and awaited identification by next of kin. In a newspaper article years later, Policeman Nelson recalled that "after they had identified their children, overcome with grief, many of the mothers collapsed and had to be carried home."[48] Nelson knew all of the children personally and cut locks of hair from some of the children's heads to give to their parents. Robert Nelson never forgot this experience and carried the image of the deceased innocents with him until his death.

The British and the Americans responded quickly and effectively to the catastrophe. Without the heroic actions of hundreds of men and women the death toll could have been much higher than 61 people. The British press praised the selfless valor of the Americans involved in the rescue work. On August 25, an article in the *Lytham–St. Anne's Express* stated:

> Great work was done by a large number of American soldiers. They came with cranes, lorries, bulldozers, ambulances, and fire-fighting appliances and set to work with typical American hustle to clear the debris in the effort to save any who were trapped. With bare hands, many of them moved hot material from the smoldering ruins which their stretcher parties entered to remove the bodies.[49]

The BAD2 Historical Report for August 1944 also credited the American servicemen with a quick and determined response. The report read: "many members of this unit performed heroic service in rescuing and treating victims of the tragedy."[50] The report continued: "Enlisted men on the scene immediately went into action aiding occupants in their escape from the buildings and in extinguishing the flames. The Station Hospital was opened to military and civilian personnel with medics working untiringly until all victims had been removed to the hospital and treated."[51] The horror of war had arrived in Freckleton with a sudden fury and the GIs at BAD2 responded with courage and valor.

The death toll of the B-24 crash eventually reached 61 souls. Thirty-eight students, two teachers, seven civilians, four R.A.F. airmen, and ten members of the Mighty Eighth died as a result of the crash. Four of the deceased were evacuees who had left their homes for the safety of Freckleton. It was the worst civilian air disaster suffered by the Allies in World War II and remained one of the most devastating air disasters until air passenger travel became popular in the 1950s and 1960s. The catastrophe wiped out nearly all of the children in the four- to six-year age range in the village of Freckleton. BAD2 was also deeply affected by the tragedy. Ten airmen stationed at the base had died. Almost one-third of the 29 deaths that occurred at the Warton base during the war happened on August 23. The Americans also shared the grief of the Freckleton families who had lost their most prized and precious possessions in the crash, their children.

The people of Freckleton and their American neighbors never forgot the events that transpired on August 23. They were now bound together by love, sorrow, tragedy and loss. Together they had fought the inferno, rescued the living and recovered the dead. In the next few days, that bond grew tighter as together they mourned their losses and buried their dead.

7

The Interment of the Innocents

"You knew the nature of war; you were prepared mentally for the fact that you were going to lose comrades. But none of us even considered that five year-old children could get killed. That's something you never forget."

—Sergeant Ralph Scott, member
of the BAD2 honor guard

The morning of August 24 confirmed that the nightmarish events of August 23 were not part of a horrific dream. The charred debris of several buildings, including the Sad Sack Café and the Holy Trinity School, were cruel reminders of the damage wrought by the crash of the B-24 into the village. Thirty-four families grieved the loss of their children, while seven more families devoutly prayed that their little ones would recover from their burns. The servicemen of BAD2, who had battled the raging inferno and led many children to safety, now felt the crushing reality of the catastrophe and the loss of several of their comrades. The Sad Sack Café, and its well liked owners and staff, were now just fond and tragic memories to the patrons who had frequented the establishment. For both American and British families there would forever be a vacant chair at the dining room table and only the memories of a lost loved one to embrace with their hearts. There are times when reality can appear to be unrealistic.

Through the night of August 23 and into the morning of August 24, American and British workers, employing searchlights and heavy equipment, removed the rubble from the Lytham Road area. The official BAD2 news entry for August 24, 1944, was succinct. It stated: "Major amount of debris cleared and traffic proceeds along at an almost normal pace. No reports of new deaths."[1] The report is inaccurate. Though workers at the crash site found no more bodies, R.A.F. Sergeant Pilot Walter William Cannell died of his burns in the Warton base hospital. Sergeant Cannell, 20, son of John and Eva Cannell of Port St. Mary, was enjoying his breakfast in the Sad Sack Café at the time of the crash. American GIs rescued him from the debris and brought him to the base hospital. He was the last of the four British airmen to die from their burns in the café inferno. One of the airmen was pronounced dead at the scene of the fire. Robert Bell and Douglas Batson, the two friends of Bone and Brooke, died earlier in the day on August 24.

At the base hospital, Head Surgeon Major Sharpley and Chief Nurse Nell Russell attended to the burn victims. Nell Russell was one of 6,500 women in the U.S.A.A.F. nursing corps. Before the United States entered World War II, Russell volunteered to go to England with an American hospital group to care for wounded British soldiers. After the Japanese attack on Pearl Harbor, she transferred to the United States Army Medical Corps. When the base hospital opened at Warton, the Army Medical Corps assigned her to BAD2 as the head nurse because of her previous experience of treating British soldiers. She was not only a skilled nurse but also a warmhearted and caring person.[2] On August 24, she was in charge of attending to the burn victims the hospital received the previous day.

Hospital personnel had ten burn victims to care for on August 24. Dr. Sharpley, Head Nurse Russell and nurses Rita Ryan and Jane Chestnutwood had six children, two R.A.F. airmen, one American GI and teacher Louisa Hulme under their care and supervision. Ruby Whittle, rescued from the infants' school by Headmaster Billington and Sergeant Stinger, was burned over most of her arms and legs. She remembers that "my arms and legs were in splints, I looked like a mummy. I was bandaged head to foot and had to sit with my arms out straight because of all the burns."[3] Dr. Sharply told Ruby that goblins inhabited the canisters that contained her bandages and medications. He instructed Ruby to keep a watchful eye on the canisters and to immediately inform him if any of the goblins escaped into the room. Through the use of this ploy, Sharpley was able to distract Ruby from the painful changing of her dressings.

David Madden, rescued from the infants' school, had badly burned legs. His first recollection in the hospital was of "a stern, older nurse" (probably Nell Russell) attending to him.[4] George Carey, another survivor of the infants' school blaze, has little memory of his first days in the hospital. He was heavily sedated because of his severe burns. Rescuers said that when they carried George out of the burning school all of his clothes had been burned off of him except the clogs on his feet.[5] Neither Sergeant Bone or Sergeant Brooke of the R.A.F. have any distinct memories of their first day in the hospital other than Bone remembering that he received the last rites and that he saw a light at the end of a dark tunnel.

British and American newspapers broke the story of the Freckleton disaster on the morning of August 24. Subscribers of *The Times* of London read about the liberation of Paris, the Soviet advance in the Ukraine, the sinking of eight German ships between Brest and Lorient as well as the Allied advance across the Falaise gap. The news from the frontlines seemed to be positive and ultimate victory over Germany within the grasp of the Allies. The headline on page two of *The Times*, however, put a damper on the jubilant stories of success emanating from the battle front. The bold print banner, "Aircraft Crash on School—35 Children Killed in Fire," quickly sobered giddy readers and put the war back into perspective.[6]

The article described the crash of the B-24 into Holy Trinity School and the Sad Sack Café. The author stated that there were 54 known fatalities at the time (an accurate count) and estimated that 30 to 40 more people might be trapped or dead in the debris of the café. The author based his estimate on the usual number of customers in the snack bar. Mercifully, the bad weather had kept patronage down on the morning of August 23. The article contained eyewitness accounts of the plane crash and the older children's escape from the school. The author conveyed the gruesome nature of the crash scene to his readers by describing the remains of some of the victims. The author wrote: "one body recovered late yesterday was so badly charred that sex could not be determined. The severe burns have hampered the task of identifying the bodies, which will be continued today."[7] The article captured in prose the heart-wrenching sight of how "mothers rushed to the scene and waited in silent, tragic groups as the victims were brought out."[8] The article did not blame the Americans for the accident but continued a trend started the day before by British rescue workers and the families of the victims who praised the American soldiers for "doing splendid rescue work."[9]

The day after the crash, *The New York Times* ran a story about the Freckleton air disaster on page eight. The inaccurate headline read: "76, Including 51 Children, Killed As U.S. Plane Hits English School." The wire service story out of London was mainly based on the account published the same day in *The Times*. The author of the wire service story, however, took the liberty of adding some of the estimated dead to the confirmed total. *The New York Times* story also included the official statement about the accident from the Headquarters of the United States Strategic Air Forces. The statement read: "A B-24 Liberator bomber on a local flight was caught suddenly in a violent thunderstorm. The pilot and two enlisted men were killed. A school and snack bar were struck."[10] Like *The Times*, *The New York Times* article offered kudos to the servicemen at BAD2. The article stated that "villagers praised highly a score of American soldiers, who rushed into the flames and carried out trapped children, wrapped them in army blankets and gave aid to the injured."[11]

On August 25, the crash claimed three more victims as the death toll rose to 59. Miss Louisa Hulme, 64, an infant school teacher, was set to retire the following week. She was an evacuee from Salford and taught at Holy Trinity School since her arrival in Freckleton. Jacky Nichol remembered seeing Miss Hulme engulfed in flames right after the crash. Rescuers pulled her from the debris of the school and rushed her to the base hospital where she received treatment for her severe burns until she died on August 25. Two children from the infants' school also passed away the same day. Joseph Threlfall, age 5, son of Christopher and Jessie Threlfall of Bush Lane, and Beryl Hogarth, age 6, daughter of William and Annie Hogarth of Kirkham Road, both succumbed to their burns.

The Times carried a follow-up story about the Freckleton air disaster on August 25 on page two. This article was only one-third of the length of the original story. The author of the article informed readers that rescuers had thoroughly searched the rubble of the demolished buildings and no longer held out hope of finding any survivors. The author also told readers that Jennie Hall died on the night of August 23 and that three young evacuees from London, John Cox (5), Sylvia Whybrow (5), and Martin Alston (4) perished in the school fire. The article reported that the official coroner's inquest would open on August 25 and that the funeral for the children killed in the crash would take place on August 26. *The Times* also reported to its readers that "United States military authorities have announced their desire to defray the funeral expenses, including the cost of the coffins. It is expected that the children will be buried in a communal grave."[12]

A short, three-paragraph article appeared on page 8 of *The New York Times* on August 26. It was an abbreviated version of the article appearing in *The Times* the previous day. The newspaper corrected its earlier stated death toll of 76 and accurately placed the number at 59 on August 25. *The New York Times* reported that "a mass burial for the children will be held in the village churchyard tomorrow."[13] It is curious that *The New York Times* version did not mention the upcoming inquest or that the United States military was going to cover the expenses of the funeral. Two days after one of the worst air accidents in history, *The New York Times* viewed the story as one of minor interest to its readership.

An article in the *Lytham–St. Anne's Express* on August 25 stated the funeral arrangements were set for the afternoon of August 26 and the "entire expenses will be met by the American authorities."[14] The burial of the children would be in a communal grave and if the "parents wanted a private grave, they will be free to make the required arrangement."[15]

The coroner's inquest began on August 25 in the Methodist Church Hall. Under British law, a coroner's inquest must be convened when a death is violent or unnatural. The coroner's role in the inquest is to identify who the deceased were, when they died, and by what means as well as in what circumstances they came by their death. The coroner has legal custody of the body of the deceased until he or she releases the body for final disposition. Once the coroner has taken the steps to identify the body and establish the cause of death, the coroner can release the body for burial or cremation. The coroner may make recommendations about how similar deaths may be avoided in the future but the recommendations are not legally binding on the involved parties. The coroner may not attribute a finding of civil liability to any individual, organization or company.[16]

Deputy Coroner L.A. Ashton opened the inquest proceedings and abruptly suspended them when he received word of the deaths of two more victims, Miss Hulme and student Beryl Hogarth. The opening of the hearing and temporary adjournment did, however, clear the way for the funeral of the children the next day.

The deputy coroner reconvened the inquest at the Kirkham Police Station on September 8. The inquest dealt with the identification and manner of deaths of the 51 British citizens killed in the air crash but did not include the ten Americans who also died in the disaster. It was left to the U.S.A.A.F. to investigate and inquire into the reasons for their demise. Relatives identified most of the dead to the coroner by providing answers to Mr. Ashton's questions or providing remnants of their beloved one's clothing. In the case of six of the deceased school children, there was no physical evidence to confirm their deaths. In each of these cases, Mr. Billington, Headmaster of Holy Trinity School, provided the morning roll call report for the coroner. The roll call report confirmed that Miss Hall and Miss Hulme had marked each of the missing students as present on the morning of August 23.[17]

At the close of the inquest, Deputy Coroner Ashton recorded a verdict of "death by misadventure" for each of the victims.[18] Death by misadventure is not technically the same as accidental death, though today British authorities treat both statistically in the same manner. Accidental death is defined as something over which there is no human control such as a tree falling on a moving car in a storm and killing the driver. A verdict of misadventure suggests a lawful human act that takes an unexpected turn and leads to death.

To return a verdict of misadventure, the coroner must be satisfied about the balance of probabilities that death occurred as a result of unexpected events and complications. Ashton recorded a verdict of misadventure in all 51 cases because a sudden and violent thunderstorm brought down a lawful flight of a B-24 from BAD2. The crew of the plane had no intent of harming the citizens of Freckleton. Some witnesses at the inquest also suggested that lightning struck the *Classy Chassis II*.[19]

The communal funeral service was set for the afternoon of August 26. The American military provided the coffins for the deceased and covered other final expenses. The GIs dug the communal grave in the Holy Trinity Church cemetery. Personnel from BAD2 also served as the honor guard for the funeral procession and as pall bearers for the children's coffins. The funeral itself consisted of a procession, services in Holy Trinity Church, and burial in the church's cemetery.

Two nights before the funeral, officers at BAD2 picked the men who would serve in the honor guard and act as pall bearers. Four servicemen stationed at Warton requested to carry the coffins of two children they had befriended in the village. Sergeant Ralph Scott was among the GIs chosen to form an honor guard that would line the path from the street to the grave. Officers selected Tom Miller to be a pall bearer. Miller does not recall why he was chosen for the honor but believes that one of the reasons was because he worked the night shift and had no obligations on the base during the day of August 26.[20] Miller was honored to be chosen as a pall bearer and he read the list of names of the children who died in the disaster to his friend, Cliff Leggett. As Miller read the list to Leggett, Tom paused at one name, Sonia Dagger. He became entranced with the name Sonia and asked Leggett if he also liked the name. The two men agreed that Sonia was a beautiful name and Miller continued to read the list.[21]

Two services were scheduled for the afternoon of August 26. The first service at 2:30 p.m. was for the children who died in the fire and their teacher, Jennie Hall. The second service at 3:30 p.m. was for the Whittles, owners of the Sad Sack Café, their daughter and the other civilians who perished at the snack bar. The coffins of the children were in the school playground. Identical wreaths of flowers adorned each of the little caskets and covered a plate that contained the name of the child in the coffin. BAD2 officials assigned two servicemen as pall bearers to carry each coffin. The exception to the rule was Warrant Officer Painter Alexander. He stood 6'8" tall and there was no other servicemen of similar height to pair with him. He, alone, bore the weight of Judy Garner's coffin in the procession.

The procession of caskets began at the burned-out school and proceeded to Holy Trinity Church. Grieving relatives and mourning neighbors lined the route five to six people deep. Doris Catlow (now Gardiner) was at the head of the procession.[22] She had come to Freckleton in 1939 after receiving training at St. Katherine's College in Liverpool. She had taught at the Holy Trinity Infants' School with Miss Hulme. She had left the school a few days before to take a position at a different institution. When her fiancée, who was serving in Burma with the R.A.F., heard about the catastrophe in Freckleton, he believed that Doris had perished in the fire.[23] Only later did he learn that she had not been at the school on the day of the crash. Throughout her entire life, Doris Catlow Gardiner never forgot the students who died in the fire or Jennie Hall, the teacher who took her place on that tragic day.

The communal funeral service took place on the afternoon of August 26, 1944. The U.S.A.A.F. assigned two servicemen to carry each of the children's caskets. The lone exception was Warrant Officer Painter Alexander. He stood 6' 8" tall and there was no other serviceman of a similar height to pair with him. Alexander, alone, carried the coffin of Judy Garner and later married her mother (photograph courtesy of BAe Systems Heritage Division).

The line of caskets processed by buildings damaged in the crash of the *Classy Chassis II*. Thousands of mourners, five to six people deep, lined the procession route to pay their last respects to the victims. Identical wreaths of flowers adorned each of the little caskets and covered a brass plate that bore the name of the child in the coffin (photograph courtesy of BAe Systems Heritage Division).

Many of the children who escaped the burning school were too trauma-tized to attend the funeral of their siblings, cousins, and friends. Most parents kept their children away from the funeral so they would not flashback to the recent events still so vivid in their active, young minds. Val Preston escaped physically unharmed from the fire but she lost her brother George in the inferno at the infants' wing. She remembers her father and grandmother send-ing her away during the time of the inquest and funeral. She recalls: "I was taken to the Isle of Man (an island halfway between Lancashire and Ireland) for a few days by our next door neighbors who were on holiday there. When I returned home, the funeral had taken place."[24] Margaret Mason, another survivor of the crash, remembers that her parents would not allow her to attend the funeral. Mason recalls that "none of the children were allowed to go to the funeral."[25] Her statement is not completely accurate. Photos of the funeral procession reveal a small number of children present at the solemn occasion.

The procession of coffins wound its way to the entrance of Holy Trinity Church. The structure was too small to fit all the caskets and mourners. American servicemen brought only the coffins of Miss Hall and one child into the church. The name of the child remained anonymous and served as a symbolic remembrance of all the members of the infants' class that died in the inferno. Since the seating capacity of the church was only 250 people, only immediate family and important dignitaries were allowed inside for the liturgical service. The Reverend J.W. Broadbent, vicar of the parish, conducted the service. He was assisted by the Reverend Knies, a chaplain from BAD2, and several local Methodist ministers. Dr. W.M. Askwith, Episcopal Bishop of Blackburn, delivered the homily. In his remarks, Bishop Askwith told the congregation that they had the condolences and sympathy of the entire country. He stated: "You are in their thoughts and prayers and they are trying to surround you with their loving comfort."[26] He also hoped that the families of the victims would not blame the calamity on God. He suggested that tragedies of this nature were the result of the free will of humans and not the result of a directive from God.[27]

Bishop Askwith expressed a similar sentiment in a personal letter he wrote to Mrs. Edna Lonsdale on September 6, 1944. Mrs. Lonsdale lost her eldest daughter Georgina in the tragedy. In his letter, Bishop Askwith wrote: "I am not going to ask you to believe that what happened was the will of God. God did not do it, and God did not will it. It is one of the tragedies that have happened through war and war is man's work, not God's."[28]

There were several moving eulogies and tributes to the children and their teachers. The congregation sang hymns such as "Loving Shepherd of Thy Sheep" and "Jesus Lives."[29] General Isaac W. Ott, the commanding officer of the Air Depot Area for the European theater of operations, represented the U.S.A.A.F. at the funeral. General "Hap" Arnold, commander of the U.S.A.A.F., was distraught and saddened by the Freckleton disaster. General Arnold cabled General Ott and directed Ott to be his personal representative at the funeral.[30] BAD2 commander Colonel Moore also attended the services.

At the conclusion of the service, mourners filed out of the church. The American servicemen lifted the tiny coffins and carried them through an honor guard formed by personnel from BAD2. The line of coffins processed the short distance from the church to the cemetery. There the American soldiers had excavated a communal grave in the form of a T. The grave was over eight feet deep. The GIs buried the children and their teacher, Jennie Hall, in the short arms of the T. The adults were later placed in the trunk of the T. More than 500 floral tributes adorned the mounds of dirt surrounding the grave site.[31] Several of the mourners fainted at the cemetery and medics from the St. John Ambulance Corps attended to them.

American servicemen were in the grave to receive and arrange the caskets. As the pall bearers approached the grave site, they set the coffin down at the edge of the grave, removed the flowers, and stepped back. The men in the grave then took the coffin from the edge and placed it in position for burial. Sergeant Tom Miller placed the coffin he was carrying on the edge of the grave. When he removed the floral wreath from the casket, he made a startling discovery. The name plate on the casket read Sonia Dagger. It was the same name that Miller and Leggett thought was so beautiful the night before.[32] Funeral organizers had randomly assigned caskets to the BAD2 ser-

At the grave site in Holy Trinity Cemetery, GIs arranged the more than 500 floral tributes that arrived in Freckleton from all over the United Kingdom. When pallbearers approached the burial site, they set the coffin down at the edge of the grave, removed the flowers from the coffin, and stepped back. Servicemen in the grave then took the casket and placed it in position for burial (photograph courtesy of BAe Systems Heritage Division).

vicemen. The coincidence that Miller bore Sonia's remains to her final resting place touched the core of Miller's soul. Miller's memories of that day are still vivid and real. In an interview a half-century later, Miller said: "I can't explain my feelings about this experience, but it has stayed with me until now. After the funeral I always wanted to let the Dagger family know that I carried their little girl. I hesitated, and didn't do it for fear they may be angry at the Americans for the tragedy."[33]

At the time of the crash, five-year-old Sonia Dagger was the only child of Clarice and Wilfred Dagger of Preston Old Road. Wilfred served with the British army in France. At the time of the crash, Dagger was hospitalized with a bad case of dysentery. While recovering from his illness in France, Dagger read about the B-24 crash in Freckleton in an article published in a British newspaper. He immediately inquired about the disaster and his superiors informed him that his daughter Sonia had died in the school fire. His officers, however, had no information about his wife Clarice. The British army discharged Dagger from the hospital and granted him compassionate leave to return home to Freckleton. When he arrived in the village, his daughter was already buried and his wife was in shock over the ordeal. Clarice and Wilfred Dagger would go on to have two children after Sonia's death, Stephanie and Tony.

Tom Miller could never erase Sonia Dagger from his memory. The experience of the crash and funeral always stayed with him. Before he married Bernadine Swindler on May 6, 1950, Miller informed her that "in event we have a daughter, her name will be Sonya."[34] The Miller's first child was born on March 12, 1953, and Tom and Bernadine named her Sonya in memory of the little girl Tom had carried to her grave.

In the funeral procession, Warrant Officer Painter Alexander carried the casket of five-year-old Judy Garner alone because of his height. Judy was the daughter of Jane and Michael Garner of Lytham Road. Relatives said that Judy had a strong resemblance to child star Shirley Temple. Judy's father Mick was the village butcher and dairyman. He enlisted in the First East Lancashire Regiment and arrived in France shortly after D-day. The war exacted a harsh toll from Jane Garner. Her daughter Judy and her two nieces, Georgina Lonsdale and Annie Herrington, all perished in the infants' school fire. Her husband Mick died in combat in Calvados, France, on August 17. Word of Private Garner's death did not reach Freckleton until the afternoon of August 23. Her family and local officials decided to inform Jane of her husband's death after the burial of her daughter and nieces. They thought the multiple tragedies would be too much of a burden for her to bear all at once.[35] One of the many strange coincidences that accompanied the disaster was that August 23, 1944, would have been Mick Garner's thirtieth birthday.

A few days after the funeral, Alexander's commanding officer encouraged Painter to comfort the grieving mother and widow. It became a common practice at BAD2 for the servicemen to console and aid the grieving families of the children lost in the fire. At first, Jane Garner refused Alexander's sympathy and assistance. As Jane's despair grew greater, family members, especially her father, encouraged her to accept Alexander's aid and consolation. Jane's father even encouraged her to join Alexander on an excursion out of Freckleton. Jane eventually started dating the tall warrant officer and the two fell in love. Alexander and Garner were married two years after the catastrophe and moved to the United States where they had a son, James, and a daughter, Hazel. The couple remained happily married until Painter Alexander died in 1979. Jane lived another 11 years until 1990 and passed away on the anniversary of her marriage to Painter. Their son James summed up his parents' relationship with this beautiful sentiment: "Just as peace follows war, love followed tragedy. They came together after a great tragedy. They stayed together celebrating a great love."[36]

At 3:30 p.m. there was a second funeral service at Holy Trinity Church for the owners and employees of the Sad Sack Café as well as the one civilian patron at the snack bar, 15-year-old James Silcock. Family and friends of the victims attended the service that included prayers, hymns and readings from the Bible. The congregation processed from the church to the cemetery while the organist played the "Death March." The seven caskets were then laid to rest in the communal grave.

The Times relegated coverage of the Freckleton funeral to page 12 in its August 27 issue. The article consisted of three short paragraphs and reported that the services "were held in a church so small that only the coffin of one unidentified child and teacher could be brought inside."[37] The article stated that 36 children and 8 adults were buried in a T-shaped grave after the service. Not only was *The Times* coverage perfunctory at best, it was also inaccurate. Only 35 children were buried on August 26.[38]

After the recovery and identification of their remains, the U.S.A.A.F. buried the American servicemen from BAD2 at the Cambridge American Cemetery just west of Cambridge, England. The Cambridge American Cemetery is the only American World War II cemetery in the United Kingdom. Cambridge University donated 30.5 acres of land in 1943 to bury American servicemen. The grounds contain the remains of 3,812 servicemen, most of whom died in the Battle of the Atlantic and the air bombardment of Northwest Europe. There, names of 5,127 GIs who went missing in action in Europe are enshrined on the Tablets of the Missing located in the cemetery.[39] After the conclusion of the war, families of nine of the servicemen killed in the Freckleton crash repatriated their loved ones to cemeteries in the United States. John Bloemendal's wife, Margaret, brought her husband's remains back to the United States and buried him in Elmhurst Cemetery in the couple's hometown of St. Paul, Minnesota. Only one American killed in the crash still remains buried in Cambridge, Arthur Rogney.

Beryl Hogarth and Joseph Threlfall, the two children who died in the BAD2 hospital on August 25, were buried later in the communal grave. So was Miss Hulme, their teacher who passed away on the same day. While suffering from her injuries and hovering near death, Miss Hulme expressed the desire to be buried with her students to hospital workers and visitors. The dedicated teacher's wish became a reality when she was finally laid to rest with her little charges in the communal grave.

When the sun set on August 26, the grim task of burying the dead was over. For all involved, one chapter of the book of their lives was now permanently closed. Another chapter was about to begin. Whether they wanted it to or not, life was going to go on for the people of Freckleton and the servicemen of BAD2. Individually and together, they would have to deal with the grief, loss, and sorrow brought on by the catastrophic crash. For many families in Freckleton, there would always be that birthday, holiday, or special occasion where there was someone missing from the dinner table. For the GIs like Tom Miller, the experience haunted them forever but made them more likely to hug their children a little tighter when they left home. For others, like Painter Alexander and Jane Garner, love grew from the ashes of the tragedy. Perhaps Sergeant Ralph Scott, a member of the BAD2 honor guard, best expressed the emotions of the day when he stated: "You know the nature of war, you were prepared mentally for the fact that you were going to lose comrades. But none of us even considered that five-year-old children could get killed. That's something you never forget."[40]

8

The Investigation

"Wisdom is not acquired save as the result of investigation."
—Sara Teasdale, American poet

There were thousands of accidents involving American military aircraft during the second World War. The accidents happened on American soil as well as abroad. Some of the accidents were minor while many involved the loss of life and severe damage to military and civilian property. During the war, no American military aviation accident was as catastrophic as the B-24 crash into the village of Freckleton. The final death toll in the tragedy was 61 people, 38 of whom were children six years old or younger.

During the war, the U.S.A.A.F. investigated and catalogued every accident involving one of their aircraft, pilots or bases. The purpose of the U.S.A.A.F. accident reports was not just to document each mishap, but to increase safety and prevent future accidents. Through careful investigation, the U.S.A.A.F. tried to determine the cause of each accident. Once U.S.A.A.F. investigators determined the cause of the mishap, similar accidents could be prevented by such measures as making structural changes to the aircraft model, retraining and closer supervision of pilots, and changes in the regulations governing the operation of air bases. The U.S.A.A.F. found it difficult to conduct thorough investigations because of the frequency of accidents, the need to keep pilots and planes in the air in wartime, and the shortage of trained, independent investigators. The accident investigation officer usually was an officer stationed at the same base as the pilot and plane involved in the accident. The U.S.A.A.F. also lacked the sophisticated technology that is currently employed by such organizations as the Federal Aviation Administration when they investigate air crashes today.

The U.S.A.A.F. accident report contained four separate sections: The data page, supporting documentation, maps, and the summary page. The data page identified the pilot(s) and plane(s) involved in the crash. The page also provided information on the pilot's training and flight hours as well as the status of the aircraft involved in the crash. The purpose or mission of the flight is also provided on the data page. Supporting documentation included weather reports, eyewitness accounts of the accident, statements by the pilots and relevant crew members, transmissions from the aircraft and other messages related to the accident. Maps of the flight route and general area around the crash were often included in the report. The summary page provided a brief description of the accident. It also contained the results of the investigation as well as the conclusions and recommendations of the investigating team. The investigators then sent the accident report to U.S.A.A.F. headquarters for review. After reviewing the report, headquarters staff would act on the recommendations they judged pertinent to the safety and welfare of military personnel as well as the civilian population.

The U.S.A.A.F. appointed Major Charles Himes as the accident investigation officer to oversee the investigation of the B-24 crash into the village of Freckleton. Himes was stationed at BAD2 and was the chief test pilot at the base. He knew John Bloemendal well and had flown several missions with him. Himes was familiar with the airfield, the weather conditions of the area, and the intricacies of flying B-24 bombers, and had witnessed the violent thunderstorm on the morning of August 23. Major Himes was no stranger to accidents and was involved in one on the base on June 17, 1944.

During the day of June 17, Himes and John Bloemendal took a newly arrived De Havilland Mosquito up for a test flight. The R.A.F. supplied BAD2 with the Mosquito so base personnel could familiarize themselves with the operation and maintenance of the aircraft. When the Mosquito reached about 3,000 feet, Himes and Bloemendal feathered out the left engine to check the aircraft's ability to perform on a single engine. The Mosquito was flying slower than expected so Himes applied more power to the right engine. The application of power caused the plane to roll to the left. Himes attempted to unfeather the left engine but the propeller would not move. Himes steered the plane toward the Warton airfield and dropped his landing gear. When the wheels dropped down, the Mosquito almost came to a stop. Himes raised the landing gear to gain speed and belly-landed the aircraft. The Mosquito came to a screeching halt with its nose buried in a hedge. Both Himes and Bloemendal were uninjured in the incident. The ensuing investigation revealed that a dead battery prevented Himes from unfeathering the left engine.[1]

Major Himes immediately launched his investigation into the crash on the afternoon of August 23. Himes conducted the investigation under diffi-cult and emotional circumstances. Himes had just lost his close friend and fellow test pilot, John Bloemendal. Nine other comrades-in-arms from BAD2 were either dead or mortally injured. Freckleton had lost almost 5 percent of its population in the crash including a generation of children. Though many individuals heard the sound of the crash and saw the ensuing fireball, only a handful of people had actually seen the plane plummet into the village. In a time of immense anxiety, complete shock, and overwhelming grief, Himes had to probe the villagers and base personnel with pertinent questions about the nature and cause of the accident. To compound these trying conditions, most of the *Classy Chassis II* was destroyed by the impact of the crash and consumed afterwards by the fire.

Major Himes investigated the crash for three days. Major Johnson and Major Schooling, along with Captain Tilli, assisted Himes in gathering infor-mation and interviewing witnesses. Himes submitted the completed accident report, including recommendations, to the U.S.A.A.F. headquarters on August 26, the same day as the mass funeral in Freckleton. U.S.A.A.F. head-quarters received the report on September 8 and endorsed the investigating team's recommendations.

The accident report included a data page, supporting documents, and a summary page but surprisingly no maps. The data page contained the type, model, and serial number of the bomber as well as the names, rank, and serial numbers of the pilot and crew members. The page also contained information about the pilot charged with the accident, including the number of hours the pilot had logged in the air. According to the report, Bloemendal had logged over 744 hours of flight time as a test pilot. He had flown B-24s over 253 hours and spent almost 108 hours flying the B-24H model. In the 90 days before the accident, Bloemendal logged over 88 hours in B-24s in the skies above Freckleton.[2] The report listed the pilot's mission as a test flight and stated that the weather at the time of the accident was thunderstorms and heavy rain with visibility at 300 yards. The wind was out of the north at 30mph with strong gusts. Himes listed the aircraft, including the engines and propellers, as a complete wreck. The data page concluded with the cause of the accident listed as unknown.[3]

In his supplementary materials, Himes and his associates included the statements of six eyewitnesses. Five of the eyewitnesses were British civilians. The other witness was an American GI headed into Freckleton at the time of the crash. Only three of the witnesses, Eric Greenwood, Vera Cartmell, and Charlotte Allsup, claimed to have seen the plane come through the village. The other three individuals only provided information about the plane after the crash itself.

Eric Greenwood, age 8, was visiting a home at 21 Kirkham Road. He said he "saw a Liberator and heard its roar right over the house. It was flying very low and I saw the right wing go down as the left came up. It seemed to be swaying in the air. I saw no flames. A moment afterward I heard a crash."[4]

Vera Cartmell, also of Kirkham Road, testified that she "saw a Liberator from my home. It was flying very low and was in a banking position—that is, the wings were straight up and down. It was flying so low I felt it would crash. The plane was not on fire when I saw it flying."[5] Mrs. Cartmell then lost sight of the bomber, heard the crash, and then observed the flames rising from the crash scene.

The two witnesses from Kirkham Road tell essentially the same story. The house that Greenwood was visiting sat opposite the Cartmell property. Both individuals saw the aircraft flying low to the ground with its wings in almost a vertical position. Neither saw the plane hit by lightning or on fire as it approached their position. It appears from their testimony that Bloemendal attempted to pull out of his landing and banked his plane to head out of the storm. This would explain the position of the wings cited in Greenwood's and Cartmell's testimonies.

The observation of the third witness, Charlotte Allsup of Clitheroes Lane, provides a different scenario for the crash. During the storm, Allsup was standing behind her house moving her chickens out of the rain. She testified to seeing "a ball of fire in the sky flash and then hit the plane, the plane spun around and hit the earth."[6] Allsup's testimony became the source of the theory that lightning destroyed the B-24 and its wreckage went careening through the village.

Army nurse Jane Chestnutwood's observations from the base hospital provide some corroboration for Allsup's testimony. About 10:45 a.m. on the morning of the crash, Chestnutwood looked out a hallway window at the base hospital. The window had an eastern exposure and provided the nurse with an excellent view of the violent thunderstorm. As she watched the bolts of lightning illuminate the dark sky, she saw the *Classy Chassis II* emerge from the clouds on a northern heading at about 600 feet above the ground. She then alleged that she saw lightning hit the B-24 Liberator at the juncture of the wing and fuselage. Chestnutwood claimed that the plane split into two pieces and then crashed into the village.[7]

Himes and his team did not include any of Chestnutwood's observations in the official accident report. It appears that Chestnutwood's version of the crash emerged after the official investigation and then embedded itself into the oral history of BAD2. The story first appeared in print in 1979 in an article written for *BAD News* (a newspaper published by the veterans association of BAD2). In the article, "The Day Freckleton Wept," author David Mayor recounts the day of the air disaster and includes Chestnutwood's version of the crash in his story. Ralph Scott has also written several articles that include Nurse Chestnutwood's observations of the crash.

The investigation team also received statements from air traffic control, the station weather officer, and First Lieutenant Peter Manassero, who flew the second B-24 on the morning of August 23. First Lieutenant James W. Harper was the flying control officer at BAD2. Harper testified that air traffic control called the weather officer for weather conditions at approximately 10:30 a.m. The weather officer informed flight control that the cloud ceiling was 1,500 feet and there was two miles of visibility. Air traffic control relayed the information to Bloemendal and Manassero with a caution to have their aircraft stay "within close contact because of the unpredictable weather conditions."[8]

The two B-24s took off from runway 08 at 10:36 a.m. Harper told investigators that at 10:40 a.m. the control tower observed low, dark clouds moving toward the airfield from the southeast. He testified "that the control tower was instructed to recall local aircraft, but the cloudburst moved in so quickly that they did not have time to land. As soon as the rain started the control tower was told to keep the planes up and away from the field."[9] Bloemendal never received this order; his plane had already crashed into Freckleton.

Tech Sergeant Doyle Shaw of Control Tower Operation provided more details about the last minutes before the crash in a sworn statement to the investigation team. He gave Himes and his team a transcript of the last communication between the control tower and Bloemendal's aircraft (the entire transcript appears in Chapter 5). The last transmission from the control tower to Bloemendal informed him that "you are clear and No. 1 to land on runway 08."[10]

Shaw informed investigators that the control tower picked up communication between Bloemendal's B-24 and Manassero's aircraft after the tower's last transmission to the *Classy Chassis II*. Bloemendal told Manassero that he was retracting his landing gear and going around the airfield again. As the storm intensified, it became unfeasible to land the planes. The control tower sent out a message to both planes "to steer north of the field and listen out for a recall after the storm passed."[11] Shaw told investigators that Manassero verified the call but the tower received no verification from Bloemendal. The control tower continued its attempt to contact Bloemendal to no avail. The black smoke rising to the northeast of the field signaled the demise of the *Classy Chassis II* and its three crew members. It also made clear to control tower personnel why Bloemendal had not responded to their transmissions. Shaw's testimony confirms that orders to stay aloft never reached Bloemendal's doomed aircraft.

Captain Zdrubek, the station weather officer, provided the investigating team with a detailed statement on the weather conditions prior to and during the flight of the *Classy Chassis II*. Zdrubek stated that "at 10 a.m. there was 100 percent cloud cover at 700 feet with 2,500 yards of visibility and continuous light rain."[12] When the *Classy Chassis II* took off, there was a temporary improvement in the weather conditions. The cloud ceiling had risen from 1,200 to 1,500 feet and there was two miles of visibility in intermittent light rain. From 10:40 a.m. to 10:50 a.m., there was a dramatic switch in the weather. Zdrubek testified that "the cloud ceiling lowered to 400 feet and the visibility to 300 yards in the thickest downpour. The wind shifted from NE at 18mph to SW at 30–35mph, then back to NE at 20mph within ten minutes."[13]

Zdrubek stated that he told the control tower that the weather would "close in" and that all pilots flying locally should stay close to the airfield. Zdrubek's statement confirmed the warning Lieutenant Harper issued to Bloemendal and Manassero. The weather officer told the investigators that though the storm was short in duration, it was the most severe ever recorded at BAD2. Zdrubek concluded his report to the investigation team by stating, "There were severe up and down drafts reported within the storm and the barometer showed a 6mb. rise and fall of pressure during its passage."[14]

A key piece of the testimony was First Lieutenant Peter Manassero's statement to the investigation team. Manassero had been in the air with Bloemendal and in visual as well as radio contact with the *Classy Chassis II*. He flew in and struggled with the same weather conditions as Bloemendal's doomed bomber. If anyone could provide clues to why the *Classy Chassis II* crashed on the morning of August 23, it was Pete Manassero.

In his statement, Manassero said weather conditions were favorable for takeoff. Once aloft, both planes headed northward. A few minutes into the flight, Bloemendal radioed Manassero and called the pilot's attention to a cloud formation to the south, southeast. Manassero reported that the cloud formation "was a very impressive sight and looked like a thunderhead."[15] Shortly after the radio communication between Bloemendal and Manassero ended, the control tower at Warton ordered the two planes to return to the base because of the approaching storm.

The two planes turned and headed back to the airfield. Manassero testified that he was about 100 yards off the right wing of the *Classy Chassis II*. As the two planes approached Warton, Manassero drew further away from Bloemendal's aircraft in order to land behind the *Classy Chassis II*. Manassero told the investigators that both pilots dropped "down to 500 feet and about four miles NW of the field we encountered rain and it became heavier with less visibility as we neared the approach to runway 08. On the base leg, Lieutenant Bloemendal let down his gear and I did the same."[16] At this point, Manassero lost visual contact with Bloemendal's plane because there was no visibility directly ahead of his aircraft.

Radio contact between the two planes continued as the *Classy Chassis II* approached Warton. As Manassero flew over Lytham and made a left turn to begin his approach to Warton, he heard Bloemendal inform the control tower that "he was pulling up the wheels and going around."[17] After hearing Bloemendal's transmission to the control tower, Manassero radioed Bloemendal and told him "they had better head north and get out of the storm. Bloemendal answered 'OK.' I then told him I would take a heading of 330 degrees. He said, 'Roger.'"[18] That radio contact was the last exchange between the two pilots.

Manassero flew about five minutes on a heading of 330 degrees before he broke out of the storm. He repeatedly tried to contact Bloemendal to see if he and his crew were safe but received no reply. Manassero radioed the Warton control tower that his aircraft and crew had safely come through the storm but that he had lost contact with Bloemendal. The control tower tried to radio Bloemendal but received no response. Manassero concluded his factual account of the mishap with a veiled comment on the reason for the accident. Manassero explained to investigators that "in my opinion the storm was too severe for the most experienced pilot. I did not have complete control of my aircraft while in the storm. I was fortunate to find ground with my aircraft in almost a level attitude and no obstructions."[19] In Manassero's view, the full fury of Mother Nature had triumphed over the considerable skills of a veteran pilot.

On April 26, Major Himes concluded his investigation and sent the accident report to U.S.A.A.F. headquarters. The summary report was brief and read as follows:

> The cause of this accident is unknown. It is the opinion of the Accident Investigating Committee that the crash resulted from pilot's error in the judgment of

the violence of the storm. The extent of the thunder-head was not great and he could have flown in perfect safety to the North and East of the field.

When the approach to land was made the pilot said conditions were to [too] bad and he attempted to withdraw, but the violent winds and downdrafts must have forced the plane into the ground before he could gain sufficient speed and altitude. The statement made by 1st Lieutenant Manassero who was flying at the same time and place describe the difficulities [difficulties] he experienced in flying back out of danger.

It is possible that in the rough air structural failure occurred, however, no conclusions could be drawn from an examination of the wreckage, as the airplane was so completely demolished.[20]

Based on its findings, the accident investigating committee made the following recommendation to U.S.A.A.F. headquarters:

That all pilots who are gaining most of their flying experience in England (subsequent to flying school) be emphatically warned about entering thunderstorms or flying under thunderheads. The dangers of such practice are easily learned in Southern United States where intense thunderstorms are frequent, but in the British Isles a pilot is led to believe that thunderstorms are mere showers, hence the rare, severe type is the most apt to trap him.[21]

The accident investigating committee concluded that the specific cause of the accident was unknown but implied that pilot error was the major factor contributing to the mishap. The committee's report stated that Bloemendal "could have flown in perfect safety to the North and East of the field." The accident report left unanswered two questions: What was the cause of the accident and was the pilot at fault?

There are several competing theories about the cause of the crash of the *Classy Chassis II* into Freckleton. The use of Occam's razor may be useful in sorting through the theories and selecting one that best explains the cause of the crash. When there are several competing theories to explain an occurrence, Occam's razor urges one to select the theory that makes the fewest assumptions and therefore offers the simplest explanation of the event. The principle applies the law of parsimony in that the simpler explanation is the better explanation. Historians attribute Occam's razor to the 14th-century logician and English Franciscan friar, William of Ocham.

The simplest and most widely accepted theory of the crash is that a downdraft from the thunderstorm caught Bloemendal's aircraft while he was aborting a landing on runway 08. It is also the theory put forth by the investigation team on the summary page of their accident report. This theory hypothesizes that as Bloemendal was on his final approach to the airfield at Warton, he and Manassero realized that attempting to land during the storm was too dangerous. Manassero decided not to land and headed north. Bloemendal pulled up his landing gear and banked right to follow Manassero. While Bloemendal was banking the B-24, a severe downdraft caught the plane and forced it into the ground and it crashed into the village of Freckleton.

Two of the three eyewitness statements contained in the accident report confirm this scenario. Young Eric Greenwood said he saw the Liberator "flying very low and I saw the right wing go down as the left wing came up. It [the plane] seemed to be swaying in the air." Greenwood's testimony appears to confirm that turbulence struck the aircraft while it was banking to the right. Mrs. Cartmell also testified that when she saw the aircraft seconds before the crash, the airplane "was in a banking position and its wings were straight up and down." In his report to the investigation team, Captain Zdrubek, station weather officer, confirmed that the thunderstorm contained severe downdrafts and gusting winds. The normal difficulty in steering and maneuvering a nose-heavy B-24H would also have hindered Bloemendal's ability to escape the clutches of a downdraft while trying to abort a landing and banking his aircraft in a severe storm.

Another possible explanation for the crash was that the plane was hit by lightning while approaching the runway at Warton. Charlotte Allsup stated to investigators that she saw "a ball of fire in the sky flash, then hit the plane. The plane spun around and hit the earth." She described the ball of fire as lightning to the investigators. Her testimony directly contradicts Greenwood's statement to the investigation team. He specifically told investigators that he did not see any flames coming from the plane just before the crash. Allsup's testimony also stands in opposition to Cartmell's report, who told the investigators that the flames occurred after the B-24 crashed into the village.

Could lightning have been the cause of the crash of the *Classy Chassis II*? David Cook, lightning researcher at Argonne National Laboratory, claims that a lightning strike on an aircraft normally does not damage the plane though it may leave a burn mark. The energy of a lightning strike usually travels through the metal skin of the aircraft. The skin of the aircraft will usually dissipate the lightning energy in a manner sufficient enough to prevent serious problems. In a small number of cases, lightning energy can damage electrical equipment in the aircraft.[22] Wendell Bechthold, a meteorologist for the National Weather Service, claims that turbulence does more damage to aircraft during a thunderstorm than lightning.[23]

Edward J. Rupke, senior engineer for Lightning Technology, reports that lightning is generally no problem because the electrical current travels through the conductive exterior skin and structures of a plane and exits at some other extremity of the aircraft such as the tail. The current, generated by a lightning strike, could cause short-lived interference with electrical instruments. The main concern is with a catastrophic fuel explosion. In this instance, a tiny spark can ignite the fuel system. Rupke's research also suggests that an aircraft can trigger lightning when flying through a heavily charged area of a cloud.[24]

A recent NASA study found that when aircraft penetrate thunderstorms at low levels of altitude, lightning strikes were found to occur in areas of moderate or greater turbulence at the edge of and within large downdrafts. The study revealed that transient electrical impulses, produced by changing electrical and magnetic fields due to lightning energy, can damage electrical systems on an airplane. The NASA study also concluded that lightning energy flowing through the aircraft could, in extremely rare cases, cause a fire and explosion in the plane's fuel tanks.[25]

The experts are in agreement that lightning strikes generally do not cause serious or catastrophic damage to an aircraft. The most likely damage is a burn mark and/or short-term interference with electrical instruments aboard the plane. They also agree that planes flying through thunderstorms, especially at low altitude and within downdrafts, could trigger occurrences of lightning. All agreed that lightning could cause catastrophic failure if it ignited a fire in the fuel tanks. The probability of this occurring, however, is small.

Was there any evidence that lightning hit the *Classy Chassis II* and if it did, was it a contributing factor to the accident? The summary page of the official accident report does not mention lightning hitting the B-24. The completely destroyed wreckage of the Liberator yielded no clues about a lightning strike. In the official report, the only account of lightning striking the *Classy Chassis II* is Charlotte Allsup's eyewitness testimony. Two other witnesses, however, contradicted Allsup's observations in their statements.

There is, however, some unofficial evidence that might substantiate Allsup's contention that lightning brought down the *Classy Chassis II* or at least played a role in its demise. When Allsup saw the B-24, it was flying at a low altitude and in turbulence. These are the exact conditions when experts claim planes are most likely to generate and be struck by lightning. Lightning strikes can also interfere with electrical instruments. Flight Test Engineer Bob Lewis was on the ground at BAD2 at the time of the accident preparing another B-24 for a test flight. Lewis claims he overheard an intercom communication emanating from the cockpit of the *Classy Chassis II* on the radio of the B-24 he was working on at the base. According to Lewis, he could hear Bloemendal's voice exclaiming just before the crash: "My altimeter and airspeed have gone crazy. I can't tell if I am right side up or inverted! My compasses are spinning! I don't know my heading! I have no control at all!"[26]

The official accident report does not contain a transcript of Bloemendal's alleged intercom transmission that Lewis claimed to overhear on the morning of August 23. In fact, there is no statement or testimony from Bob Lewis in the report. There was no one else working at the Warton base that morning who claims to have heard the intercom transmission from the cockpit of the *Classy Chassis II*. In fact, Lewis' account does not appear in print until David Mayor published his story about the Freckleton air disaster in *BAD News* in 1979. The impaired instrument story has only one source and may be an apocryphal reenactment of what Lewis thought might have occurred in the cockpit in the last seconds prior to the crash. If true, however, the events lend credence to Allsup's assertion that lightning struck the *Classy Chassis II* because one of the consequences of lightning striking an aircraft is electrical interference with the plane's instruments. If lightning hit the B-24 and knocked out its instruments just as Bloemendal was banking right in a downdraft, the unfortunate chain of events would have been responsible for the catastrophic accident.

Nurse Jane Chestnutwood also claimed to see Bloemendal's plane hit by lightning. Her account differs from Allsup's in that she alleged that the bolt of lightning struck the *Classy Chassis II* at the juncture of the wing and the fuselage. The lightning strike caused the B-24 to split in two pieces and it fell 600 feet into the village. Chestnutwood's testimony is not contained in the official accident report and also does not appear in print until Mayor's article contained in *BAD News* in 1979. All three official eyewitness accounts contradict her version of the crash. Greenwood and Cartmell both saw the plane intact seconds before the crash. Allsup also saw the plane intact but on fire. Chestnutwood's account also runs counter to what experts expect to happen when lightning strikes an aircraft. In almost all instances, the lightning energy is dissipated by the exterior skin. Catastrophic failure usually occurs from a fuel tank explosion not by a lightning bolt cutting a plane in half like a buzz saw.

Chestnutwood's version of the crash found one supporter, Colonel Paul Jackson. Colonel Jackson was the Chief of Maintenance at BAD2 and he sometimes served as an accident investigation officer. In his career in the Air Force, he logged almost 8,000 hours as a command and test pilot. He also flew a plane that had been struck by lightning. Jackson said of Chestnutwood's report that "I have read and re-read Nurse Seale's [Chestnutwood's married name] statement and the more I study it, the more I am convinced that she was correct in her description of the fatal strike."[27] Jackson, a veteran pilot, put aside his experience and knowledge of experts in the field when he continued with his defense of Chestnutwood's story. Jackson said: "I don't believe that I have ever read an eyewitness account of an aircraft being destroyed by lightning before. In any case, after re-reading Chessie's account, I am sure that it is accurate."[28]

After examining all of the evidence and accounts provided by eyewitnesses and experts, the simplest explanation of the accident remains the most reliable and the one that best fits the majority of the known facts. Evidence and testimony show that the control tower at BAD2 recalled the two B-24s to base because of severe weather conditions in the immediate area. As the *Classy Chassis II* and the other Liberator began their final approach to runway 08, both pilots realized that conditions were too dangerous to attempt a landing. Bloemendal's plane was extremely low and when he attempted to bank right and abort the landing, a downdraft hit the plane. Once caught in the downdraft, Bloemendal lost control of the normally hard-to-maneuver B-24 and crashed into the village. The other theories about the crash maybe partially or fully accurate, but they lack the simplicity and corroborating evidence of the downdraft hypothesis. The dearth of eyewitnesses, the complete destruction of the aircraft, and the succinctness of the accident report will always make the cause of the Freckleton air disaster speculative at best.

The final question is if this crash could have been prevented. The strange irony of this catastrophic event is that the accident was the result of a tragic twist of fate. John Bloemendal and Peter Manassero were scheduled to test fly the B-24s at 8:30 a.m. on August 23. Though the weather was not perfect, visibility was decent and there were no thunderstorms or strong winds in the vicinity of the airfield. Bloemendal was the Officer of the Day and just before takeoff, administrative duties called him away from his role as a test pilot. He postponed the test flight until later in the morning at 10:30 a.m. If Bloemendal and Manassero had taken their aircraft aloft at 8:30 a.m., there would not have been an accident. Thirty-eight children would have reached adulthood and the promise of their potential. Ten American and four British servicemen would have returned to the happiness, security, and love of their families after the war. The Sad Sack Café might have remained a popular fixture in post-war Freckleton. One teacher would have retired while another began a rewarding career. The village of Freckleton would have become an obscure footnote in the history of the Allied air war against Germany, a position Freckletonians and Americans would have gladly accepted in exchange for the 61 lives lost in the infamous disaster. When lives are measured in years, who would have thought two brief hours would be so important?

The official accident report states that "the crash resulted from the pilot's error in judgment of the violence of the storm." The accident investigating committee placed the burden of the accident squarely on the shoulders of John Bloemendal. Should Bloemendal bear all the responsibility for the mishap? The storm itself appeared to be a freak of nature. Though the storm was short in duration, it moved quickly and packed a violent punch. The storm was also an extremely unusual weather event for the Freckleton area. Most local observers said they had never witnessed a storm of this nature in their lifetimes. Manassero, who did not attempt to land his plane but headed north, said in his report that he almost lost control of his plane and was lucky to escape the clutches of the storm. His statement that the storm "was too severe for a most experienced pilot" is an indictment of the weather rather than Bloemendal's skills or judgment. Lewis' and Chestnutwood's accounts of the crash, whether apocryphal or not, blame the weather rather than the pilot for the accident.

Air traffic control at Warton ordered the two planes to return back to the base and land. From the official transcripts of the transmissions between the control tower and Bloemendal's plane, it is clear that Control Tower Operation had a better idea of the weather conditions than the pilots. In fact, Bloemendal had to ask the tower for the reason for the planes being ordered back to Warton. Instead of ordering the planes to head northward, the control tower cleared the *Classy Chassis II* to land despite telling Bloemendal that ceiling and visibility were rapidly decreasing around the airfield. By the time the control tower sent out a general call instructing the pilots of the B-24s to steer north of the airfield out of the storm, it was too late. As Bloemendal made his final approach to land, without updated reports about local weather conditions or changed orders from the control tower, he aborted the landing, banked right, and got caught in a downdraft and crashed into the village.

Flight Control Operations must shoulder some of the blame for the accident. They possessed the updated weather forecasts, knew the ferocity and track of the storm, and could visibly see the impact of the weather conditions on the immediate vicinity. Upon receiving the storm warning from Burtonwood, the tower should have immediately ordered the planes to fly northward away from the storm and await recall to the Warton airfield. Instead, the control tower ordered the two planes to land in the teeth of the thunderstorm. Nowhere in the official accident report were the control tower operators held accountable for their fateful decision. Nowhere in the recommendations was there any suggestion that Flight Control Operations should keep planes in the air and away from a storm in similar situations in the future. John Bloemendal did not fully comprehend the weather conditions he was flying into until it was too late. Tower operators, who were in the midst of the storm, didn't radio Bloemendal to stay aloft because of the severe weather until after the crash. Despite tardy warnings and decisions from Flight Control Operations, the accident investigating committee cited Bloemendal for "poor judgment of the violence of the storm."

On the morning of August 23, Colonel Britton was the temporary base commander. Britton was not a pilot. He was the officer in charge of personnel and training at BAD2. When General Ott sent word from Burtonwood about the approaching storm, he told Britton to recall any Warton aircraft and immediately have them land. Britton, with no experience as a pilot, did as Ott instructed and phoned the control tower to recall the B-24s. The tower operators, in turn, followed Britton's orders. Colonel Paul Jackson normally would have been the temporary base commander but he was not at Warton on August 23 because of official business elsewhere. Jackson was a skilled and experienced pilot. Several years after the crash, Jackson told Ralph Scott at a BAD2 reunion that if he had been at Warton and in command of the base that August morning, he would have ordered Manassero and Bloemendal to head out of the storm and fly north to Scotland. Jackson believed that the weather conditions were too severe to risk a landing and Britton should have kept the planes out of the vicinity until the storm passed through Warton.[29] No mention or criticism of Britton's command decision to land the planes appeared in the official accident report.

On December 5, 1944, Colonel Hutchins, the base commander, received the recommendations from the U.S.A.A.F.'s Aircraft Accident Board about the August 23 accident. Colonel Hutchins replaced Colonel Moore in November and was not stationed at Warton at the time of the accident. The board recommended that the station flying control officer and the station operations officer be the same person. The officer corps at Warton thought the recommendation from the board reflected poorly on the officers on duty at the time of the crash. Colonel Hutchins, after discussion with his officers, notified the Base Air Depot Administration that he was not going to put the recommendation into effect. Instead, Hutchins appointed a pilot to be the operations officer and the flying control officer would be a ground officer and a graduate of flying control school.[30] The board's recommendations and Colonel Hutchins's modifications suggest that both Flight Operations and Flying Control had a role to play in the crash and could have provided Manassero and Bloemendal with more timely information about the weather and landing their B-24s.

Timing, the weather, the plane, the pilot, the base commander on duty, and air traffic control all played a role in this accident. No one at BAD2 committed an unlawful act or made a deliberate mistake to cause the mishap. Every American stationed at Warton bore the grief and burden of the disaster. A freak storm, cruel fate and difficult split-second decisions resulted in the deaths of 61 people. No accident investigating committee or its report could bring the victims back to life. No matter what its cause was, the crash had still shattered many lives. Now it was time to begin the process of piecing those shattered lives back together again.

9

The New Normal

"Time heals and life goes on."—Val Preston Whittle,
survivor of the Holy Trinity School fire

August 27 was the first day of the last week in August. It was also the first day after the mass funeral in Freckleton and the start of a new work week at BAD2. The day before, the accident investigating committee had completed its report on the crash and sent their findings to U.S.A.A.F. headquarters. Seven victims of the accident remained in the base hospital in critical condition. The tragic accident of August 23 affected every person stationed at the base and living in the village of Freckleton. The cruel reality of the situation was that the living had to continue on with their lives despite the air disaster. At the base, planes need to be maintained, modified and repaired as the war ground into its sixth year. In the village, Freckletonians still had to work to feed, house, and clothe their families. The children had to return to school. In the midst of sorrow and grief, daily life continued its relentless pace.

On Sunday afternoon, August 27, BAD2 held a memorial service for the victims of the catastrophe in the base theater. Seven army chaplains conducted the service and the Reverend Knies delivered a moving eulogy. American soldiers, bereaved families, and grieving villagers sang hymns such as "Rock of Ages" and "Abide with Me." In the evening, the Methodist Church on Kirkham Road also held a memorial service that featured musicians and singers from the Warton base. Sergeant Buckle played the organ while a quartet of BAD2 servicemen sang "Beyond the Shadows." Sergeant le Paquet followed the hymn with a solo rendition of "Open the Gates of the Temple."[1]

At BAD2, base personnel lined up on payday to contribute to the Freckleton Memorial Fund. The BAD2 historical report for September 1944 stated that the donations were to "be used to erect a memorial to the kids who lost their lives in the tragic Freckleton plane crash last August."[2] The report also stated that the "latest report indicated that officers and men were responding with characteristic Yankee generosity."[3] The American servicemen initially raised $44,000. Some of the donations were used to defray the expense of the mass funeral while the Americans turned over the balance of the money to local authorities to fund a memorial in honor of the deceased children.

Lieutenant General Carl Spaatz, commander of Strategic Air Forces in Europe, sent a letter of regret and condolence to Lord Derby, Lord Lieutenant of the County of Lancashire, on August 29. In the letter, Spaatz expressed his, and the American Air Army Forces,' regret "for the distressing accident which occurred at the village of Freckleton."[4] Spaatz wrote that early indications pointed to weather conditions as the primary cause of the crash. He expressed his sympathy for the families who lost loved ones in the accident. Spaatz concluded the letter by writing that he regretted "more than I can say that our Air Forces should have been involved in such a blow to our British ally."[5] Even at this point of the war, Spaatz was keenly aware of the importance of good relations between the Americans and British and did not want this tragic accident to impair the alliance.

Lord Derby replied to Spaatz the same day. In his letter, Lord Derby thanked Spaatz for his regrets and condolences. He informed Spaatz that he would forward the American general's letter to the authorities in Freckleton and endeavor to make known "to all those whose families suffered from this unfortunate accident the kind message of sympathy which you have been good enough to send me."[6] Lord Derby also sought to maintain the cordial relations between the two allies.

On August 30, exactly a week after the accident, base personnel received the distressing news that Private George Brown died from the injuries he sustained when the *Classy Chassis II* crashed into the Sad Sack Café. Brown was the last American servicemen to die as a result of the crash. After the war, his mother Jennie repatriated her son's remains from the American cemetery in Cambridge and buried them in the Long Island National Cemetery in Farmingdale, New York.

Singer and entertainer Bing Crosby raised base morale when he and his troupe visited Warton on Friday, September 1. Harry Lillis Crosby's career as a singer and entertainer took off when NBC asked him to take over its faltering radio program, *The Kraft Music Hall*. Crosby resurrected interest in the show by combining his unique voice and style with a variety of music genres including pop, jazz, opera, and classical. *The Kraft Music Hall* soon became the prototype for other broadcast variety shows.[7]

During the war, Crosby's radio show attracted more than 50 million listeners. The singer became a spokesperson for the American war effort. Crosby sold war bonds, personally answered letters from servicemen and their families, and toured military facilities in the United States and abroad. At the end of the war, a poll taken by *Yank* magazine declared Crosby to be the entertainer who had done the most to raise American morale during the war. Crosby coveted this achievement even more than his academy award.[8]

Crosby's signature song was his rendition of Irving Berlin's "White Christmas." He first sang the song on the radio on Christmas Day 1941. Crosby again sang the song in the movie *Holiday Inn*, released in 1942. Crosby finally recorded "White Christmas" on October 3, 1942. It reached the top of the charts as the number one song on October 31 and stayed there for the next 11 weeks.

Crosby arrived at Warton with a troupe of well-known entertainers including Earl Baxter, Buck Harris, Darleen Garner, Jean Darnell, Joe Doretta, and Robert Ratford. Crosby and his fellow entertainers performed for thousands of BAD2 personnel crowded into hangar #7 and a portion of hangar #6. From 10:00 a.m. to 11:05 a.m., the performers entertained the audience with jokes, songs, and dance. Crosby and the others sang popular tunes such as "Easter Parade," "Swinging on a Star," "If I Had My Way," and "Sweet Lelani." During the performance, Crosby called Corporal Joe Fogarty onto the stage. Once on stage, Jean Darnell, a former silent movie star, held Fogarty in her arms and drew him closer to her for a kiss. The peck on the lips brought a rousing cheer from the crowd of GIs.[9]

At the conclusion of the performance, Crosby and the other entertainers signed autographs for base personnel. Crosby then headed to the base hospital. The Special Services Division had informed Crosby about the accident in Freckleton and the burn patients still in the hospital. Crosby wanted to visit with the patients and personally sing to them. When he came to Ruby Whittle's room, the crooner went to Ruby's bedside and held her fingers protruding out of the bandages. Crosby then asked Ruby what song she would like him to sing. The only songs that Ruby could think of were "White Christmas" and "Don't Fence Me In."[10]

When Crosby attempted to sing to Ruby and the other children in the room, the notes stuck in his throat and he broke down in tears. Years later, in an interview in *Stars and Stripes*, Ruby recalled that "the sight of us lying there was too much for him. He couldn't sing a note. So he got up and went into the hall for a moment."[11] In the hall, Crosby composed himself and returned to the doorway of the room. There he stood, and without going back into the room, sang his signature holiday carol "White Christmas" and the popular tune "Don't Fence Me In." The thought of Bing Crosby singing to her is one of the few vivid memories Ruby Whittle recalls from her stay at the base hospital at Warton.

Ray Brooke, the R.A.F. serviceman who suffered extensive burns to his face, hands and right leg at the Sad Sack Café, also remembered Bing Crosby's visit to the hospital at Warton. Brooke, in an interview published in the *Lancashire Evening Post* in May 2007, said that "a surprise visit from Bing Crosby will always stick in my mind. He was entertaining American troops but he came in and stood at the bottom of my bed. That was really a great morale boost seeing him. I believe he sang to some of the children who had been burned at the school."[12] Bill Bone, another R.A.F. servicemen badly burned at the snack bar, also remembers Crosby's visit to Warton. Bone said that "it was a great feeling to see and meet him."[13]

Bing Crosby

Singer and entertainer Bing Crosby visited BAD2 on September 1, 1944. At the conclusion of his performance, Crosby headed to the base hospital to sing to the patients burned in the air disaster. When he attempted to sing to the severely burned children, the notes stuck in his throat and he began to cry. The crooner composed himself and sang his iconic hit "White Christmas" from the doorway of the children's hospital room (photograph courtesy of BAe Systems Heritage Division).

Shortly after Crosby's visit to BAD2, Maureen Denise Clark died at 5:30 p.m. on September 4, 1944. The six-year-old was the last person to die as a result of the Freckleton crash. The death toll from the accident was now permanently fixed at 61 persons.

On September 13, another celebrity arrived at Warton. The celebrated fighter Billy Conn returned to the base as he promised back in July. This time, however, Conn was without Joe Louis. Special Services erected a boxing ring in hangar #7 and at 4 p.m. Conn put on a demonstration of his considerable boxing skills. Conn delighted the crowd when he sparred with several of the servicemen stationed at the base.[14]

Accidents and death continued to stalk the base in the month of September. The most serious incident occurred on Monday, September 25. Private Edward Farrow of the Maintenance Division was working the night shift when he inadvertently walked into a spinning propeller of a P-38. Base doctors attributed death to a compound fracture of the skull.[15] The fragility of life and one's tenuous grip on it once again became apparent to the GIs of Warton.

The conditions of the surviving burn victims began to stabilize in September and base doctors decided to transfer them out of Warton to facilities that could provide more advanced care and treatment. Dr. Archibald McIndoe of the Blond-McIndoe Center based in Queen Victoria Hospital in East Grinstead examined Bill Bone and Ray Brooke at the Cosford R.A.F. hospital just north of Wolverhampton. The American doctors had transferred the two British airmen to the Cosford facility after their conditions had stabilized.

Dr. McIndoe was a famous plastic surgeon. He was born in Dunedin, New Zealand, on May 4, 1900. He graduated with a medical degree from Otago University with a specialty in surgery. McIndoe left New Zealand and studied pathological anatomy in the United States. In 1930, he went to London. There, he took a position as a clinical assistant in the department of plastic surgery at St. Bartholomew's Hospital. In 1938, the R.A.F. appointed McIndoe as their chief consultant on plastic surgery. In 1939, McIndoe started to work at a clinic that eventually became known as the Blond-McIndoe Research Center at Queen Victoria Hospital in East Grinstead.

When World War II began, McIndoe attended to severely burned R.A.F. pilots who came to his research center. McIndoe knew that the key to dealing with loss of function and disfigurement due to deep burns was early use of skin grafts on the patient. The main problem with skin grafts, however, was rejection of the grafts by the patient. Through trial and error, McIndoe developed new skin graft techniques to improve function, appearance and to prevent rejection. Since many of his techniques were new and experimental, McIndoe nicknamed his pilot patients the "guinea pigs." McIndoe also provided the burn victims with psychological rehabilitation to help them overcome depression and despair as well as to aid them in regaining their self-esteem. To help integrate his patients back into society, McIndoe, and his friends Neville and Elaine Blond, encouraged families in East Grinstead to host recovering pilots as guests in their homes.[16]

Medical personnel transferred Ray Brooke from Warton to Queen Victoria Hospital in East Grinstead. Dr. Gerry Moore of the Blond-McIndoe Research Center was his principal surgeon. Moore himself was an R.A.F. pilot before he became a plastic surgeon. Over the next five years, Brooke underwent almost 50 surgeries on his face, hands, and right leg. In 1949, Brooke was finally released from medical care.[17] Brooke became a member of the Guinea Pig Club. This club is open to men who have been burned in a plane crash and had plastic surgery at Queen Victoria Hospital. Club membership is also open to the doctors and scientists who worked at the Queen Victoria Hospital as well as friends of the Guinea Pig Club. Friends include people who have contributed to the club financially or in any other manner. The Guinea Pig Club still meets on a yearly basis at various sites in the United Kingdom.

Bill Bone remained at Cosford where Dr. Henry performed several skin grafts on him. The R.A.F. later transferred Bone to its Haltom Hospital facility near Aylesburg. Here, Dr. Matthews performed more skin grafts on Bone's legs and right hand. After 15 skin grafts, Bone went to Marchwood Park on Southampton Bay to convalesce. Bone said that the Marchwood facility "was intended to fight off depression of an unknown future. Carousing was the outcome and we were the scourge of all mothers with daughters of practically any age."[18] Bone completed his medical treatment in January 1947 and the R.A.F discharged him from active service as a temporary warrant officer in good standing.

David Madden, the five-year-old who had moved with his mother from Brighton to Freckleton, stayed in the Warton hospital for less than a week. He was moved to a hospital in nearby Preston and from there was transferred to the burn unit at Queen Victoria Hospital. McIndoe and his associates grafted skin from Madden's thigh to his shin. Madden claims that "today the grafted area is completely indistinguishable from the unaffected skin elsewhere."[19]

Ruby Whittle spent three months in the base hospital before she was transferred to the British military hospital near Manchester. She spent the next two years having skin grafts and numerous outpatient visits until she was fit to go back to school. George Carey spent four painful years in and out of hospitals enduring dozens of skin grafts to repair his burned body. Ruby and George were the only two children in their age group from Freckleton to survive the infants' school fire.

In the village it was time for the children to return to school. Unlike today, there were no grief counselors to meet with the children and help them come to terms with their sense of loss and to reduce their fears and anxiety.

Almost all of the children returning to school had lost a friend, close relative or a sibling in the school fire. The school and the fixtures were unusable in their present state and stood in silent testimony to the devastation and death that took place within its walls. After a tragedy, nothing is ever completely the same again. The best that anyone can hope for is to establish a new normal out of the chaos of catastrophe. Children attending school in the fall and returning to lessons and homework was a step toward that new normalcy.

While repairs began on Holy Trinity School, the village used the Methodist Church Hall as a temporary classroom building. The makeshift school lacked proper desks, chairs, books, and supplies. Val Preston, whose brother George died in the school fire, returned home from her brief stay on the Isle of Man. Val remembers continuing her education very soon after her return to Freckleton and recalls that she "went to classes in the chapel on Preston Old Road. I had to continue with writing in my exercise book in pencil as there were no inkwells in the chapel. The biro [ballpoint pen] hadn't been invented."[20] Workmen completed repairs on Holy Trinity School on October 30, 1944, and the students returned to their old venue. The infants' rooms were missing from the building and were no longer needed.

The children of the village had a lot to cope with as a result of the crash. They had to deal with the loss of friends and family. They had to comfort and console grieving parents. The children had to eventually face the fear and anxiety of returning to the same school where the fire took place. Lightning and thunder struck a primal fear in their young minds. Later, some of the children had to face survivor's guilt: why did I live while my cousin died? The fact that almost all of the survivors grew up to live normal, productive lives is living testimony to the strength and resilience of the human spirit.

Val Preston talked about coping with the loss of her brother and the changed circumstance of the village. She said: "Naturally I missed my brother. I was left without siblings as my mother died when I was two and a half years of age and my father never remarried."[21] She also recalls that her father's hair went gray in a matter of days after the accident. She went on to say "the children in the immediate vicinity of my house were all older than me and they were all boys. In view of this, I learned to play their games and when we went fishing, I was the one who always had to dig up the worms."[22] Sixty-eight years after the tragedy, Val speaks for almost all of the survivors when she states that "time heals and life goes on."[23]

The arrival of autumn meant the beginning of football season. The Warriors, the BAD2 football team, opened their schedule with a tightly contested 6–0 victory over the Burtonwood Bearcats. The two teams played the game at the home field of the Blackpool Football Club. Over 30,000 people watched the defensive struggle and donated over £500 to the R.A.F. benefit fund. The Warton Warriors went on to an undefeated season and captured the league championship.[24]

The servicemen at BAD2 continued to repair, modify, and maintain P-51s and B-24s. Since February 1944, base personnel had worked 12 hour shifts, seven days a week with no leave. The sweatshop workload took a toll on the physical and mental health of the GIs. In September, Colonel Moore issued passes for leave to boost the morale of the servicemen. GIs received passes for three to seven days of leave. In October, the base commander cut the work week from seven to six days. Despite the time off, BAD2 personnel still processed 542 planes in the month including 87 B-24s. In November, Colonel Moore cut the work shift from twelve to eight hours. The need for better health and morale as well as the increased efficiency of base personnel led to Colonel Moore's decision to reduce the workload.[25]

On Thursday, October 5, there were three aircraft accidents at BAD2, all on runway 15.[26] Flight Operations rarely used the short runway and normally it was filled with parked aircraft. On this day, Flight Operations used the runway because of an unusual wind pattern. There was a slight depression in runway 15 right where it intersected runway 08. A pilot landing an aircraft on runway 15 had to exercise caution at the intersection or the plane could become airborne again and sail off the runway. On October 5, a B-24 coming in for a landing at Warton hit the depression at the intersection and glided off the end of runway 15. The impact ripped off the nose wheel and left the Liberator sitting helpless in the grass.

Twelve minutes later, the control tower cleared an A-20 Havoc to land after informing the pilot about the depression and the crippled Liberator. Despite the warning, the A-20 hit the depression, slid off the runway, and narrowly missed the helpless B-24. The control tower continued to land planes on runway 15 with two crippled aircraft bent and dented in the grass at the edge of the runway.

Three minutes later, a P-51 Mustang followed the same flawed pattern of the previous two aircraft. Once again the Mustang just missed the two stranded planes and was rendered incapacitated in the grass off runway 15. In less than 15 minutes, three planes crashed in the same manner on the same runway. Fortunately, all the pilots and crews walked away from the debacle without serious injury. The accident investigating committee concluded that strong winds, the runway depression, and the pilots' unfamiliarity with the airfield all acted in synergy to cause the mishaps.[27]

In November, the Warton Warriors continued their winning ways and were a great source of pride and entertainment for the troops. The month also brought sad news to the GIs stationed at the base and saw tragedy return to Warton. On November 9, the U.S.A.A.F. informed Colonel Moore that he was being transferred to U.S.A.A.F. headquarters in Washington, D.C. Moore had commanded BAD2 for 13 months. Under his command, Warton became the most productive air depot in BADA. His motto of "It can be done" became the mantra of every GI stationed at the base. Moore not only increased the productivity and efficiency of the operations at BAD2, he also boosted the morale of the servicemen under his command. Moore provided the base with compassionate leadership during its most difficult hour, the Freckleton air disaster. Base personnel admired and respected Colonel Moore and he trusted and relied on them. This symbiotic relationship propelled the success of BAD2.

Colonel Donald L. Hutchins assumed command of Warton on November 25. On November 29, just four days after Hutchins took command, two A-26 Invaders collided together in the skies above Warton. The A-26s were part of the 641st squadron of the 409th Bomb Group of IX Bomber Command stationed in Bretigny, France. The 641st was exchanging their A-20s for new A-26s. Pilots from the 641st flew their old A-20s to Warton in mid–November. During their stay at BAD2, the pilots familiarized themselves with their new A-26s prepped at the base. There were about 24 planes scheduled to return to their base in France on November 29. At about noon, there were approximately 20 A-26s circling the airfield at Warton waiting for the remaining four planes to join the formation. Two of the circling A-26s collided in the air and crashed into the tidal mud flats of the River Ribble estuary.[28]

The accident claimed the lives of Second Lieutenant Norman Zuber, Second Lieutenant Kenneth Hubbard, and Private John Guy. Both planes were total wrecks and became embedded in the mud flats of the estuary. BAD2 salvage crews were unable to remove the planes and their wreckage remains mired in the mud today. The fatal crash was reminiscent of the Freckleton disaster and reinforced in the villagers the danger of living so close to a busy air base.

The U.S.A.A.F. transferred Sergeant Ralph Scott to London in the fall. Scott had been a member of the base honor guard at the communal funeral in Freckleton in late August. In London, Scott worked for the military publication, *Stars and Stripes*. In his new position, Scott was in charge of a small radio unit located 185 feet underground. The unit sent stories about the

8th and 9th Air Forces to *Stars and Stripes*. In the spring of 1945, the U.S.A.A.F. sent Scott to a small airfield in St. Dizier, France, where he worked in radio communications. Scott stayed in France until the end of the war but his heart and loyalties remained with BAD2.[29]

In December, two events, one real, the other rumored, caused trepidation and anxious moments for the servicemen of BAD2. The first event was the Battle of the Bulge. On December 16, Hitler launched a last ditch counteroffensive against the Allies in Belgium, Luxembourg, and France. The German attack employed three armies in an attempt to split in half the British and American armies moving forward toward Germany. Hitler hoped to capture Antwerp, a Belgian port through which the Allies shipped a large amount of their supplies and then encircle and destroy four Allied armies. Hitler believed that a German victory would force the Allies to negotiate peace on the western front. This would then allow the Germans to concentrate their forces in the east against the Soviet onslaught.

At first, the German offensive went well. The Germans were able to punch a hole in a weak spot in the Allies' defensive position. The Germans advanced 60 miles in two days of combat. A spirited defense by the U.S. 101st Airborne Division around the Belgian town of Bastogne slowed the German advance and disrupted their timetable. Poor weather prevented Allied air power from attacking German armored divisions and their supply routes. The weather also kept reinforcements from reaching beleaguered Allied troops.

On December 22, the weather began to clear and the Allies launched a counterattack on the Germans. Allied planes bombed German supply routes and chewed up German tanks. Allied reinforcements, led by General George S. Patton's Third Army, blunted the German offensive and forced them to retreat toward Germany. By January 25, 1945, the Germans were in full retreat and the Battle of the Bulge was over. The Germans suffered more than 100,000 casualties and were never able to muster a strategic offensive again in the war. The price of victory for the Americans alone was almost 81,000 GIs killed, wounded, captured, or missing in action.[30]

As Christmas Day approached, the servicemen at BAD2 were deeply concerned about what a German victory in Western Europe would mean to the Allied war effort. The concern grew more intense when a rumored German plot to attack the base at Warton surfaced on Christmas Eve. The British military detained nearly 28,000 German prisoners of war in camps near Warton. Many of the German prisoners were pilots and crew members who served in the *Luftwaffe*. British and American military officials were concerned that if there ever was a mass breakout from the prisoner of war camps, the escapees might head to Warton and commandeer American aircraft for transportation back to Germany.[31]

At 4:30 p.m. December 24, the U.S.A.A.F. informed Colonel Hutchins that military intelligence had discovered a plot that German prisoners in the vicinity around BAD2 were planning a mass escape during the Christmas holiday. The German escapees planned to destroy Allied military bases in the area to support the ongoing German offensive in Western Europe. Hutchins ordered the base on full alert and armed the GIs to protect the facility. Two days later, the U.S.A.A.F. downgraded the alert, though the base remained vigilant for German saboteurs throughout the winter. The alert was partially triggered by the early success of the German winter offensive in Western Europe and Germany's use of cunning, secrecy, and deception to achieve the element of surprise in their attack on the Allies. The over 825 planes housed at Warton also made BAD2 a tempting target for German sabotage.[32]

The arrival of 1945 brought new hope for an Allied victory over Germany. The Americans and British had thwarted the German offensive in Western Europe and began to advance to the Rhine River. In Eastern Europe, the Soviet Red Army steadily advanced toward the German homeland. Final victory seemed to be within the grasp of the Allies. To continue the assault on Germany, the Americans had to quickly replace the soldiers they lost in the Battle of the Bulge. Beginning in January 1945 and continuing through April, SHAEF (Supreme Headquarters Allied Expeditionary Forces) began transferring GIs from administrative and support positions to combat infantry divisions on the frontlines in Europe. In the first three months of 1945, SHAEF transferred approximately 1,700 servicemen from BAD2 to frontline combat units. The transfer reduced base personnel by almost 17 percent. The loss of servicemen forced Colonel Hutchins to eliminate most of the night shift.[33]

Accidents also continued to occur during the first three months of 1945. On January 2, a B-24 heading from Seething to Warton for overhaul work crashed into Burn Fell, a hillside near Slaidburn. Four of the 17 people aboard the aircraft died when the plane's navigation system failed to properly function. On January 3, Flight Officer Edward Johnston died when the P-51 he was delivering to the 361st Fighter Group crashed in Essex. On January 11, there was another fatal P-51 crash. First Lieutenant Leonard Johnson died when the Mustang he was delivering from Warton to Debden crashed near Spurtstow. On February 19, a crew from BAD2 participated in a rescue mission involving a B-24 that crashed near Burnley. On arrival, the men pulled four survivors from the wreckage and rushed them to the base hospital. Three of the rescued crew members later died of their injuries. First Lieutenant Charles Goeking, the pilot, was the only one of the four rescued men to survive the accident.[34]

The workload at BAD2 continued unabated despite the reduction in personnel. The servicemen continued to modify B-24s with pilot replacement seats and refitted B-24s headed for the 15th Air Force with ball turrets. They refurbished P-38s, harmonized gun-sight cameras on P-51s and overhauled C-47 transports. The BAD2 crew also assembled Waco CG-4A gliders for combat duty in Europe while base machinists produced hinges for the new forward entrance doors of B-17s. The men at BAD2 continued to take great pride in their work and remained highly productive and extremely efficient despite the loss of personnel. "It can be done" was more than a motto for base personnel; it was a collegial commitment to perseverance and excellence in all their endeavors.

March 7, 1945, was a dramatic day for the Allies. The 9th Armored Division of the American First Army captured the bridge over the Rhine River at Remagan before the German army could blow it up. The First Army, under the command of General Courtney H. Hodges, used naval landing craft as well as the bridge to cross the Rhine. Once on the east bank of the river, the First Army secured the highway to Munich. On March 22, General Patton's Third Army crossed the Rhine at Oppenheim. The British 23rd Army moved across the Rhine the following day. Once across the Rhine, the Allies encircled the Germans in the Ruhr region and captured more than 325,000 prisoners. By April 18, organized German resistance ceased in the Ruhr and Allied armies drove deeper into Germany.

As the German military crumbled before the advance of the Allies, joy turned to mourning when news of President Roosevelt's death on April 12 reached the troops on the western front. Roosevelt had returned in poor health from the wartime conference held in February in Yalta. He decided to go to the "Little White House" in Warm Springs, Georgia, to recuperate and regain his vigor. After he contracted polio in 1921, Roosevelt often visited Warm Springs to rejuvenate his health and refresh his spirit. His winter home there provided a sanctuary away from the constant politics and pressures of Washington, D.C. On this visit to Warm Springs, Roosevelt not only rested, but he also prepared himself for the inaugural United Nations conference set for San Francisco.

In the early afternoon of April 12, Roosevelt was sitting for a portrait by artist Elizabeth Shoumatoff. During the sitting, Roosevelt grabbed his head and exclaimed, "I have a terrific pain in the back of my head."[35] The president then slumped in his chair and became unconscious. His valet and butler carried him to his bedroom where he died of a massive cerebral hemorrhage.

Roosevelt's sudden death plunged the American public into a state of national mourning and sorrow not witnessed since the assassination of the Great Emancipator, Abraham Lincoln. Roosevelt had been president for 12 years. The American people had elected him to an unprecedented four terms in office. He led the American people through and out of the Great Depression. Roosevelt navigated his nation through the dangerous shoals of World War II. Now, just before he could bring the ship of state safely into port, he passed into history and immortality. Like Lincoln before him, Roosevelt's death sealed his legacy and his place in the pantheon of American heroes.

The night before he died, Roosevelt worked on a Jefferson Day address that he was going to deliver to the nation during a radio broadcast scheduled for April 14. In the last words he ever wrote, Roosevelt captured the confidence, optimism, and hope for the future that he used to motivate the American people through the Great Depression and a horrific world war. Roosevelt concluded his undelivered radio address with these words: "The only limit to our realization of tomorrow will be our doubts of today. Let us move forward with strong and active faith."[36]

Colonel Hutchins held a memorial service for President Roosevelt at BAD2 on Sunday, April 15. Only servicemen who were off-duty could attend the service. The transfer of personnel to combat units in Europe made it impossible to interrupt the work schedule at Warton. The memorial service was well attended, but many GIs who wanted to honor their fallen Commander-in-Chief were denied the opportunity to do so by the demands of war.[37]

On April 26, Colonel Hutchins suffered a massive stroke while in his living quarters. Orderlies took him to the base hospital, where doctors treated his condition. The stroke left him paralyzed in his left leg and unable to discharge his duties as base commander. On May 4, the U.S.A.A.F. placed Colonel Thomas W. Scott in command of BAD2. Colonel Hutchins remained in the base hospital until May 23 when he was transferred to the U.S. Army's 157th General Hospital in Birkenhead. After recuperating at Birkenhead, Colonel Hutchins returned home to the United States for further treatment and physical therapy.[38]

The day before Colonel Hutchins took his stroke, the Allies reached another milestone in the war. American and Soviet troops linked together along the Elbe River at Torgua, Germany, on April 25. There no longer was a western and eastern front. On the same day, the Soviet army encircled the German capital of Berlin. In Italy, Italian resistance fighters killed Benito Mussolini and his mistress. Sensing complete and utter destruction of the Third Reich, Adolf Hitler committed suicide on April 30 in his underground bunker in Berlin.

Hitler had promised the German people that his Third Reich would last a thousand years. On the first day in May, Hitler's Reich lay in smoldering ruins after 12 horrendous years of Nazi rule. German General Adolph Jodl, Chief of the Operations Staff of the Armed Forces' High Command, signed an unconditional surrender document at Allied headquarters at Rheims, France, on the morning of May 7. This document formally ended the war between the Allies and Nazi Germany. The Americans and British proclaimed Tuesday, May 8, 1945, as V-E Day (Victory in Europe) because the surrender documents signed at Rheims became effective on this date at 11:01 p.m. Central European time.

At 12:30 p.m. on May 8, Colonel Scott announced to the servicemen at Warton that the war in Europe was officially over. The GIs at Warton greeted the news with a euphoric cheer and hugged each other in celebration of the Allied victory. Scott ordered all but essential work to stop on the base for 35 and a half hours to commemorate V-E Day. In his address to base personnel, Scott asked the GIs to remember all the military personnel who had died or been wounded in the war to destroy fascist tyranny. The commanding officer was quick to remind the men that the war with Japan was not over and they needed to continue to give their best effort until the Allies defeated the Japanese.[39]

The base chaplains held church services to offer thanksgiving for the Allied victory and to memorialize the individuals who had lost their lives in service to their country. On the evening of May 8, Colonel Scott hosted a V-E Day party in the Technical Area Mess Hall and lit a bonfire, comprised of the wood from the glider crates, behind the base headquarters.[40] The GIs at Warton had a lot to celebrate that evening. Base personnel had played an important role in the Allied victory over Germany. Through their around the clock efforts, the Eighth Air Force had the aircraft to establish air superiority in the skies over Western Europe. Allied air superiority led to a successful invasion of France and ultimate victory over Nazi Germany.

In the midst of their celebration, there were also sobering memories.

The servicemen of Warton had lost 29 of their own number during the war. They also remembered the tragic morning of August 23, 1944, when a B-24 bomber on a test flight from Warton crashed into the village of Freckleton, wiping out a generation of children. Not one GI based at BAD2 at the time of the crash would ever forget the sight of the procession of the tiny coffins, carried by their comrades, winding its way through Freckleton. They would always carry with them the memory of the coffins being lowered into their final resting place at the Holy Trinity Cemetery. Every victory comes with a price tag. The bill paid by Freckleton and the servicemen of Warton was steep indeed.

10

The Playground Memorial

"Memorials become relics if they do not stir our modern conscience."
—Henry Waxman, United States
Representative from California

When the V-E Day celebration ended at Warton, the base resumed its normal workload with renewed vigor. The Allied war effort against Japan in the Pacific and on the mainland of Asia continued in earnest. By May 1945, the Americans and their allies had recaptured the Philippines and had won a costly victory on the island of Iwo Jima. On Easter Sunday, April 1, 1945, the Americans launched an amphibious assault on the Japanese island of Okinawa. The Americans wanted to use Okinawa as a base for air operations preceding the planned invasion of Japan. The battle for Okinawa raged for 82 days and ended in an expensive victory for the Americans. Nearly 12,500 Americans died in the battle and more than 62,500 more were wounded in combat. In the spring of 1945, the American navy lost 27 ships to Japanese kamikaze planes. A new British offensive on the mainland of Asia pushed the Japanese out of Burma. B-29 bombers conducted daily raids against Japan and heavily damaged Tokyo and other Japanese cities with incendiary bombs. As the Allies closed in on the Japanese homeland for the final offensive, scientists in Los Alamos, New Mexico, continued to work under a shroud of secrecy on the ultimate doomsday weapon, the atomic bomb.

At Warton, base personnel continued to work on and overhaul B-24s and C-47s. GIs also prepared P-51s for their return trip to the United States. Planes were not the only thing being shipped home. On May 14, the U.S.A.A.F. sent an order to Colonel Scott to begin sending some GIs stationed at Warton home. The U.S.A.A.F. command based the transfer of personnel back to the United States on a point system. Servicemen who had accumulated enough points were first in line to return home. GIs received points based on their time in the service, time overseas, marriage, children,

136

other dependent relatives or hardship. The first Americans to return home shipped out from Warton on May 18.[1]

Some GIs never made it home. On the same day as the first contingent of Americans left Warton, Lieutenant James Allen took off from BAD2 in an A-20. Allen was headed for Langford Lodge when the aircraft exploded and crashed into the Irish Sea. Rescue workers searched the water for two days. They were able to find parts of the wreckage but never recovered Allen's body. In an ironic and fatal accident, a pilot who had survived the ravages of war perished in the first week of peace in Europe.[2]

In June, the Supply Division began to ship stock to the Occupational Air Force in Germany. The Supply Division crated the remaining stock and shipped it back to the United States or to R.A.F. bases to support American aircraft flown by British pilots.[3] The U.S.A.A.F. continued to send servicemen home to the United States or transfer them to the Occupational Air Force in Germany.

Sergeant Ralph Scott, who had been transferred first to London and then to France, went to Germany after V-E Day. The U.S.A.A.F. first assigned him to Gross Gerau and then moved him to the American airbase at Schweinfurt. There, he was promoted to Master Sergeant and made the Base Communication Chief. At Schweinfurt, he was in charge of the message center, the radio station, and the telephone switchboard. German prisoners of war helped Scott run and maintain the communications network at the airbase. While in Germany, Scott was able to visit the town of Oberstetten where his grandmother Waldmann lived as a child before immigrating to the United States. While in Oberstetten, Scott met several of his stepmother's cousins and he stayed at the family's ancestral farm house. In April 1946, the U.S.A.A.F. finally discharged Scott after five years of service, three of them overseas.[4]

Also in June, BADA sent word to Colonel Scott that Warton would receive 22 B-24s that landed in neutral Sweden during the war. Pilots often sought refuge in Sweden for their crew and planes badly damaged on bombing missions against German targets. For crew members of crippled aircraft, this was a safer option than parachuting out of the plane over Nazi-occupied territory or ditching the aircraft in water. From 1943 to the end of the war, over 140 wounded American aircraft landed in Sweden.[5]

At first, the Swedes repatriated American airmen on a one-to-one basis with German flyers who also landed their damaged aircraft in Sweden. As the Allies intensified the air war against fuel plants and the aircraft industry in northern Germany, the number of American planes landing in Sweden dramatically increased. This ended the one-for-one repatriation program because American airmen greatly outnumbered their German counterparts. The Swedes were unprepared for this "American Invasion" and did not possess adequate internment facilities to house the more than 14,000 American airmen stranded in their country.[6]

In villages such as Rattvik, Korsnas, Alvida, and Loka, the Swedes turned guesthouses and health spas in to internment camps. These camps had very few restrictions. There were guards and a 10 p.m. curfew but few other rules pertaining to the internees. Many of the internees remained at Swedish airfields and repaired and maintained their impounded aircraft. The reason for the relatively humane treatment of American internees was an agreement between the United States and Sweden that gave Sweden the right to convert and use nine B-17s as courier planes.[7]

Swedish authorities informed the American government that they would repatriate all American airmen "as soon as possible" after the Americans landed on Swedish soil. Many Americans remained in Sweden for several months until they were flown out of Sweden on one of the courier planes. After V-E Day, the Swedes released all remaining airmen to the United States. During the war, a total of 40 Americans airmen died in Sweden, most from wounds received in aerial combat. All of them were buried in the town of Malmo. By 1948, 38 of the deceased were moved by their families and buried in U.S. military cemeteries or private burial plots.[8]

The job of BAD2 servicemen was to travel to Sweden and repair the B-24s so that American pilots could fly them back to Warton. Once the planes arrived at the base, they were thoroughly overhauled and redeployed to bomber squadrons.[9]

The Warton base commander gave Sergeant Tom Miller two options. He could either go to Sweden and work on the B-24 project or be sent to France and assigned to the 99th Troop Carrier Squadron based in Villacoublay, France. Miller chose France. Twice a week, he flew to Berlin in a modified B-25 moving troops and supplies to and from Germany. The trips proved financially lucrative for Miller. The American government issued two cartons of cigarettes each week to each GI. Miller did not smoke and he sold his cigarette ration for $25 a carton to willing consumers in Berlin. Military regulations only allowed servicemen to send the amount of their pay home. Miller's profits on the sale of his cigarette ration allowed him to send his entire pay of $110 home each month to his mother. When Miller returned home from the war to Louisiana, he had amassed a $2,500 nest egg (equivalent to about $27,000 today).[10]

In the fall, the U.S.A.A.F. reassigned Miller from France to the American airbase at Wiesbaden. In December 1945, his commanding officer chose him to be part of a B-17 crew headed to Palestine. The crew's mission was to bring back 13 rabbis who had volunteered to attend to the spiritual needs of the Jewish people released from concentration camps in Germany. Work crews at Wiesbaden had modified the B-17 into a transport plane by installing seats in the bomb bay. The B-17 flew from Wiesbaden to Paris, then to Rome and onto Athens. After refueling in Athens, the B-17 headed to Cairo where it blew out a tail wheel while landing on the runway. After repairs in Cairo, the B-17 headed to Tel Aviv.[11]

Miller and the rest of the crew stayed in Tel Aviv for three days. Their Jewish hosts took them on a tour of the Holy Land, including visits to the Church of the Nativity in Bethlehem, the Dead Sea, Jericho, and Jerusalem. After their brief pilgrimage to the Holy Land, the crew and the Rabbis departed for Germany. On the return trip, the plane stopped in Tunis and the crew spent the day sightseeing in the city. After departing Tunis, the crew flew over Corsica, Italy, and the Swiss Alps. When the plane arrived at Wiesbaden, the control tower did not clear the B-17 for a landing because of ice and fog. The air traffic controllers instead directed the plane to a small airfield near Hanou, Germany. The Hanou field had a steel mat runway rather than one made of concrete. The B-17 landed on the runway at an odd angle and the holes in the steel mat cut the tires of the aircraft. The plane teetered and wobbled continuously on landing until the aircraft slid to a stop near the end of the runway. A shaken crew and 13 terrified rabbis safely emerged from the B-17.[12]

The following week, Sergeant Miller received the ultimate Christmas present, his orders to return home. He boarded a ship in Antwerp and after 21 days at sea arrived in New York City. From New York, he went to Camp Shelby in Hattiesburg, Mississippi, where he was discharged from the army on February 11, 1946, after almost four years of service. When he stepped off the Greyhound bus in Oak Grove, Louisiana, his proud parents were there to welcome their son home. Of his time in the service, Miller says: "I consider myself very fortunate, especially when you think of the ones that went over and never returned, and those that did return who may be far from the way they were when they went into the military."[13] While serving at BAD2, Miller and a Canadian airman exchanged dollars for good luck. On the Canadian dollar, Miller wrote down all the places he had visited during the war. He brought the dollar home with him as a memento of his time in the service. The memory of Sonia Dagger and her short life also returned home with

Miller. Her name was not on the dollar because it was already etched on his heart.

In June and July, BADA continued to reduce the force at BAD2 through redeployment home or to other facilities. The Maintenance Division saw a 38 percent reduction in production in June and July. In the Production Planning Section every production line came to a standstill and over 50 percent of the men working in the section were transferred back to the United States. The Engine Repair Department ceased operation at the end of June. B-24s carrying troops home, stopped to refuel at Warton on a daily basis. On August 2, the last plane to be repaired at Warton, ironically a B-24 Liberator, departed Warton to join its squadron. Work now began on closing the base down.[14]

On July 16, 1945, the nature of war changed forever. At 5:29 a.m. (mountain war time), the Americans detonated the first atomic bomb at Los Alamos, New Mexico. "The Gadget" (the code name for the weapon) illuminated the New Mexico sky and sent an orange-red pulsating fireball 30,000 feet into the morning air creating a classic mushroom cloud of radioactive vapor. The atomic age was born!

"The Gadget" was the end product of several years of research and testing conducted by the scientists working on the Manhattan Project. On August 2, 1939, Albert Einstein wrote a letter to President Roosevelt and informed him of German efforts to build an atomic bomb. Shortly after receiving Einstein's letter, Roosevelt commenced a secret project to build a viable atomic weapon for the American government. The original headquarters for the project was in an office in a federal building located at 90 Church Street in Manhattan, hence the origin of the code name for the mission, the Manhattan Project.[15]

At first, the project moved slowly with little progress. When the United States entered World War II, the project gained momentum. In 1942, Major General Leslie Groves took administrative control of the project and theoretical physicist J. Robert Oppenheimer directed the scientific research. The top secret project employed 130,000 people and spent over two billion dollars in building the bomb. By 1942, the project was no longer housed in Manhattan. The Manhattan Project had three primary sites: a plutonium production facility in Hanford, Washington; a uranium enrichment facility at Oak Ridge, Tennessee; and a weapons research and design laboratory in Los Alamos.[16] The culmination of the Manhattan Project's work, "the Gadget," was successfully tested at Los Alamos on the morning of July 16.

President Truman received the news of the successful atomic test while he was attending the Potsdam Conference in Germany. Truman, as vice president, had no knowledge of the Manhattan Project until he became president after Roosevelt's death in April. Truman informed British Prime Minister Clement Atlee and Soviet leader Joseph Stalin at the conference that the Americans now possessed a weapon of awesome power. The three leaders agreed that this new weapon should be employed against Japan if the Japanese did not accept the surrender terms put forth by the Allies. The leaders at the conference issued an ultimatum to Japan that called for immediate surrender or "face prompt and utter destruction."[17] The Japanese did not reply to the Potsdam ultimatum.

On July 25, President Truman issued orders to the XX Army Air Force to prepare to drop atomic weapons on Japan at the first favorable moment after August 3 if the Japanese did not accept the Allies' surrender proposal. On August 6, the *Enola Gay*, a B-29 Superfortress commanded by Colonel Paul Tibbetts, departed from Tinian and headed for the Japanese city of Hiroshima. Aboard the *Enola Gay* was a four-and-a-half-ton atomic bomb nicknamed "Little Boy." At approximately 8:15 a.m. in the morning, the *Enola Gay* dropped its payload on Hiroshima. Upon impact, an area of one-half mile was immediately vaporized, killing more than 70,000 people. Over time, another 70,000 people died of radiation poisoning and burns. After the attack on Hiroshima, the Allies called for the Japanese to surrender. Once again, Japanese authorities did not respond to the Allies' demands.[18]

On August 9, a second B-29, *Bockscar*, commanded by Major Charles Sweeney, headed for Nagasaki carrying an atomic bomb known as "Fat Boy." Sweeney dropped the device on Nagasaki at about noon. The bomb destroyed about half of the city and eventually killed over 140,000 people.[19] On August 10, Japanese authorities asked for terms of surrender. On August 14, the Japanese agreed to terms of surrender with the Allies and hostilities in the Pacific theater of war came to a halt. The Japanese and Allies signed the formal surrender documents on the deck of the American battleship, the USS *Missouri*, on September 2 in Tokyo Bay. World War II was over; the Allies had defeated the Axis powers. Now came the task of building the peace in the post-war world.

At Warton on August 14, Colonel Scott announced to the servicemen that Japan had accepted the Allies' terms of surrender and that the war was over. Jubilation resounded among the GIs stationed at the base.[20] They were now certain that they would be headed home rather than assigned to the Pacific theater. Their futures had begun! Throughout the day and night, religious services and secular celebrations commemorated the end of the scourge

The GIs stationed at BAD2 built and paid for a playground in Freckleton in loving memory of the victims of the air disaster. On August 20, 1945, more than 2,000 civilians and U.S. servicemen turned out for the playground's dedication ceremony. At the conclusion of the event, Colonel Scott removed the parachute silk that covered the seven ton granite rock and its commemorative plaque. Today, the memorial and playground still bear silent witness to the tragic events of August 23, 1944. The plaque reads: This playground presented to the children of Freckleton by their American neighbors of Base Air Depot No. 2 U.S.A.A.F. in recognition and remembrance of their common loss in the disaster of August 23rd 1944 (photograph courtesy of BAe Systems Heritage Division).

of war and the beginning of peace. Hope had finally triumphed over despair with the complete defeat of the Axis powers.

On Monday, August 20, more than 2,000 people, including the GIs still stationed at Warton, turned out for the dedication of a memorial playground in Freckleton. The servicemen of BAD2 built and paid for the playground in loving memory of the victims who lost their lives in the B-24 crash the year before. The GIs donated $10,400 for the building of the playground and provided $5,700 for its maintenance. More than 600 GIs from BAD2 also contributed their time and effort to build the playground. Working with private contractors, the servicemen built sliding boards from salvaged airplane parts, mixed concrete, plowed and graded the cricket and football fields and seeded the lawns.[21]

To open the dedication ceremony, the BAD2 band played traditional children's songs. Chaplain Lewandowski, from the Warton base, read a selection from Mark 10:14–16. The opening verse of the reading is: "Suffer the little children to come unto me and forbid them not, for such is the kingdom of God." During the ceremony, BAD2 commander, Colonel Scott, officially turned the playground over to the Freckleton Parish Council represented by the vicar of Freckleton, the Reverend J.W. Broadbent. In a moving speech, Scott asked the people of Freckleton to accept the playground as a symbol of Anglo-American unity.[22] After he completed his remarks to the gathering, Colonel Scott removed the parachute silk covering the seven-ton granite rock bearing a bronze commemorative plaque. The plaque reads:

> This playground presented to the children of Freckleton by their American neighbors of Base Air Depot No. 2 U.S.A.A.F in recognition and remembrance of their common loss in the disaster of August 23rd 1944.

The short but emotional ceremony was punctuated by American servicemen and British civilians standing together at silent attention while the BAD2 band played the national anthem.[23] Common loss and common affection had bound the two communities together in remembrance of their loved ones. The BBC and USO radio mobile units recorded the ceremony for broadcast across the United Kingdom and for American troops stationed in England.

On September 1, the Eighth Air Force officially closed BAD2. Some personnel remained to dispose of the supplies and property remaining on the base. BADA turned the base over to the American Technical School. The purpose of the school was to train servicemen with marketable skills that could be used in the civilian job market back in the United States. The military provided training in 18 trades, such as surveying, automotive repair, operation of heavy machinery, and electronics. Students took courses over an eight-week period and then returned to the United States. The technical school at Warton closed on January 11, 1946, when the U.S. military transferred its operation to occupied Germany. The Americans completely vacated Warton in February and returned the facility to the R.A.F.[24]

The production figures of BAD2 provide testimony to the productivity, ingenuity, and perseverance of the servicemen stationed at Warton. From 1943 to 1945, the base processed and delivered 10,068 aircraft to operational units. It repaired and overhauled 38,430 aircraft guns. The Radio and Signal Section repaired 146,626 radios and other communication devices. Mechanics repaired and overhauled 6,164 engines while technicians worked on and fixed 375,383 flight instruments. The Manufacture and Repair Section built 742,800 modification kits.[25] The production records in areas not mentioned above are equally as impressive.

Colonel Scott, in his farewell message to the servicemen of BAD2 on August 29, 1945, captured the essence of the men's contribution to the war effort when he wrote: "You have at all times been exceptionally loyal to your purpose, your country and your commanding officer. You have cooperated among yourselves in a superior manner in your combined efforts to attain the highest degree of success in all your achievements. We have done our part in bringing the great conflict to a victorious conclusion."[26]

11

Remembrance

"There are stars whose light only reaches the earth after they have fallen apart. There are people whose remembrance gives light in this world, long after they have passed away."
—The Talmud

The war ended with a decisive and thorough Allied victory over the Axis powers. The human cost of the war staggers the imagination. Never in the annals of history had so many human beings perished in war in such a short period of time. Estimates of the number of people killed during World War II range from 53,000,000 to 162,171,000. Depending on the estimate, the war claimed 8.7 million to 10.4 million people each year. The war was catastrophic for the Soviet Union. Somewhere between 20,600,000 (10.4 percent of the population) to 23,400,000 (13.9 percent of the population) Soviets died in the war with Germany. The Allies killed 6,850,000 Germans, about 9.5 percent of the population of Germany.[1]

Though every life is precious and dear, the war was far less costly in human lives for the British and Americans. British losses in World War II ranged from 388,000 soldiers and civilians to 458,000 or from 0.8 percent of their population to 0.94 percent. The Americans, who bore most of the responsibility for combat in the Pacific, lost somewhere between 418,500 to 500,000 individuals in the war, or about 0.32 percent to 0.4 percent of their population.[2]

No one has been able to place an exact price tag on the financial cost of the war. Rough estimates place the cost of lost property and war material at approximately one hundred trillion dollars in today's currency. World War II cost the Americans about 296 billion dollars, the equivalent of 4.4 trillion dollars today.[3] The British spent the equivalent of £2 trillion on the war.

For the Americans, World War II ushered in great changes and a new era. War production brought the Great Depression to an end. Conversion of

145

defense industries to peace-time production, along with the release of pent-up consumer demand, fueled exceptionally strong post-war economic growth. The American Gross Domestic Product (GDP) increased 50 percent from 1940 to 1950.[4] The automobile, aviation, and electronics industries provided new jobs and new products for the American public. GIs returning from overseas started families and used their veteran's benefits to purchase homes, creating a housing boom. The growing middle class witnessed the United States becoming the world leader in both manufacturing and technology.

The war was also a catalyst for social change in the United States. Civil rights and integration began to move to the center stage of American politics. In 1941, President Roosevelt issued Executive Order 8802. The order prohibited discriminatory employment practices in defense industries. It established the Committee on Fair Employment Practice to investigate alleged racial discrimination and eliminate it. This was the first presidential directive dealing with civil rights since Reconstruction. It was also the first directive to deal with discriminatory employment practices in private industry.

In 1947, Jackie Robinson broke the color line in Major League baseball when he played for the Brooklyn Dodgers. President Truman issued Executive Order 9981 to integrate the American Armed Forces in 1948. In 1954, the Supreme Court struck a fatal blow against segregation in public schools in the landmark case *Brown vs. the Board of Education of Topeka.*

The American social fabric saw other changes as well. Automobiles and new highways made the American people more mobile. People could now abandon the crowded cities for the more bucolic suburbs. Feminism had a rebirth due to the shifting roles of women during the war. As disposable income increased, Americans became more materialistic and purchased merchandise they wanted rather than needed. GIs returning from war were eager to regain the lost days of their youth. The result was marriage and a baby boom. In 2010, the U.S. Census Bureau listed the number of baby boomers in the United States as 78,058,246; about 26 percent of the American population.[5] According to the U.S. Census Bureau, the baby boom began in 1945 and ended in 1964.

World War II ushered in a new world order. The Allies occupied the conquered Axis powers, Germany, Italy and Japan. The war caused a serious decline in the power and stature of France and the United Kingdom. The United States and the Soviet Union emerged from World War II as the world's most powerful countries. From 1945 to 1949, only the United States possessed atomic weapons. American atomic dominance changed on August 29, 1949, when the Soviets successfully tested their first nuclear device on their testing range on the Kazakhstan steppe. By this time, most European countries were either under the domination of the Soviets or were under the protection of the American nuclear shield. The war had thrust the United States to the center of the world's stage. Americans could no longer retreat into the cocoon of isolationism. American foreign policy now rested on the cornerstones of containing communism, rebuilding Europe, promoting free trade, and providing our allies with a nuclear umbrella.

Though victorious, the United Kingdom emerged from World War II in far worse shape than the United States. The British spent almost one-quarter of their national wealth on the war and lost over 12 percent of its productive capacity in the air war with Germany. For six years, defense needs drove the British economy and it took a substantial period of adjustment to reorganize industry to peacetime production. To pay for the war, the British borrowed heavily from their own citizens and the Americans. In 1947, the British national debt was an astounding 238 percent of the British GDP.[6]

The Labor government of Prime Minister Clement Atlee introduced an austerity program from 1945 to 1951 to deal with the debt crisis. Wartime rationing continued until 1953, the year of Queen Elizabeth II's coronation. The Labor government also nationalized some British industries, causing more turmoil in an already tenuous economy. State direction of the economy had the unintended consequence of stifling entrepreneurship and this placed the United Kingdom at a competitive disadvantage in the global economy.

British economic woes, coupled with declining military power, led to the erosion of the British Empire beginning with independence of India in 1947. The end of the empire meant not only a decline in stature in the international community, but also a loss of markets and resources for British industry.

In Freckleton, the end of the war brought its citizen soldiers back to the village. Fathers, sons, brothers, and sweethearts now returned home from North Africa, Europe, Asia, and the Pacific Islands to resume their lives interrupted by six years of war. The Americans had left their base in Warton and returned home. For almost three years, Freckleton had been a bustling hub of activity, hosting both American and British servicemen in its community. Though Freckletonians desperately wanted to return to their normal lives, they were still haunted by the specter of war. The absence of a generation of children was a constant reminder of the cost of the victory over the forces of evil.

Almost immediately after the communal funeral, the question arose in the village about what would be the best way to permanently memorialize the victims of the crash, especially the children. Donations for a memorial came in from American servicemen stationed at Warton, local donors, and patrons from across the United Kingdom. Everyone in the village agreed that a monument should be erected over the communal grave to commemorate the victims of the crash. The Americans decided to build a memorial playground for the children of Freckleton. The servicemen completed construction of the playground in August 1945 and dedicated the facility on August 20. Controversy arose, however, between the Church Council and the Parish Council over whether a new school or village hall should be erected in memory of the victims.

The Church Council of Holy Trinity Church met on August 30, 1944, to discuss plans for a fitting memorial for the victims of the crash. The Church Council is the executive body of a Church of England parish. The council is responsible for the financial affairs of the church and cooperates with the vicar to promote the parish's mission. At the meeting, the vicar of Holy Trinity Church, the Reverend J. W. Broadbent, and the Church Council endorsed the establishment of two funds, one for the building of a new church school in memory of the victims of the crash and the other for a monument for the communal grave. The Church Council sought to raise £1,000 for the monument on the grave and £15,000 for the construction of a memorial school.[7] The vicar believed that the building of a new school would not only provide for the educational needs of the community but would also "comfort all that mourn" and allow "triumph over misfortune."[8] Broadbent also believed that a new school would provide Freckleton with a powerful symbol of recovery as well as hope and trust in the future.

The Freckleton Parish Council, the local, elected political authority, convened a special meeting on September 8, 1944, to discuss the memorial issue. The Parish Council decided to use the funds it had collected to build a memorial hall in honor of the victims. In a September 10 letter to the editor of the *Lancashire Daily Post*, Matthew Armstrong, chair of the Parish Council, wrote that the village hall "will be non-political and non-sectarian, and will be free to all who wish to avail themselves of the amenities which we hope will be provided."[9] Armstrong and the Parish Council saw the hall as a center where young people could participate in activities that led to "the betterment of their physical and moral lives."[10] The Parish Council also created the Village Memorial Hall Committee to oversee the construction and management of the hall. The council permitted each religious and public body to appoint one member to the memorial committee to insure a wide representation of constituencies in the village.

Within weeks after the tragedy, both the Church Council and the Parish Council had drawn clear lines in the sand over the memorial issue. The Reverend Broadbent, the Church Council and most Anglicans wanted to build a memorial school and had started to collect donations to fund the project. The vicar and his supporters believed they were entitled to rebuild their partially demolished school or have it replaced by a new structure. Holy Trinity had provided the only elementary school in the village for more than 100 years. The doors of the school were open to children of all faiths. The insurance policy on the school did not cover war damage and the British government's war damage compensation payment was not enough to repair or replace the building. The vicar and Church Council also reasoned that since the church school bore the brunt of the catastrophe, a damaged building and 38 students and two teachers killed, a memorial school would be a fitting tribute to the deceased.[11]

The Parish Council, consisting of many Methodists, saw the Church Council's memorial proposal to build a new church school as a blatant sectarian attempt to benefit Holy Trinity Church and its parishioners. The Parish Council felt its proposal to build a village hall would provide the community with a secular memorial that would benefit everyone in Freckleton regardless of their faith. Matthew Armstrong, chair of the Parish Council, argued that his group should make the decision about the memorial because they were the duly elected representatives of the people. Armstrong stated that the memorial should not be "a new church school. A village hall for all the people would be more suitable."[12] Walter Rawsthorne, a long-standing member of the Parish Council, contended that "Freckleton's memorial should have nothing to do with the providing of elementary education."[13] Rawsthorne suggested that if Freckletonians wanted a new school, they should build a council school funded by taxpayer money.

The memorial that was meant to unite the village and comfort its sorrow now began to divide the community. The clash between sectarian and secular interests was exacerbated by the division of Anglicans and Methodists on the subject. Three separate funds existed for memorial projects. There was an American fund intended to provide maintenance for the playground. The Church Council maintained a fund for a new school while the Parish Council collected money for a village hall. Competition for donors and no clear memorial plans hindered the Parish Council's and Church Council's appeals for donations. As a result, each organization's envisioned tribute for the victims languished for years.

The one thing everyone in the village could agree on was that they needed to erect a monument at the communal grave of the air crash victims. The Church Council raised £1,300 in donations from the families and friends of the deceased. The cost of the monument was £1,100. The Church Council set aside the remainder of the donations, £200, for maintenance of the gravesite.

The monument, built by the village, sits in front of the T-shaped communal grave and is a tall cross seated on a square base. There are sloped stone panels flanking both sides of the square pedestal. On closer inspection, the monument resembles an aircraft that has crashed to earth with its nose section buried in the ground. The cross represents the tail section and fuselage of the aircraft. The square pedestal is a continuation of the fuselage. The sloped stone panels coming out of the square pedestal symbolize the plane's wings. The nose of the aircraft appears buried in the ground along with the victims of the air tragedy. The inscription on the square base of the monument reads:

> Sacred to the memory of the two teachers, 38 scholars and seven civilians who lost their lives when an American Liberator Bomber crashed during a thunderstorm and destroyed part of the adjoining school and other property on the 23rd August, 1944. This monument was erected over their grave by public subscription.
> "In God We Trust"

The two sloped panels on either side of the square pedestal contain the names of the children, teachers, and civilians who lost their lives in the crash.

The Parish Council dedicated the monument on May 24, 1947. Hundreds of people crowded Holy Trinity Church and the cemetery to take part in the ceremony. The service commenced in the church with the choir singing "Through the Night of Doubt and Sorrow" by Bernhardt S. Ingeman. The lyrics of the hymn point out Christ's blessings upon those who will be the chosen few laborers in God's plentiful harvest at the end of the world. Following the hymn, lecturers read Psalm XXIII ("The Lord Is My Shepherd") and Matthew XVIII, verses 1–14 (a selection about children).[14]

After the readings, the congregation sang "Let Saints on Earth in Concert Sing," written by Charles Wesley in 1759. This is a jubilant, uplifting piece that joins the living and the dead in communion with each other. The congregation then recited the "Our Father" and other prayers. The Bishop of Blackburn, Wilfred Marcus Askwith, delivered a consoling homily to the congregation followed by the hymn, "Jesus Lives!" This song is about resurrection and eternal life and is often sung at Easter services.[15]

At the conclusion of "Jesus Lives!" the congregation processed out of the church to the communal grave. Once at the gravesite, the Reverend Broad-

On May 24, 1947, the Parish Council dedicated the monument that commemorates the victims buried in the T-shaped communal grave in Holy Trinity Cemetery. The cost of the monument was 1,100 British pounds sterling. The monument's shape resembles an aircraft nose-diving into the ground. The two sloped panels on either side of the square pedestal contain the names of the teachers, students, and civilians who lost their lives in the tragedy (photograph by Judy Hedtke).

bent recited a series of versicles, short, prayerful verses, to which the congregation offered their response. The Archdeacon of Lancashire then stepped forward and said: "We have come together to unveil and dedicate this memorial to the 38 students, their two teachers and the seven neighbors who lost their lives in the airplane disaster on 23rd August, 1944."[16] He then invited James Stanley Barlow, village leader and grandfather of several of the victims, to step forward and unveil the monument.

With the new monument revealed to the congregation, Bishop Askwith dedicated the memorial with the following words: "In the faith of Jesus Christ, we dedicate this cross in the memory of the children and the others of this parish who died on 23rd August, 1944: In the name of the Father, and of the Son, and the Holy Ghost, Amen."[17]

The choir, joined by the rest of the gathering, sang a final hymn, "Abide with Me." Henry Francis Lyte wrote the lyrics for this song while he lay dying of tuberculosis in November 1847. He completed the work three weeks before his death. The hymn is often sung at funerals and is regularly performed on Remembrance Day in the United Kingdom. Since 1927, the first and last verses are traditionally sung before the kick-off of the final FA Cup match. The dedication service concluded with a traditional Anglican blessing.[18]

On the last page of the dedication ceremony pamphlet, the Reverend Broadbent continued to make his argument for a memorial school. He wrote that "the work of education in this parish has been left in the hands of the Church of England for more than 100 years, and its record has never been in dispute or questioned."[19] He went on to say that the most fitting memorial for the air crash victims would be a school. He concluded his remarks by writing that the memorial school "is our mission and opportunity, and we hoped that it would be shared by others. Alas! A chapter of frustration and sabotage has followed which can only be closed by opening a new one of practical sympathy and good will."[20]

Over the next decade, the vicar pursued his vision of a memorial school and continued to solicit funds for the project. In 1954, construction on the new school began, financed by funds solicited for the memorial school and help from the Church of England. The first phase of the building project included the construction of three infants' rooms. In 1959, the second phase of construction began with the addition of an assembly hall, staff rooms, and kitchens. The school was finally completed in 1970 with the addition of four junior classrooms and playing fields for the students. In 1979, Holy Trinity demolished the old school hit by the B-24 bomber and transferred its cornerstone to the new facility.[21] The demolition crew removed a tragic reminder of Freckleton's loss with the destruction of the old school building. The new school provided hope for a brighter future for a new generation of children living in the village.

Shortly after suggesting the building of a memorial hall, the Parish Council turned over the donations it had collected and stewardship of the project to the Village Hall Committee created by the council. The committee, in turn, placed the funds in a charitable trust, where the trustees had sole control over how to invest the money. As the decades passed, the memorial hall remained unbuilt because of insufficient funds, the lack of a centrally located site, and continued harassment by villagers who opposed the project.[22]

33 years after the air disaster, the village finally built a memorial hall in 1977 on the site of the old Hodgson Institute. The stated purpose of the

Freckleton Memorial Hall, as listed by the Charity Aids Foundation, is that the hall is "for the use of the inhabitants of the parish of Freckleton without distinction of political, religious, or other opinions. The hall's uses include meetings, lectures and leisure-time occupations with the object of improving conditions of life for said inhabitants. Special regard shall be paid to the needs of youth residents in the area of benefit."[23] The mission of the hall has remained true to the original concepts put forth by the Parish Council in 1944. The memorial hall has become a central landmark in the social lives of Freckletonians and provides space for club meetings, concerts, and other community activities.

The controversy concerning memorial funds spilled over into the 21st century. In November 2000, Freckleton Parish Council member Trevor Fiddler helped to uncover £110,000 cash legacy in a private limited company run as a charity by anonymous trustees.[24] During the contentious debate over the format for the memorial, the Parish Council had transferred donations they received for the memorial to the trust. Some of the money in the charitable trust was used to construct the memorial hall in 1977, while another portion of the money was used to underwrite the annual village music festival. The rest of the donations remained in the trust accruing interest. The discovery of the money rekindled smoldering passions from the original memorial debate because most of the anonymous trustees turned out to be Methodists opposed to the school project. At a public meeting, upset villagers demanded that the funds in the charitable trust be transferred back to the control of the Parish Council.

The Parish Council eventually reached a compromise solution that restored harmony in the village and doused the flames of resentment. The funds remained in a charitable trust but run by a more inclusive board of trustees in a more transparent manner. The trustees must now include clergy from the Church of England, the Methodist Church, and the Roman Catholic faith as well as three members of the Parish Council.[25] The income from the fund must be used in a non-discriminatory fashion to benefit the community with an emphasis on programs for the youth of the village. When Ruby Whittle Currell, one of the infant school survivors, heard that the argument over the charitable trust had been amicably settled, she told a *Daily Mail* reporter that "it is wonderful news and it will be nice to see things done for the village where I grew up."[26]

In the United States, veterans who had served at Warton formed the BAD2 Association in 1977. Servicemen like Richard McClune, Ralph Scott, David Mayor, and Tom Miller organized the BAD2 Association to perpetuate the history of the base, to encourage reunions of BAD2 veterans, and to insure that the memory of their comrades, who gave their lives for their country, did not perish with them. Membership in the organization is open to all military personnel and civilians who served at Warton. Other interested individuals could join as associate members. Until 2010, the association published *BAD News*, a quarterly publication that provided information and stories of interest to its membership.[27] The association held its first reunion in 1978. Until age and health took their toll, association members returned to the Freckleton/Warton area on a regular basis to renew old friendships and to honor and remember the victims of the air tragedy.

Valerie Preston Whittle became an associate member of the BAD2 Association in August 1986. As a seven-year-old, she escaped the flames of Holy Trinity School but lost her brother George in the fire. She now wanted to meet some of the servicemen who had helped her to safety on that tragic day. In his letter that extended membership in the association to Mrs. Whittle, Richard McClune, chair of the membership committee, expressed the close ties that still bound American servicemen to Freckleton. McClune wrote: "Words are just not adequate to express the feeling we have when an individual from England asks to join our association."[28] He continued: "We, whom have strong memories of our days in England, do not consider you as a foreigner but as a member of *our family* [McClune's emphasis] that lives many miles away. All the children who were in the school the day of the disaster have an exclusive spot in our hearts and their memories will live forever."[29] The children, who are now adults, also have a special place in their hearts for the Americans who selflessly came to their rescue on that tragic August morning.

The BAD2 Association donated £704 in 1993 to buy ten new seats for Holy Trinity Church. Association members dedicated the chairs to the doctors and nurses of the base hospital who treated the children burned in the school fire.[30] The medical staff at Warton was able to save three children pulled from the wreckage of the school.

More than 800 people gathered at the Freckleton C.E. (Church of England) school's playground at 7 p.m. on August 23, 1994, for a memorial service to commemorate the 50th anniversary of the air disaster. The Freckleton Brass Band played several hymns including "Praise My Soul" and "Abide with Me." David Mayor, the founder of the BAD2 Association, recited his vivid account of the tragedy "The Day Freckleton Wept," and then the names of each victim were read to the congregation. Ruby Whittle Currell broke down in tears as she listened to the names of her classmates killed in the school fire. Moments later, she bravely composed herself to read a selection from the Book of Micah.[31]

The Reverend Stephen Brian, vicar of Holy Trinity Church, gave the homily. Brian said the village should always remember the victims but should also look to the future with hope. He told the congregation: "It was probably the worst day in the history of Freckleton, and the community still bears the scars today."[32] At the conclusion of the prayer service, the Royal British Legion flags were lowered as a sole trumpeter played "Last Post" (a song used in British army camps to signal the end of the day). The pupils from Freckleton C.E. School then sang "We'll Meet Again," a selection from a musical of the same name about a World War II evacuee.[33] The evening concluded with refreshments served in Memorial Hall.

Earlier in the day, a group of about 40 mourners held their own unofficial tribute to the victims at the communal gravesite. Some of the individuals present were upset with the Reverend Brian and did not want to attend the evening service conducted by the vicar. Others simply wanted to defy Brian by holding their own service without him present but also went to the evening ceremony. The villagers were angry with Brian because he refused to allow nicknames, such as dad or mum, on the headstones in Holy Trinity Cemetery. The vicar said the guidelines of the diocese and the Council for the Care of Churches did not allow the use of such monikers on monuments in Church of England cemeteries. A Church of England consistory court upheld the vicar's ruling citing the *Council for the Care of Churches Handbook*. The handbook states: "Nicknames or pet names (Dad, Mum, Ginger) inscribed in stone would carry overtones of the dog cemetery unsuitable for the resting place of Christian men and women."[34] The vicar's decision and the ruling by the church tribunal caused dissension in the village and displeasure with the Church of England.

The unofficial ceremony took place at 10:45 a.m., the approximate time of the airplane crash. As the tribute began, grey storm clouds gathered and rain poured down on those honoring the victims. The irony of the weather conditions was not lost on those gathered at the gravesite. Gwen Smith, who had been in Holy Trinity School the day of the crash, said: "It was just like this on the day it happened. The skies were dark just as they are today as we were all trying to scramble out of school."[35] Barbara Cunpsty commented that "every year we remember what happened but today has been especially poignant."[36] The highlight of the tribute was when Una Higgins, who organized the ceremony, placed a wreath at the base of the memorial at the communal grave.

At 10:30 a.m. on August 23, 1997, the Mighty Eighth Heritage Museum held a dedication ceremony for the BAD2 garden on the museum's grounds in Pooler, Georgia. The ceremony commenced at the exact time that the *Classy Chassis II* took off from Warton 53 years earlier. The 25-foot-by-25-foot square garden contains bushes and flowering plants as well as two plaques. One plaque commemorates the victims of the Freckleton crash and all the servicemen who died at Warton during the war. The other plaque provides a brief history of BAD2 and a succinct description of the events of August 23, 1944. The garden also contains a stone monument that reads: "To the memory of the following who died when an American B-24 crashed destroying the Freckleton Church of England School on the 23rd August, 1944."

The memorial lists the 38 students and the two teachers who died in the crash. The stone also contains a dedication that comes from the poem, "For the Fallen" written by Laurence Binyon, a poet from Lancaster, England. Binyon wrote the poem in memory of soldiers who died in World War I. The dedication on the monument reads:

> They shall not grow old, as we
> That are left to grow old.
> Age shall not weary them nor
> The years condemn.
> At the going down of the sun
> And in the morning,
> We shall remember them

Though most of the veterans of BAD2 have now passed away, their memories of the children of Freckleton are forever etched in stone in Pooler, Georgia.

Ralph Scott, the secretary of BAD2, gave the keynote address at the memorial garden's dedication. Scott told the gathering that "out of the ashes of that terrible day has sprung a bond between those of us on both sides of the ocean that is strong and, hopefully, will be carried on by those who succeed us."[37] In dedicating the garden, Scott told the gathering "we are remembering those who were lost to us many years ago. They shall not grow old as we have done and we shall remember them as they were, young men, young women and small children."[38] Scott concluded his remarks by trying to make sense of tragedy with a plea that we should all remember that the people "who died while wearing the uniforms of our two countries, the civilians who were killed and the innocent children who were lost to us were all part of the price paid to assure our present day freedoms."[39]

The ceremony concluded with Richard McClune laying a wreath at the stone monument. Following the wreath-laying ceremony, the Right Reverend Henry Louttit, the Episcopal bishop of Georgia, formally blessed the garden. The group walked from the garden to a reception in the Museum Art Gallery as Dan Ailes appropriately played "Blest be the Tie that Binds Us" on his bagpipes.[40]

August 23, 2004, marked the 60th anniversary of the air disaster. The squabbles over the charitable trust and the headstone controversy were now past history. Three remembrance services, two in Freckleton and one in the United States, were held to honor and commemorate the victims. At the Mighty Eighth Air Force Heritage Museum, members of the BAD2 Association laid a wreath at the stone memorial honoring the crash victims. At 10:40 a.m. in Freckleton, BAD2 Association members from both the United States and the United Kingdom placed a wreath on the communal grave in Holy Trinity Cemetery. Among the Americans at the wreath-laying ceremony was Ernest Bloemendal from Stillwater, Minnesota. Ernie's brother John was the pilot of the *Classy Chassis II*. Ernie himself had been stationed at Warton in 1943. After the ceremony Bloemendal told a reporter for *The Blackpool Gazette* that he was "touched to see so many people turn out to honor the memory of my brother and all those who were killed."[41]

The evening service in Freckleton started at 7 p.m. Clergy representing Anglicans, Methodists, and Roman Catholics offered prayers and remarks in remembrance of the victims. Once again, Ruby Whittle Currell read a passage from the Bible and the Freckleton Brass Band offered musical accompaniment for the hymns. For many members of the BAD2 Association, this was their last trip to Freckleton and their final opportunity to memorialize the victims of the air crash. Time was finally gaining ground on the "greatest generation."

In 2007, the BBC did a short documentary on the Freckleton air disaster. The piece aired on the BBC's *Inside Out—North West* on January 26, 2007. While the crew was filming the documentary, they asked residents why there was no plaque at the site where the B-24 crashed into the school. Residents working with the film crew could offer no reason why there was no fitting tribute at the crash site. With a nudge from Harry Latham and other residents of the village, the Parish Council and the charitable trust provided the help and financial support to place a commemorative plaque on the old school site.

In a brief ceremony on Wednesday, May 2, 2007, two children from the Freckleton C.E. School unveiled the plaque. One of the children was 11-year-old Mary Thompson. She is the great-great-niece of disaster survivor

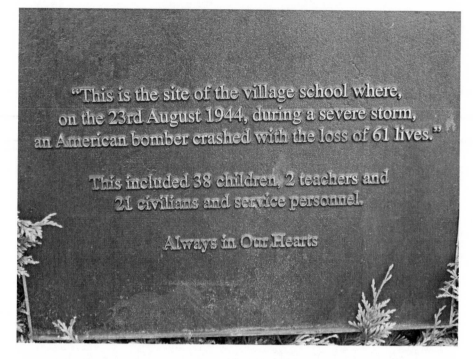

"This is the site of the village school where, on the 23rd August 1944, during a severe storm, an American bomber crashed with the loss of 61 lives."

This included 38 children, 2 teachers and 21 civilians and service personnel.

Always in Our Hearts

In 2007, the BBC produced a short documentary on the Freckleton air disaster. The crew filming the documentary could not find the site where the *Classy Chassis II* crashed into the Holy Trinity School. The original edifice had been demolished and the village had not placed a marker to indicate the former location of the school. The Parish Council remedied this situation when it dedicated a commemorative plaque on May 2, 2007, at the site of the old school (photograph by Judy Hedtke).

Ruby Currell. The Reverend Peter Ford, the vicar of Warton, dedicated the plaque and the Freckleton Brass Band provided the musical interlude. The plaque reads: "This is the site of the village school where, on the 23rd August 1944, during a severe storm, an American bomber crashed with the loss of 61 lives. This included 38 children, 2 teachers and 21 civilians and service personnel. Always in Our Hearts." Harry Latham, crash survivor, remarked about the plaque: "This is something we should have done a few years ago. I hope it will be there for generations to come."[42]

The memorial service to mark the 65th anniversary of the air disaster featured an ecumenical service that focused on the familiar Christian themes of salvation and resurrection. Anglican, Methodist, and Roman Catholic clergy conducted the service held at 6:30 p.m. at the Freckleton C.E. School campus. The Freckleton Brass Band, under the direction of Paul Daulton, provided the music for the ceremony. After a brief welcome by the Reverend Percival of Holy Trinity Church, the congregation sang "Thou Whose Almighty Word." This missionary anthem, written by John Marriot, calls on Christians to spread the Gospel and God's word throughout the world.

After the opening hymn, the Reverend Scholz, also of Holy Trinity Church, led the gathering in prayer. Ruby Whittle Currell then read a short reading from the Gospel according to St. Mark. In the passage, Jesus admonished his apostles not to prevent children from coming to him because the Kingdom of God belonged to children and those who became like children. The reading stresses the innocence of children, a theme of the 1944 funeral and all of the ensuing remembrance services. The Reverend Hartley, from St. Paul's Church in Warton, read a selection from Romans, chapter eight, that stresses preparing the way for the Lord.[43]

After the readings, the Reverend Ruddick, a Methodist minister, and Father Burns, a Catholic priest, told the gathering the story of the tragic crash 65 years ago. Following their recitation, the congregation sang "Great Is Thy Faithfulness." The hymn, written by Henry Lyte, stresses the loyalty and fidelity of God to the true believer. The choir of Westminster Abbey sang this hymn at the wedding of Princess Elizabeth and Phillip Mountbatten, the Duke of Edinburgh, on November 20, 1947.[44]

An awed silence descended on the gathering as the clergy read the names of the fatalities from the air crash. When the last name was read, the clergy joined together and recited the stanza from Laurence Binyon's poem "For the Fallen" that appears on the memorial for the crash victims in Pooler, Georgia.

The congregation finally broke their silence when they sang "Thine Be the Glory." George Handel wrote this hymn and it is often sung during Easter liturgies because of its powerful theme of resurrection. The service concluded with benediction offered by the Reverend Ruddick. Following the service, there was an exhibition of 1940s photos of Freckleton, including pictures from the tragic day 65 years before.[45]

The legacy of the Freckleton air disaster runs deep in the village of Freckleton and in the hearts and souls of its inhabitants as well as the GIs who served at BAD2. Unfortunately, the breadth of the legacy is not very wide. Outside of Lancashire, most British people are unaware of the tragedy that befell Freckleton on August 23, 1944. In the United States, the catastrophe is virtually unknown unless you are a relative of an individual who served at BAD2 or have strolled through the memorial garden at the Mighty Eighth Air Force Heritage Museum.

In Freckleton, there is a memorial service conducted every August 23 in remembrance of the crash victims. The local press covers the ceremony and usually runs a background story about the tragic events of 1944. On the milestone anniversaries, there is often national coverage by the BBC. The only memorials to the crash in the United Kingdom are located in Freckleton. In the United States, there is a wreath-laying ceremony at the stone monument in the memorial garden at the Might Eighth Air Force Heritage Museum every August. The only plaques in the United States that commemorate the incident are also located in the museum's garden.

In over 65 years, there has only been one book written about the disaster. Joyce Turner, a local librarian, published *The Freckleton Tragedy, 1944* in 2007. The work is the size of a pamphlet, only 62 pages in length, and provides the reader with a succinct account of the events of August 23, 1944, and the immediate aftermath of the catastrophe. Turner's book received some local notoriety, but a search of the World Cat database reveals that only five libraries, all located in the United Kingdom, possess the work. Harry Holmes has published two excellent works on BAD2, *The World's Greatest Air Depot* and *Warton in Wartime*. Both books, however, only devote a single chapter to the tragedy. Fred West wrote an excellent article about the crash in the Harrington Aviation Museum's publication, *The Dropzone*. His article "Classy Chassis II" presents the reader with a solid synopsis of the crash. Other works, such as James Dodson's *Final Rounds*, mention the disaster in passing but do not offer a significant description or analysis of the tragedy. Local histories provide only limited coverage of the crash. Very little has actually been written about the Freckleton air disaster and what literature exists does not command a wide audience in either the United States or the United Kingdom.

There have been two poems written about the Freckleton air disaster. Helen Richardson of Preston wrote the first poem, "With Deepest Sympathy to Freckleton," shortly after the disaster in late August 1944. In her work, the poet described the demise of the *Classy Chassis II* as it crashed into the village and destroyed Holy Trinity School. In sentimental verse, she laments the deaths of the children, teachers and crew of the plane. She ends her work by offering her deepest sympathies to the families of the victims. The poem remains unpublished and is housed in the BAe North West Heritage Group Museum in Warton.

David Carr has written the only published poem about the Freckleton catastrophe. Carr's uncle and namesake, David, perished in the infants' school fire at the age of six. The older David's father, Jim Carr, was at sea serving in the British navy at the time of the disaster and returned to Freckleton on compassionate leave after the communal funeral. Carr's wife Agnes and their older son William (the poet's father) were left with the unenviable task of identifying and burying David's remains. Dave Carr, the poet, remembers that his grandmother Agnes kept a Hummel figure of a boy with a satchel on her mantelpiece. She told her grandson not to touch the figure because it was very precious to her. Agnes said it reminded her of another little boy, one lost in a fire many years before. Carr remembers his grandmother's eyes filling with tears as the memories of her lost son came streaming back to her as she gazed at the figurine.

Carr's poem, "The Freckleton Air Disaster," tells the story of the crash and funeral in a ballad format similar to the style employed by Gordon Lightfoot in his song the "Wreck of the Edmund Fitzgerald," The poet captures the pathos and horror of the tragic day in verse. Carr also pays tribute in his poem not only to his grandparents and uncle but to all the parents who lost a child in the tragedy. The poem is Carr's attempt to understand his grandmother's tears and keep the memory of her son David, and all the other victims, alive.

David Carr is an electrical engineer who writes prose and poetry as a hobby. Carr's poem, written in December 2006, appears below in its entirety with the poet's permission.

The Freckleton Air Disaster

In mid Forty Four came the turn of the war:
Our troops had advanced up the Seine,
And Hitler withdrew as the allies pushed through,
Growing strong since the D-Day campaign.

Jim thought of his boys as he worked the convoys
And patrols in the South China Sea.
Not sure if or when, he would see them again,
Back at home where he longed to be.

In a town on the Fylde, Agnes finally smiled
As she heard that her Jim would return.
After months without news of the ships and their crews
Things had finally taken a turn.

On the twenty third of August they heard
That Paris was soon to be freed.
The day started bright for a U.S. test flight
And the two planes came up to speed.

The Lancashire base was warned of the pace
Of a storm moving up from the south.
From all the reports, they'd agreed to abort
As they searched out the dark Ribble mouth.

They heard one airmen say that they must turn away
As suddenly day turned to night,
For the other plane's crew it was too late, they knew,
As the storm clouds shut out the light.

From out of the black came an ungodly crack
As a fireball of lightning struck.
The huge burning plane roared on down through the rain
'Till the wing hit a tree and broke up.

The Sad Sack Café was just carried away
As the great metal carcass swept past.
Further over the road it was seen to explode
As the school took the brunt of the blast.

The wreckage became a huge ocean of flame
As rescuers battled the blaze.
With increasing dread they recovered the dead
In a mission that lasted for days.

Of the children inside, some thirty eight died
And the grim news seeped out through the nation.
The stunned disbelief soon dissolved into grief
As they mourned for a lost generation.

So poor Jim returned as soon as he learned
That his young son had died in the school.
He had lived with the threat to his own life and yet
The direction of fate can be cruel.

Can you close your eyes tight and imagine the sight,
Tiny coffins row after row?
Can you see parents left standing torn and bereft?
Can you feel the tears start to flow?

There were many who tried to understand why,
And questioned their faith that day.
And some would hear screams evermore in their dreams
As Freckleton's nightmare replayed.

Now a place to reflect and pay their respects
Marks the graves where the victims all lay.
A memorial cross tells the world of their loss
When the dark angel passed by that day.

Coverage of the disaster on the internet is also very thin. There are only two websites completely dedicated to the air catastrophe. Wikipedia maintains one of the sites. The Lancashire Aircraft Investigation Team maintains the other site, "The Freckleton Disaster." This organization researches the history of World War II air crashes that took place in northwest England. It is also actively involved in the recovery of artifacts from the crash sites. The organization's website about the Freckleton crash is primarily based on U.S.A.A.F. records of the accident and provides little critical analysis of the crash itself. A Google search reveals fewer than 100 other websites that mention the disaster. Most of these sites only contain a paragraph or two about the crash or are succinct news stories about the survivors or coverage of the memorial services on the anniversary of the disaster.

BAD News, the publication of the BAD2 Association, often contained stories about Warton and the Freckleton disaster. David Mayor published his often cited article, "The Day Freckleton Wept," in *BAD News* in 1979. His story became the cornerstone for all further research on the air crash. David Madden first published his survivor's story in *BAD News* in 2009. Though *BAD News* is a treasure trove of eyewitness accounts about the tragedy, its readership is confined to members of the association and their friends and relatives. *BAD News* went out of publication in 2010.

Newspapers, past and present, are a source of knowledge about the tragedy. At the time of the crash, the catastrophe was the leading stories in local paper like the *Lytham–St. Anne's Express*, *The Blackpool Gazette*, and the *Lancashire Daily Post* (later the *Evening Post*). National papers, like *The Times*, relegated coverage of the Freckleton story to the back pages. Only large American papers, like *The New York Times*, carried articles on the tragedy. Through the 1950s, whenever there was a plane crash, newspaper reporters compared the death toll from the accident with the Freckleton catastrophe. The Freckleton comparison disappeared in the 1960s when planes became larger and air accidents claimed more victims. Today, the local Lancashire newspapers run stories about the crash on milestone anniversaries and cover the annual memorial services. In 2007, the BBC produced and broadcasted a short documentary about the Freckleton air disaster on their Inside Out—North West program. This is the only documentary that has been filmed about the crash.

Why is the Freckleton air disaster not widely known in the United Kingdom and the United States? The overwhelming death and destruction of World War II overshadowed the tragic events of one day in a small English village. Epic stories like the D-Day invasion, the liberation of Paris, the Holocaust, and the detonation of the atomic bomb pushed the Freckleton catastrophe from the main stage to the local theater. The air disaster received limited national press coverage in the United Kingdom and the United States. The liberation of Paris, Soviet gains on the eastern front and Allied progress in the Pacific took precedence over a single bomber crash in northwest

England. The story never made it to the front page and remained buried in the back pages of the major papers.

The citizens of Freckleton bore their suffering and mourned their dead in silent dignity. They did not seek to blame the Americans for the accident and did not want to create an international controversy that could damage Anglo-American relations and impair the Allied war effort. Instead, they joined the Americans in a bond of affection to honor and bury the dead. The lack of controversy, litigation, and bitter acrimony, as well as the desire to return to normal village life, helped to take the disaster out of the spotlight.

As the years passed, other tragedies, such as Aberfan and Lockerbie, supplanted the Freckleton air disaster in the British collective memory. The tragedy at Aberfan in South Wales occurred on October 21, 1966, when a tip of coal waste slid down a mountainside into the Welsh mining village. The

Elsie Barlow (now Dollin) gave Pearl Whittle a scarf for her 15th birthday. Pearl died with her parents, Allan and Rachael, when the *Classy Chassis II* crashed into the Sad Sack Café. Several days after the crash, Elsie was walking by the debris that once was the eatery and spotted Pearl's charred scarf in the rubble. She retrieved it and kept the remnants of the scarf as a memento of her friendship with Pearl. The scarf appears in this picture along with a photograph of Pearl Whittle taken shortly before her death (photograph by Judy Hedtke).

slide first destroyed a farm cottage and killed all of its occupants. It then engulfed the Pantglas Junior School and 20 houses in the village. The deadly slide left 144 people dead including 116 students and five of their teachers. About 50 percent of the children enrolled in the junior school died that Friday morning.[46]

On December 21, 1988, a Boeing 747 crashed into the village of Locker-bie, Scotland, and killed 270 people. Pan Am Flight 103 was a transatlantic route that originated in Frankfurt, Germany, and was destined for Detroit, Michigan, with stopovers in London and New York City. After takeoff from Heathrow Airport in London, the plane exploded mid-air in the skies over Lockerbie. A bomb planted by Libyan terrorists, seeking to avenge American air attacks on Libyan leader Moammar Gadhafi, brought down the aircraft. All 259 people aboard the Boeing 747 died in the explosion. Debris from the aircraft fell on several houses in the Scottish village and killed 11 more people on the ground. The final death toll from the terrorist attack was 270 people.[47]

The compelling story of the Freckleton disaster is not widely known outside of northwest England but it is a tale worth telling. The tragedy is a cautionary story about the harsh realities and the brutal costs of war. Both the Americans and British realized that the ultimate blame for the accident rested on the shoulders of the fascists who initiated the war. The Americans and British also understood that the Freckleton disaster was part of the hefty price paid for freedom and democracy. That is why there was no blame, no recrimination and no acrimony over the mishap.

The most enduring legacy of the Freckleton air disaster is the remembrance of the victims. Their names are not only enshrined on monuments in Freckleton and Pooler, Georgia, but also in the hearts and souls of all those who know their story. In the end, the only guarantee we have of immortality is that someone remembers us and who we once were. As long as their story is told, the victims of the air disaster at Freckleton will continue to live on into the future they lost on the morning of August 23, 1944.

12

Freckleton Today

"We should never forget those children and adults who died. I certainly never will."

—Ruby Whittle Currell,
survivor of the infants' school fire.

Since World War II, the population of Freckleton has grown from approximately 1,000 to 6,045 people. This is an increase of approximately 600 percent over the past 70 years. Suburban sprawl, the desirability of living in a quaint English village, and the availability of employment opportunities in the aircraft industry are all important factors in Freckleton's growth. Despite the rapid increase in population, Freckleton has remained a relatively homogeneous English village.

Freckleton is overwhelmingly white and British. About 99 percent of the population describe themselves as Caucasian and of British ancestry. The remaining 1 percent are people of color, mostly Asians from China or India.[1] Freckleton residents tend to be more Christian (82 percent) than the general British population (71.7 percent). The majority of villagers consider themselves to be either Anglican or Methodists. About 16.5 percent of the residents do not practice any religion.[2] According to the most recent census, residents of Freckleton are middle-aged, middle class, and tend to be in good health. The median age for the village is 41, which is close to the median age for the entire United Kingdom.[3] Nearly 54.4 percent of the residents are in the upper and middle classes with 24.3 percent of the population working in upper- or intermediary-level managerial or professional positions. The working class comprises about 45.6 percent of the population, with 14.8 percent working as skilled manual laborers. Approximately 22.2 percent are semi-skilled or unskilled workers with the remaining 14.7 percent on state benefits or unemployed.[4] Only about 20 percent of the population suffers from long-term or chronic illnesses that would limit their employment.

The overwhelming majority of Freckletonians (81.5 percent) own their homes. Approximately 24.7 percent of the villagers live in single homes while 62.6 percent are in semi-detached houses.[5] The average house in Freckleton has 5.5 rooms and the average number of people in each household is 2.35 persons. Freckletonians tend to work close to home, the average commute is 7.3 miles, and they travel to work by car rather than public transportation.[6] The average work week for men in the village is 41 hours. Women tend to put in fewer hours in the workplace, averaging about 31 hours a week.[7]

Though the population of Freckleton has dramatically increased since 1945, the core aspects of the village have remained the same. Freckleton is still a white, Christian, English village where middle- and working-class families live in modest owner-occupied houses. Its citizens still work close to home and the community remains a central aspect of their lives. Club Day, the Freckleton Brass Band, the music festival and the commemoration of August 23 are as important and vital to the community today as when the war ended in the summer of 1945.

Today, Freckleton has two elementary schools, Freckleton C.E. (Church of England) Primary School and the Freckleton Strike Lane Primary School. Freckleton C.E., located on Church Lane, is the former Holy Trinity School. It is now an aided Church of England school for children aged four to eleven. An aided school is state funded but a foundation or trust owns the school buildings and has substantial influence over the curriculum and the operation of the institution. The school is attached to the Blackburn Diocese and has close links to Holy Trinity Church where the students attend services throughout the school year. The curriculum is broad and progressive and gives priority to the "acquisition of basic academic skills."[8] The school bell that Headmaster Billington rang at Holy Trinity School on the fateful morning of August 23, 1944, is housed at Freckleton C.E. Primary School and is prominently displayed for all to see when entering the building. A plaque near the bell commemorates the date of the tragedy.

In 1965, Freckleton opened a second school. The Freckleton Strike Lane Primary School is a community school that provides parents with a secular option to educate their children. The concept of a community school in the village dates back to the debate over the crash memorial in the summer of 1944. At that time, Matthew Armstrong, chair of the Parish Council, and other council members argued in favor of establishing a community school in Freckleton. Their idea came to fruition 21 years later with the opening of the Strike Lane School. The school is open to all pupils and provides students with a wide range of academic and extracurricular activities. Both schools maintain strong ties to the community and integrate the history of the crash into all levels of the curriculum. The children of the community also participate in the memorial services held on August 23.

In 1993, Holy Trinity Church went through a major renovation and restoration project. Contractors installed a new floor and removed most of the pew boxes. Builders extended the sanctuary, removed the signature brass communion rails, and moved the altar forward. A plaque in the porch way records the major benefactors for the refurbishment project. These benefactors included the airmen of the BAD2 Association and British Aerospace.[9] In the rear of the church rests the *Memorial Book*. In 1985, Angela Proctor compiled this book for her mother, Edna Lonsdale, who lost her eldest daughter, Georgina, in the air disaster. *The Memorial Book* contains photographs of the victims, letters of condolence, and press clippings about the catastrophe. Sylvester Till crafted the bookcase that houses the *Memorial Book* from wood salvaged from Holy Trinity School. The verger's wand is dedicated to the memory of Lt. John Bloemendal, the pilot of the doomed Liberator that crashed into the village.

BAe Systems now owns and operates the former BAD2 base at Warton. BAe Systems came into existence in November 1999 when British Aerospace merged with another British corporation, Marconi Electronics. Today, BAe Systems is the world's third largest defense company employing more than 105,000 people in its worldwide facilities. BAe Systems produces and delivers a full range of products and services for air, land, and sea military forces. The corporation has customers in more than 100 countries and its annual sales exceed £20 billion.[10]

The BAe Systems facility at Warton employs more than 6,550 workers. Approximately 20 percent of the residents in the Fylde, who are employed in manufacturing, work at Warton. An Oxford economics study found that the Warton facility contributed an additional 8,700 support jobs and added over £300 million to the regional economy.[11] The BAe facility in Warton is partially responsible for the dramatic increase in the population of Freckleton and for the middle-class nature of the village.

The Warton plant serves as BAe Systems' headquarters and major assembly/testing facility for the corporation's Military Air Solutions Division. The projects at Warton have included the building and testing of the Tornado, the Nimrod MRA4, and the Typhoon. The Tornado is a twin-engine, variable sweep wing combat aircraft. BAe systems built approximately 990 of the multi-role planes that saw service in the First Gulf War as well as the Bosnian and Kosovo conflicts. The Nimrod MRA4 is a surveillance aircraft mainly

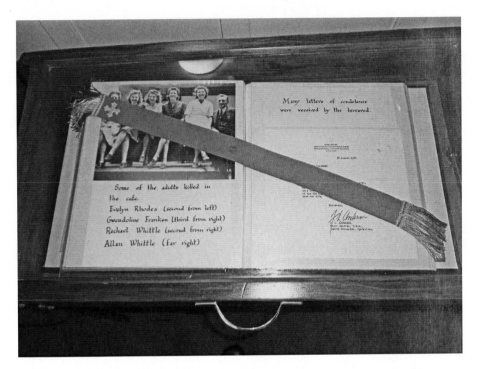

In 1985, Angela Proctor compiled the *Memorial Book* for her mother, Edna Lonsdale. Mrs. Lonsdale had lost her eldest daughter, Georgina, in the air disaster. The book contains photographs of the victims, letters of condolence, and press clippings about the catastrophe. Sylvester Till crafted the bookcase that houses the *Memorial Book* from wood taken from Holy Trinity School. The *Memorial Book* now resides in the rear of Holy Trinity Church (photograph by Judy Hedtke).

used in maritime and reconnaissance missions. The plane can be armed with Sting Ray anti-submarine torpedoes, Sidewinder missiles for aerial combat, and Harpoon anti-ship missiles. The Nimrod is powered by four Rolls-Royce engines. The R.A.F. withdrew the plane from service in 2006 after a crash in Afghanistan killed 14 servicemen. An investigation revealed that a faulty hot-air duct was responsible for the mishap. The Ministry of Defense cancelled the Nimrod program in 2010.

Warton also serves as one of the four assembly lines for the Typhoon Eurofighter. The Typhoon is a twin-engine, multi-role fighter that contains one 27mm Mauser cannon, air-to-air missiles, air-to-surface missiles, and six 500-pound bombs. The Warton plant is responsible for the final assembly of the fighter and more than 300 aircraft are in service today. Almost 70 years later, the old BAD2 facility still rolls out aircraft for combat duty and the sight and sound of planes in the skies over Freckleton is a common occurrence.

The experiences of life at BAD2 and the memories of the Freckleton air disaster remained with the men stationed at Warton for the rest of their lives. Ralph Scott returned to Wilmington, Delaware, after his discharge from the service in 1946 and resumed employment with the *News Journal*. He wanted to become a sportswriter but the *News Journal* had other plans for him. The company assigned Scott to his father, the plant engineer, as an electrician. He worked on the electrical parts of the company's linotypes and printing presses. When his father retired from the company, the *News Journal* promoted Scott to his father's former position of plant engineer. Scott held this post for 23 years despite not having a college degree. Like many servicemen, Scott married shortly after his return home. He and his wife, Virginia, had two children, a daughter Patricia and a son Ian, who died soon after his birth.[12]

Scott was very active in his parish, the Church of the Nativity. He was a lay reader and assisted at communion. He also took communion to shut-ins and presided at funeral services. Scott had a lifelong interest in painting and was a talented artist. He preferred to work in either oil or pencil. In the last years of his life, Scott did pencil sketches of children at local craft fairs. Shortly before his death, Scott had begun a self-portrait of himself and his beloved cat Sebastian.[13] The portrait remains unfinished.

His service at BAD2 and his role as an honor guard at the funeral of the Freckleton crash victims always remained fresh and vivid in Scott's memory. In 1977, Scott was one of the founders of the BAD2 Association. From 1983 until his death in 2010, Scott served as the secretary and newsletter editor for the association. He helped to organize and arrange several reunions of BAD2 veterans and crash survivors in both the United States and in Freckleton. He was a keynote speaker at the dedication of the BAD2 memorial garden and the Freckleton memorial in Pooler, Georgia. Every August 23, if Scott was not in Freckleton, he placed a bouquet of flowers on the altar of the Church of the Nativity and attended mass in memory of the crash victims.[14] It was a tradition that Scott maintained for 64 years until he passed away at the age 93 on February 9, 2010.

Tom Miller returned to Baton Rouge, Louisiana, in the winter of 1946. He resumed his job at the Louisiana Creamery where he worked in the office posting milk deliveries for the route men. Shortly afterward, his uncle, Earl Miller, secured a job for Tom at the Wolf Baking Company. Miller rented a room at Mrs. White's boardinghouse located at 433 North 7th Street in Baton Rouge from the time of his return from the war until his marriage in 1950.

On May 6, 1950, Miller married the love of his life, Bernadine Swindler. Even before he married Bernadine, Miller informed her that if they ever had a daughter they would have to name her Sonya, after the young girl whose coffin he carried on August 26, 1944, Sonia Dagger. The Miller's first child was a girl born on March 12, 1953. Bernadine and Tom named their daughter Sonya.[15]

Miller had always wanted to contact the Daggers to let them know that he had carried Sonia's coffin the day of the funeral. He did not contact the Daggers because he felt they would be angry at Americans for the tragic crash and the loss of their daughter. The memories of Sonia and the funeral continued to haunt Miller even after the birth of his daughter, Sonia's namesake. Miller did not know how to get in touch with the Daggers and he was still unsure what their reaction to his contacting them might be. As the years rolled by, the task of contacting the Daggers became more daunting to Miller.

In 1962, the Wolf Baking Company hired an English woman, Mrs. Winnie, as a secretary. Miller told Winnie the story of the crash and the funeral. Mrs. Winnie offered to help Miller contact the Daggers. She suggested that Miller write a letter to the vicar of Holy Trinity Church and explain the entire situation. About a month later, Miller received a letter back from the Dagger family thanking Miller for his correspondence. The Daggers informed Miller that they had no resentment or anger against Americans since the accident "was an act of God."[16] Three generations of Millers and Daggers have exchanged correspondence and visits since the original communication in 1962.

The Millers and Daggers finally met each other in person in 1979 when Tom and Bernadine visited the Dagger family in Freckleton. Tom later wrote that this was the first time that he and his wife had ever stayed in someone else's home overnight.[17] In June 1995, Tom and his wife returned to England for a BAD2 reunion. This time the Millers brought their daughter Sonya with them to meet the Daggers. During her visit to Freckleton, Sonya Miller met the Dagger's two children, Stephanie and Peter. Sonya also placed a bouquet of flowers on her namesake's grave. Shortly after the Millers' visit to Freckleton, Wilfred Dagger passed away on August 21. He had been extremely ill before the Millers' arrival, but the anticipation of meeting Sonya Miller rallied his strength and kept his spirits high throughout the Millers' visit. Ironically, Mr. Dagger was buried on August 23, 1995, exactly 51 years after Sonia's death. The Miller and Dagger families, bound together by tragedy, hope, and two children bearing the same name, continue their circle of friendship today.

Bill Bone, the badly burned R.A.F. airman who survived the Sad Sack Café inferno, returned to Dorsham in 1947. He worked during the day and attended South East London Technical School in the evening. In 1950, at the age of 27, Bone married a woman whom he describes as "a lady of little character and less ambition."[18] The marriage started out in an inauspicious manner when Bone had to go out and search for the vicar on his wedding day. It seems that the vicar failed to remember the date of the wedding and had to be roused from his garden to perform the ceremony. Soon after the birth of his first child, Bone journeyed to Canada alone in search of employment opportunities. He booked steerage class aboard the *Queen Mary* and shared a small cabin with three other men including a 300-pound Belgian farmer whose sturdy frame occupied most of the available space in the room.[19]

Once in Canada, Bone found work with Ontario Hydro in Windsor, Ontario. His wife and daughter joined him from England but Mrs. Bone never adjusted to life in Canada. In 1958, Bone divorced his wife and she returned to England with their child. In 1965, Bone left Canada and went to Ghana to work on the Volta River Project. The project's primary purpose was to provide electricity for the aluminum industry in Ghana by damming the Volta River. The hydroelectric project originally produced an output of 912 megawatts of power for southeastern Ghana.

Bone returned to Windsor after two years of working in Ghana and met his second wife Margaret Mary. Margaret was from Dearborn, Michigan, and was a gifted musician. She played the harp, flute, piccolo and piano.[20] The couple wanted to live in a warmer climate and start a family so Bone took a job with the Bechtel Corporation and the couple moved to Irvine, California. They immediately started a family and they had two children, Steve and Mary. For the next three decades, Bone worked on many nuclear and fossil fuel generating stations in the southern United States.[21] Bone is now retired and still lives in Irvine. He has only returned to Freckleton once since the crash. His wife of 42 years, Margie, died on February 10, 2011.

The survivors of the crash continued to bear the memories and the scars of that fateful August morning. Doris Catlow Gardiner was a teacher at the Holy Trinity Infants' School. She was not in her class on the morning of August 23 because she had just left her job at Holy Trinity School to take another position. If she had been present, she certainly would have died with her colleague Louis Hulme and her students. Instead she survived and her replacement, Jennie Hall, perished in the raging inferno. This thought haunted Doris Catlow Gardiner for the remainder of her life. Fraser Gardiner,

Doris' son, said: "My mum never really liked to talk about the air disaster, I think she found it painful to remember. In a way she must have felt blessed that her life had been saved but I know she never forgot those children who lost their lives or the teacher who was covering for her, who also died."[22]

In 1946, Doris married David Gardiner and they moved to Scotland where she enjoyed a successful teaching career. She taught at the Bankhead School in Glasgow and then several other schools in the area. In 1970, she and her husband ran Park Lodge, a combination nursery and preparatory school close to Loch Lomond in Dumbartonshire. In 1976, the Gardiners retired and moved back to the Fylde Coast where they purchased a house in Lytham. It had been more than 30 years since Doris had last been in the Freckleton area, and after a lifetime of service to children, she finally felt able to come to terms with the disaster. Mrs. Gardiner attended several of the memorial services for the crash victims. She also continued her passion for teaching and taught Sunday school at the White Church in Lytham. She was a tireless worker for charitable causes and did volunteer work for Oxfam (an international organization working to find lasting solutions to poverty) for almost two decades.[23] Doris Gardiner died, with her son Fraser at her side, on June 30, 2010. She was 91 at the time of her death.

Harry Latham was a nine-year-old evacuee from Salford at the time of the crash. He escaped the burning school through the boys' cloakroom. After the war ended, Latham's family remained in the village. Latham married Edna Sudell, another survivor of the catastrophe. He made a living as an egg merchant and became an active member of the Freckleton community. He served as a trustee and chair of the memorial fund and was an avid supporter of the Freckleton Brass Band. He was involved in Club Day, the music festival, and a wide variety of community events. He was also the unofficial caretaker of the communal grave and one of the survivors interviewed for the BBC documentary on the air disaster.

On the 60th anniversary of the air disaster, Latham shared his thoughts on how the tragedy affected his life with a reporter for the *Blackpool Gazette*. Latham told the interviewer that "the terrible experience of that day never leaves myself and the other surviving pupils and villagers. A lot of the girls, and the boys if they will admit, are always a little concerned when there is thunder and lightning outside. The memory will stay with me until my dying day."[24] Harry Latham died on August 30, 2012, in the presence of his daughters. He is buried in Holy Trinity cemetery near the victims of the air disaster.

Val Preston Whittle escaped the burning school unharmed but lost her brother George in the fire. At seven and a half years old, she had already lost her mother and only sibling. Val continued on at Holy Trinity School until she was 11. She then gained entrance into Queen Mary School, a grammar school for girls in Lytham St. Anne's. She describes her teenage years as "typical and filled with dancing, tennis, and boyfriends."[25] At the age of 21, she started work for a commercial company in Lytham and worked there in various clerical jobs until she was appointed the secretary for the Director of Finance. After 29 years with the company, she left it to become a stay-at-home housewife. When her husband retired, the couple traveled extensively in Europe, Africa, the Caribbean Islands, and North America. According to Val, their favorite vacation destination is the United States.[26] Val is an associate member of the BAD2 Association and attends meetings held in England.

On July 27, 2012, Jackie and Peter Martin hosted an afternoon tea in their home in Freckleton. Present were some of the survivors of the air disaster who met and chatted with the author. In the back row from left to right: Jack Nichols, Brenda Sidebottom, Barbara Hall, Judy Hedtke (the author's wife), and Peter and Jackie Martin. In the front row from left to right: Elsie Dollin, Val Whittle, Jim Hedtke, Ruby Currell, and Joan Richardson (photograph by Judy Hedtke).

Almost 70 years after the crash, Val says, "I look back on the events of August 23, 1944, as a tragic accident and with sadness for the young lives lost and the suffering caused. At the same time, I realize that because of those events great friendships have been made and close bonds forged between the people of Freckleton and the servicemen of BAD2. Time heals and life goes on."[27] It is this sense of common loss and the need for remembrance that has helped heal the wounds inflicted by the disaster while insuring the constant memory of its victims.

Ruby Whittle Currell is one of the three children who survived the fire in the infants' school. She is the most prominent of the three survivors because of her courageous willingness to grant interviews and the eloquence of the voice she provides for the victims. She also participates on a regular basis in the memorial services held in Freckleton on August 23. Ruby spent

First Lieutenant John Bloemendal, from St. Paul, Minnesota, is seated in the cockpit of a P-51 waiting for takeoff at Warton. Bloemendal enlisted in the U.S.A.A.F. on March 25, 1942, and after he earned his wings, the Army Air Forces assigned him to BAD2 as a test pilot. He logged over 740 hours in the air test-flying a variety of aircraft. On the morning of August 23, 1944, Bloemendal took a refurbished B-24 on a test flight. The Liberator crashed into the village of Freckleton during a violent thunderstorm, immediately killing Bloemendal and two other crew members. This poor quality image is the only known existing photo of Bloemendal.

nearly two years receiving skin grafts to repair her badly burned body. In 1947, she returned to school in Freckleton. Almost all of her classmates had perished in the fire and the absence of children her age in the village was a constant reminder of the catastrophe. Ruby remembers being upset when mothers, who lost their children in the fire, would look at her and try to imagine what their children might have looked like if they had survived the fire that tragic August morning. One mother would cry every time she saw Ruby, while others would longingly and lovingly run their fingers through Ruby's hair.[28]

Tragedy continued to stalk Ruby. When she was nine, her father died. Five years later, her mother passed away. Ruby's fortune changed when she met Brian Currell at the age of 17. A year later, Ruby, now 18, married Brian and the couple left Freckleton. Brian became Ruby's rock. The burns had left scars on Ruby's arms and she would not wear clothes that exposed them in public. Brian convinced her that "it did not matter what was on the outside but it is what is on the inside that counts" and she is now comfortable with wearing short-sleeved clothing.[29] Sadly, Brian Currell passed away in April 2013. The couple was married for 51 years, a testimony of their love and devotion to each other.

Mrs. Currell regularly participates in memorial services for the victims. She says she can still see her classmates' faces and she comes back to the ceremonies to honor their short lives. Her story of survival has appeared in newsprint on the anniversaries of the crash and she was the focal point of the BBC documentary on the air disaster. She has participated in several BAD2 reunions in England and has made several trips to the United States to reunite with American servicemen and medical personnel stationed at Warton. Ruby says that she has made many wonderful friends through the reunions but "unfortunately they are fast leaving me behind and going to the reunion in the great blue yonder and I miss them so much."[30]

In 2003, after Ruby's husband Brian recovered from a serious illness, the Currells left the Isle of Wight and returned home to live in Freckleton. Since the Currells had no family on the Isle of Wight, Brian insisted that they come back to the village so Ruby could be near her family in case anything happened to him.

Ruby does not blame anyone for the crash or for her personal ordeal and she never received any compensation for her injuries from the American government (nor did any of the other victims of the crash or their families). She sees her survival as a link between the living and those killed in the disaster. The key element in the link is the remembrance of the victims. In February 2012, Ruby wrote: "It was a terrible tragedy and as long as there is breath in my body I will love and remember all those who perished that day for I am sure that is why I was spared."[31] For almost 70 years, she has continued to remember and honor her fallen classmates. They are always in her heart.

In the 20th century, humans tried to sanitize warfare by introducing euphemisms to conceal its horror and devastation. The military no longer killed civilians; they eliminated counter-value targets. Authorities referred to the unintentional deaths of civilians as collateral damage. Statistics and serial numbers replaced names and faces and anesthetized the public to the personal tragedy of war. The human toll of war can easily fade from the collective memory of society without the dead having names or faces. In turn, it is this collective memory that provides the first line of resistance to countries capriciously engaging in war with each other.

In Freckleton, the victims of the air disaster have faces and names. In Holy Trinity Church, there is a book that contains the photographs of all the children who died in the crash. The innocent faces of young children instantly remind the viewer of the true horror and cost of war. In the adjacent cemetery stands the memorial cross over the communal graves. The base of the monument contains the names of all the children and civilians who died in the catastrophe and personalizes the suffering and loss of each of the victims, their families, and their communities. In Pooler, Georgia, the stone memorial pays homage to the dead and captures the pathos of the disaster.

The citizens of Freckleton and the former servicemen of BAD2 have chosen not to sanitize war. Instead, they have chosen to remember the terrible costs of warfare and the expensive price of freedom. Seeing the faces and reading the names of the victims reminds us to exhaust all of the other possible alternatives of achieving our country's foreign policy before we employ the use of violence. We must also be positive that our actions are vital to our national security. Without remembering its personal costs, we are doomed to relive the ultimate perversion of war, parents burying their children.

Remembering the victims also gives them life in our collective memories. It allows us to see them with eyes still young. Remembrance gives their lost lives meaning and binds the past, present and future together. They are a reminder of the cost of war and the need to strive for peace. As long as we remember them, they will live. On the 60th anniversary of the disaster, Ruby Whittle Currell said: "We should never forget those children and adults who died. I certainly never will."[32] On the same occasion, Harry Latham commented that "it is important that the whole village is never allowed to forget the victims."[33] In conclusion, it is important that none of us forget the victims, for if we do, they would surely die and the loss of their lives would have been in vain. Remembrance of their lives is all that keeps darkness and war from conquering light and peace.

Epilogue

History sometimes has a tragic way of repeating itself. On the night of January 7, 2012, fire and death again stalked the village of Freckleton. This time, however, the disaster was not an accident, it was murder. Michelle Smith, the mother of nine children, was celebrating her 36th birthday at her home on Lytham Road with family and friends. Her newly renovated bungalow is just down the street from the site where the *Classy Chassis II* crashed into the village 68 years ago. At approximately 11:20 p.m. a fire broke out in a wardrobe containing children's clothes and toys in one of the two attic bedrooms. Asleep in the rooms at the time were Smith's four-year-old twin girls, Holly and Ella, and her youngest child Jordan, age two. The smoldering fire emitted intense smoke that quickly enveloped both bedrooms. The house was equipped with smoke detectors but they failed to sound an alarm.[1]

The party-goers left the house when the odor of smoke permeated the bungalow and one of them made an emergency call for help. Mrs. Smith remained in the house seeking the source of the smoke. Her 19-year-old son Reece, who had temporarily left the bungalow, raced back inside when he realized his twin sisters and younger brother were not outside. He quickly ran up the stairs, entered the attic bedroom, and immediately was overcome by the smoke. Reece's 16-year-old brother Andrew also re-entered the structure, but the intense smoke kept him from climbing the stairs.

When police and firefighters arrived, the outside of the house showed no apparent signs of fire. They were also confronted with a chaotic scene in front of the bungalow as dazed and distressed party-goers milled around in the road. Six firefighters entered the house. They first led Andrew and his mother to safety. The firefighters then went up the stairs to the attic and found Reece and his siblings unconscious in the bedrooms. Some of the crew extinguished the fire while the rest attempted to resuscitate the victims. The firemen removed the four siblings from the bungalow and rushed them to Royal Preston Hospital.[2] All four of the Smith children died there. The twins, Holly and Ella, would have celebrated their fifth birthday later in the month. The results of the coroner's postmortem tests revealed that all four victims died of smoke inhalation.

Police and fire officials immediately opened an investigation to determine the cause of the fire. The initial findings revealed that the smoke alarms were not working in the house. As a result of this finding, the Lancashire Fire Service started a program of handing out free fire alarms and provided free safety checks of existing alarms. On Saturday, January 24, the fire service gave out 11,000 free alarms at fire stations, shopping centers, food markets, and playing fields.[3]

Investigators also found that the fire was deliberately set and treated the deaths as murders. Detective Superintendent Dermott Horrigan of the Lancashire Constabulary revealed that the fire in the wardrobe was deliberately started by a naked flame. There was no evidence that any accelerant, such as gasoline, was used to initiate the fire. Horrigan stated that "the children were in bed at the time of the fire. Whoever did it knew children were inside that room."[4]

Several days after the fire, the police arrested 18-year-old Dyson Allen of Lytham on suspicion of murder. The alleged arsonist is reputed to be an acquaintance of Reece Smith. After the fire, Allen posted messages of condolence and sympathy for the victims on his Facebook account.[5] The court freed Allen on police bail. Under police bail, a suspect is released from police custody without being officially charged with a crime but must return to the police station at a given time. Meanwhile, law enforcement officials continued their investigation into the suspected murders.

On February 8, Blackpool coroner Anne Hind reopened the inquest into the deaths of the four Smith children. After a second postmortem, she confirmed the cause of death as smoke inhalation. Her findings confirmed the first autopsy report and she released the bodies for burial. After an excruciating month of waiting, the Smith family could finally put their loved ones to rest.[6]

The funeral for the Smith children took place on February 16, five weeks after the fire. The funeral procession began at 12:45 p.m. in front of the family's burned bungalow. Two horse-drawn carriages each carried a coffin. One coffin carried the remains of Reece and Jordan. It was draped in a Blackpool F.C. flag, the symbol of Reece's favorite soccer team. The other coffin contained the four-year-old twins, Holly and Ella. Their coffin was draped in pink. Led by the carriages, the funeral entourage processed from the family home to St. John the Divine Church in Lytham. Mourners lined the entire route and crowded into the church for the service.

Pall bearers, wearing orange ties to represent the colors of the Blackpool F.C., carried the caskets into the church. The Reverend Jack Wixon presided over the service. Michelle Smith, accompanied in church by her surviving five children, delivered an emotional and tearful eulogy. She said of her oldest son Reece: "You were not only my first born but my best friend, my rock and big brother to your little sisters and brother." She described Holly and Ella as "my beautiful girls." She called Jordan, nicknamed "Banger" because of his tendency to walk into almost anything, "my little man with piercing eyes and a very cheeky personality." She concluded the eulogy by saying: "You were all my heart, my life, my babies. God bless my little man Jordan, my beautiful twins, Holly and Ella and Reece my hero."[7]

As the pall bearers carried the coffins from the church, the congregation sang the Blackpool F.C. anthem, "Glad All Over" by the Dave Clark Five.[8] The funeral procession continued to the Lytham Crematorium for a private ceremony.

Police arrested Dyson Allen again in December 2012 for suspicion of murder in the deaths of the fire victims. On March 4, 2013, Allen pleaded not guilty to the murder charges in Preston Crown Court. The court set Allen's trial date for June 4. In July 2013, a jury at Preston Crown Court convicted Allen of four counts of manslaughter. He was sentenced to life in prison and must serve a minimum of nine years and three months behind bars.

Events in history are like snowflakes; they may look similar but no two are ever truly identical to each other. The Freckleton tragedies, separated by nearly 70 years, bear some similarities. In both calamities, fire snuffed out young lives before they ever had a chance to fulfill their dreams. In each of the incidents, heroes emerged and selflessly risked their lives to save others. The media coverage in both instances touched the heart strings of both a national and international audience. In each circumstance, the community came out to mourn its loss. The fires were even in close proximity to each other.

The differences between the two calamities also clearly manifest themselves. The Smith fire was more contained and there was less loss of life than in the B-24 crash. The second fire devastated a family but did not destroy an entire generation of children in the village. The greatest and most meaningful difference, however, is in the causes of the two tragedies. The Freckleton air disaster was the result of an accident in wartime. The unintentional act occurred while the Americans and British were fighting the evil of fascism. The Allied victory over the Axis powers helped to preserve freedom and democracy. The victims of the Freckleton air disaster paid part of the immense cost of that victory. The sacrifice of their lives was not in vain. Our continued freedom serves as a permanent memorial to their existence.

The deaths of the Smith children were an intentional, despicable act by a cowardly, depraved individual. The killer cut short four young lives before the victims ever had a chance to fulfill themselves. It is too soon to make any sense out of this tragic loss of life and maybe we never will. One is left to wonder how many more tragedies this little English village must endure and how many more times the community will be called upon to bury their children.

Appendix

Individuals Killed in the Freckleton Air Disaster

STUDENTS (AGE)

Howard Allanson (5)
Martin Peter Alston (4)
Edna Rae Askew (5)
Sylvia Bickerstaffe (5)
Kenneth George Boocock (6)
Jean Butcher (6)
David Carr (6)
Maureen Denise Clarke (6)
John Cox (4)
Sonia Dagger (5)
Peter Danson (6)
John Hargreaves Foster (4)
Judith Millicent Garner (4)
John Hardman (4)
Annie Lonsdale Herrington (4)
Beryl Hogarth (6)
William Hilton Iddon (4)
Elizabeth Isles (5)
Vera Christine Jones (5)
Georgina Lonsdale (4)
Thomas Frank Mullen (4)

Gillian Parkinson (5)
June Parkinson (5)
George Preston (5)
Michael Probert (5)
Thomas Rawcliffe (4)
Alice Margaret Rayton (5)
Malcolm Scott (5)
June Stewartson (6)
Dorothy Sudell (5)
John Sudell (6)
Joseph Threlfall (5)
John Townsend (6)
Barrie Brown Truscott (4)
Lillian Marjorie Waite (4)
Alice Sylvia Whybrow (5)
Alan Wilson (5)
Richard William Wright (5)

TEACHERS

Jennie Hall (21)
Louisa Hulme (64)

CIVILIANS

Kathleen Forshaw (22)
Gwendolyn Franken (age unknown)

183

Evelyn Rhodes (21)
James Silcock (15)
Allan Whittle (50)
Pearl Whittle (15)
Rachel Whittle (50)

R.A.F. AIRMEN

Sergeant Douglas Batson (20)
Sergeant Robert Bell (20)
Sergeant Pilot Walter W. Cannell
(20)
Sergeant Eric Newton (23)

U.S. AIRMEN

Private George C. Brown (35)
Corporal Herbert G. Cross (31)

Private Minas P. Glitsis (38)
Private Samuel A. Mezzacappa
(35)
Sergeant Theodore E. Nelson (31)
Corporal Arthur Rogney (26)
Sergeant Frank L. Zugel (28)

CLASSY CHASSIS II CREW

First Lieutenant John A. Bloemen-
dal (27)
Sergeant Gordon W. Kinney (26)
Tech Sergeant James M. Parr (25)

Chapter Notes

Chapter 1

1. Richard Spencer, *Reminiscences of Freckleton* (Preston, UK: G.W. Whitehead, Ltd., no date), 2.

2. Richard Spencer, *Freckleton in Old Picture Postcards* (Zattboomel, Netherlands: European Library, no date), 1.

3. Peter Shakeshaft, *A Short History of Holy Trinity Freckleton* (published in aid of the Church Restoration Fund, 1977), 1.

4. Spencer, *Freckleton in Old Picture Postcards*, 11.

5. Ibid., 54.

6. Allan Crosby and Peter Shakeshaft, "History of a Village: Freckleton," http://www.bbc.co.uk/history/trail/local_history/village/history_of_a_village_01.shtml (accessed 12 September 2011).

7. Spencer, *Freckleton in Old Picture Postcards*, 52–53.

8. Ibid., 64.

9. "Freckleton in 1934," http://www.a-mounderness.co.uk/freckleton_guide_1934.html (accessed 12 January 2012).

10. Spencer, *Reminiscences of Freckleton*, 7–8.

11. Allan Brack, "Friendly Freckleton," *Lancashire Life* (January 1985), 23.

12. Ibid.

13. Ibid.

14. Shakeshaft, *A Short History*, 1.

15. Ibid., 2.

16. Ibid., 3.

17. Ibid.

18. Peter Shakeshaft, *History of Holy Trinity* (Lancaster, UK: Scotforth Books, 2012), 48.

19. Spencer, *Freckleton in Old Picture Postcards*, 2.

20. Spencer, *Reminiscences of Freckleton*, 5.

21. Julie Armitage to James Hedtke, 13 January 2012, "RE: Hodgson Institute," personal email.

22. Spencer, *Freckleton in Old Picture Postcards*, 68.

23. John A. Vickers (ed.), *A Dictionary of Methodism in Britain and Ireland* (London: Epsworth Press, 2000.

24. Spencer, *Reminiscences of Freckleton*, 30–33.

25. "The Ship Inn," http://theshipinnfreckleton.co.uk (accessed 12 January 2012).

26. Spencer, *Reminiscences of Freckleton*, 18.

27. Ibid., 19.

28. "Band of Hope," http://www.hopeuk.org/about-us (accessed 17 January 2012).

29. Ibid.

30. "Freckleton Brass Band," http://www.freckletonband.co.uk/History.php (accessed 23 December 2011).

31. Ibid.

32. Spencer, *Reminiscences of Freckleton*, 26.

33. Freckleton War Memorial Committee Book, Lancashire Record Office, Preston, UK, reference #Pr501018.

34. Ibid.

35. "Freckleton War Memorial," http://freckletonmemorial.webs.com (accessed 30 November 2011).

Chapter 2

1. Neville Chamberlain, speech given in Defense of the Munich Agreement, 1938 (*Parliamentary Debates*, Commons, vol. 339, 3 October 1938).

2. Samuel Elliot Morrison and Henry Steel Commager, *The Growth of the American Republic*, vol. 2 (New York: Oxford University Press, 1962), 762.

3. Harry Holmes, *Warton in Wartime* (Stroud, UK: Tempus Publishing Limited, 2006), 7.

4. Ibid.

5. Morrison and Commager, *The Growth of the American Republic*, 776.

6. Harry Holmes, *World's Greatest Air Depot* (Shrewsbury, UK: Airlife Publishing Ltd., 1998), 19.

7. Ibid.

8. Ibid., 141.

9. Donald Miller, *Masters of the Air* (New York: Simon and Schuster, 2006), 7.

10. Holmes, *World's Greatest Air Depot*, 72.

11. Holmes, *Warton in Wartime*, 8.

12. Holmes, *World's Greatest Air Depot*, 8.

13. Ibid.

14. Ibid., 28.

15. Ibid., 143–144.

16. Ibid., 30.

17. Ibid., 31.

18. Ibid., 35.

19. For more information, see Ben Parnell, *Carpetbaggers: America's Secret War in Europe* (Waco, TX: Eakin Press, 1987).

20. Holmes, *World's Greatest Air Depot*, 37.

21. Ibid., 40–43.

22. Miller, *Masters of the Air*, 243–249.

23. Ibid., 248.

24. Ibid., 291.

25. Interrogation of Field Marshal Wilhelm Kietel, 1945, 519.619–23, Air Force Historical Research Agency, Maxwell Air Force Base, Alabama.

26. Ralph Scott to James Hedtke, personal letter, 18 August, 2008.

27. Thomas Miller to James Hedtke, personal letter, 7 August 2008.

28. Holmes, *World's Greatest Air Depot*, 53–54.

29. Scott letter.

30. Holmes, *Warton in Wartime*, 11.

31. Richard Bak, *Joe Louis: The Great Black Hope* (Dallas, TX: Da Capo Press, 1998), 113–171.

32. Paul F. Kennedy, *Billy Conn: The Pittsburgh Kid* (Bloomington, IN: Author House, 2007), 153–178.

33. U.S. Air Force Records, Military Administrative Division, BAD2 Historical Reports, September 1945, Air Force Historical Research Agency, Maxwell Air Force Base, Alabama.

34. For more information, see O.B. Keller, *The Bobby Jones Story: The Authorized Biography* (Chicago, Triumph Books, 2003).

35. George T. Simon, *The Glenn Miller and His Orchestra* (Dallas, TX: Da Capo Press, 1974), 105.

36. Ibid., 88.

37. Ibid., 327–338.

38. Holmes, *World's Greatest Air Depot*, 73–74.

39. BAD2 Historical Report, August 1944.

Chapter 3

1. Thomas Miller to James Hedtke, personal letter, 7 August 2008.

2. Ralph Scott to James Hedtke, personal letter, 8 August 2008.

3. For the complete story of the 1943 race riot in Detroit, see Stephen Thernstrom and Abigail Thernstrom, *America in Black and White* (New York: Simon and Shuster, 1997).

4. Scott letter.

5. Ibid.

6. Stephen E. Ambrose, *The Wild Blue* (New York: Simon and Schuster, 2001), 52. Also see Donald Miller, *Masters of the Air*

(New York: Simon and Schuster, 2006), 165.

7. "Army Air Corp Training in World War II." http//www.scharch.org/Dick_Baer/_RFB%20AAF%Training.AAF.htm (accessed 1 February 2012).

8. Ibid.

9. Miller, *Masters of the Air*, 166.

10. Wesley Frank Craven and James L. Cates, eds., *The Army Air Forces in World War II*, vol. 6, *Men and Planes* (Chicago: University of Chicago, 1955), xxxiv.

11. Ernest Bloemendal, BAD2 serviceman, interview by author, 12 June 2008.

12. Ibid.

13. War Department, Washington, D.C., "Instructions for American Servicemen in Britain," printed in 1942.

14. Miller, *Masters of the Air*, 222.

15. "Instructions for American Servicemen in Britain."

16. Ibid.

17. Thomas Miller letter.

18. *Meet The Americans* (London: Martin Secker and Warburg, 1943).

19. "Opinion on America," Mass-Observation Archive, University of Sussex, UK (February 1942), 11–13.

20. Ibid.

21. Jerry Scutts, *Republic P-47 Thunderbolt: The Operational Record* (St. Paul, MN: MBI, 1998).

22. Ibid.

23. Ibid.

24. Ray Wagner, *Mustang Designer: Edmund Schmeud and the P-51* (Washington, DC: Smithsonian Press, 1990), 113–118.

25. "Combat Record P-47s, P-38s, P-51s in UK," *Air Force Historical Research Agency*, Maxwell Air Force Base, Alabama.

26. Robert Goebel, *Mustang Ace: Memoirs of a P-51 Fighter Pilot* (London: Zenith Press, 2004).

27. "Combat Record of P-47s, P-38s, P-51s in U.K."

28. Holmes, *Warton in Wartime*, 14.

29. Holmes, *World's Greatest Air Depot*, 66–67.

30. James S. Nanney, *Army Air Forces Medical Services in World War II* (Washington, DC: Air Force History and Museums Program, 1998), 20.

31. Ambrose, *The Wild Blue*, 79.

32. Ibid., 77.

33. Ibid., 78.

34. Holmes, *World's Greatest Air Depot*, 149.

35. Jeffery L. Ethell, *World War II Nose Art in Color* (St. Paul, MN: MBI, 1993), 77–79.

36. Robert Morgan with Ron Powers, *The Man Who Flew the Memphis Belle: Memoir of a World War II Bomber Pilot* (New York: Dutton, 2001), 97–98.

37. Ibid.

38. Ethell, *World War II Nose Art in Color*, 120–121.

39. Holmes, *World's Greatest Air Depot*, 47–48.

40. Ibid., 49.

41. Ibid., 50–51.

42. Ibid.

43. Ibid., 52.

44. Ibid.

45. Roger Freeman, *The Mighty Eighth, a History of Units, Men and Machines of the U.S. 8th Air Force* (London: Cassell and Company, Ltd., 2000), 260–261.

46. David G. Mayor, "The Day Freckleton Wept," *BAD News*, vol. 2, no. 2 (March 1979), 2.

Chapter 4

1. Anthony J. Mireles, *Fatal Army Air Forces Aviation Accidents in the United States 1941–1945* (Jefferson, NC: McFarland and Company, Inc, 2006), 7.

2. Holmes, *World's Greatest Air Depot*, 25.

3. Ibid., 40.

4. Ibid., 37.

5. Ibid.

6. Ibid., 54–55.

7. Ibid., 60–61.

8. Ibid., 63–64.

9. Information provided by Myrna Barnes, Director of the Morton County Historical Society to author in a personal letter, 14 February 2012.

10. "Morton County World War II Pilot Honored in England," *Southwest Daily Times*, 10 June 1999.

11. Ibid.

12. Holmes, *World's Greatest Air Depot*, 72.

13. U.S. Air Force Records, Military Division, BAD #2 Historical Report (19 August 1944).

Chapter 5

1. Joyce Turner, *The Freckleton Tragedy, 1944* (Blackpool, UK: Landy Publishing, 2007), 13. Also see David G. Mayor, "The Day Freckleton Wept," *BAD News*, vol. 2, no. 2 (March 1979), 3.

2. Mayor, "The Day Freckleton Wept," 3.

3. War Department, U.S. Army Air Forces Report of Accident, AAF Station 582, Accident Report no. 104 (26 August 1944), Air Force Historical Research Agency, Maxwell Air Force Base, Alabama.

4. Mayor, "The Day Freckleton Wept," 3.

5. "Village Recalls Day of Horror," *Blackpool Gazette*, 23 August 2004.

6. Ibid.

7. "56 Dead in Plane Crash," *Lytham St. Anne's Express*, 24 August 1944.

8. "When Death Fell from the Sky," *Lytham St. Anne's Express*, 25 August 1994.

9. David G. Madden, "A Day I've Remembered," *BAD News*, vol. 33, no. 1 (January, 2009), 1.

10. Ibid., 2.

11. Ibid.

12. Ibid.

13. "When Death Fell from the Sky."

14. Joan Richardson, school survivor, interview with author, 7 February 2012.

15. Barbara Hall, school survivor, interview with author, 4 February 2012.

16. William Bone to James Hedtke, personal letter, 19 June 2008.

17. Ibid.

18. Ibid.

19. "Remembering the Freckleton Air Disaster," *Lancashire Evening Post*, 23 May 2007.

20. Accident report, statement by Captain J. E. Zdrubek, station weather officer.

21. Ibid.

22. Accident report, statement by First Lieutenant Peter Manassero, test pilot.

23. Mayor, "The Day Freckleton Wept," 6.

24. Ibid.

25. Accident report, Zdrubek statement.

26. Accident report, statement by First Lieutenant James W. Harper, flying control officer.

27. Mayor, "The Day Freckleton Wept," 6.

28. Ibid., 1.

29. "Village Recalls Day of Horror."

30. Madden, "A Day I've Remembered," 3.

31. "When Death Fell from the Sky."

32. "Day Death Fell Out of the Sky: The Survivors," *Lancashire Evening Post*, 21 August 2004.

33. Ibid.

34. Accident report, statement by Tech Sergeant Doyle Shaw, control tower operation.

35. Accident report, Manassero statement.

36. Ibid.

37. Mayor, "The Day Freckleton Wept," 5.

38. Ibid., 1.

39. Accident report, Shaw statement.

40. Accident report, statement by Eric Greenwood, eyewitness.

41. Accident report, statement by Charlotte Allsup, eyewitness.

42. Accident report, statement by S.J. Rockey, eyewitness.

43. Accident report, statement by William Banks, eyewitness.

44. Accident report, statement by Vera Cartmell, eyewitness.

45. Mayor, "The Day Freckleton Wept," 6.

46. Ibid, 5.

47. Ibid, 5–6.

Chapter 6

1. David G. Mayor, "The Day Freckleton Wept," *BAD News*, vol. 2, no. 2 (March 1979), 5.
2. David G. Madden, "A Day I've Remembered," *BAD News*, vol. 33, no. 1 (January, 2009), 1–3.
3. Ibid., 3.
4. Ibid.
5. Ibid.
6. Ibid.
7. Ruby Whittle Currell, infants' room survivor, interview with author, 12 February 2012.
8. "56 Dead in Plane Crash," *Lytham–St. Anne's Express*, 24 August 1944.
9. "Village Recalls Day of Horror," *Blackpool Gazette*, 23 August 2004.
10. Ibid.
11. John Nichol, school survivor, interview with author, 27 July 2012.
12. Ibid., 24.
13. Ibid.
14. Barbara Hall, school survivor, interview with author, 4 February 2012.
15. Ibid.
16. Valerie Whittle, school survivor, interview with author, 8 February 2012.
17. Ibid.
18. Ibid.
19. Joan Richardson, school survivor, interview with author, 7 February 2012.
20. Ibid.
21. "When Death Fell from the Sky," *Lytham–St. Anne's Express*, 25 August 1944.
22. "Day Death Fell Out of the Sky: The Survivors," *Lancashire Evening Post*, 21 August 2004.
23. Ibid.
24. Ibid.
25. Ibid.
26. "56 Dead in Plane Crash."
27. "Day Death Fell Out of the Sky."
28. Ibid.
29. "Village Recalls Day of Horror."
30. "Day Death Fell Out of the Sky."
31. Ibid.
32. Elise Dollin, villager, interview with author, 10 February 2012.
33. WW2 People's War." http://www.bbc.co.uk/ww2peopleswar/stories/60/a2963360.shtml (accessed 23 May 2007).
34. William Bone to James Hedtke, personal letter, 19 June 2008.
35. Ibid.
36. Accident report, statement by Warrant Officer Jerald C. Andrews.
37. Bone letter.
38. Mayor, "The Day Freckleton Wept," 6.
39. Ibid.
40. Joyce Turner, *The Freckleton Tragedy, 1944* (Blackpool, UK: Landy Publishing, 2007), 26.
41. Irene Cottam, firefighter with the National Fire Service, interview with author, 5 February 2012.
42. Mayor, "The Day Freckleton Wept," 6.
43. Ibid.
44. James Dodson, *Final Rounds* (New York: Bantam Books, 1996), 60–61.
45. Mayor, "The Day Freckleton Wept," 6.
46. Ibid.
47. Ibid.
48. Turner, *The Freckleton Tragedy*, 36.
49. "56 Dead in Plane Crash."
50. U.S. Air Force Records, BAD2 Daily Historical Report, 23 August 1944.
51. Ibid.

Chapter 7

1. U.S. Air Force Records, Military Administrative Division, BAD2 Historical Reports (August 1944), 3.
2. David G. Madden, "A Day I've Remembered," *BAD News*, vol. 33, no. 1 (January, 2009), 4.
3. "Day Death Fell Out of the Sky: The Survivors," *Lancashire Evening Post*, 21 August 2004.
4. Madden, "A Day I've Remembered," 4.
5. Ralph Scott, "BAD2 Recalls English Tragedy," *Stars and Stripes*, 3 January 1985.
6. "Aircraft Crash on School—35

Children Killed in Fire," *The Times*, 24 August 1944.

7. Ibid.

8. Ibid.

9. Ibid.

10. "76, Including 51 Children, Killed as U.S. Plane Hits English School," *The New York Times*, 24 August 1944.

11. Ibid.

12. "54 Bodies Recovered at Freckleton," *The Times*, 25 August 1944.

13. "Plane Crash Dead Now 59," *The New York Times*, 26 August 1944.

14. "56 Dead in Plane Crash."

15. Ibid.

16. Inquests after a Disaster. *When Disaster Strikes*. http://www.disasteraction.org.uk/support/da_guide13.htm (accessed 10 March 2012).

17. Joyce Turner, *The Freckleton Tragedy, 1944* (Blackpool, UK: Landy Publishing, 2007), 37–38.

18. "Lightning Caused Disaster," *The Times*, 9 September 1944.

19. Ibid.

20. Thomas Miller to James Hedtke, personal letter, 7 August 2008.

21. Ibid.

22. Kenneth Shenton, "Doris Gardiner: The Teacher who survived the wartime Freckleton air disaster," *The Independent*, 25 August 2010.

23. Ibid.

24. Valerie Whittle, school survivor, interview with author, 8 February 2012.

25. "Everything seemed to be burning," *Blackpool Gazette*, 23 August 2004.

26. "U.S. Soldiers Carry Coffins of 36 Infants," *Lancashire Daily Post*, 26 August 1944.

27. Ibid.

28. Personal letter from Bishop Askwith to Edna Lonsdale, 6 September 1944 contained in the Memory Book, Holy Trinity Church, Freckleton, UK.

29. "U.S. Soldiers Carry Coffins of 36 Infants."

30. David G. Mayor, "The Day Freckleton Wept," *BAD News*, vol. 2, no. 2 (March 1979), 7.

31. BAD2 historical report, 26 August 1944.

32. Thomas Miller letter.

33. Ibid.

34. Ibid.

35. Doug Gross, "Victims of '44 Honored," *Savannah Morning News*, 24 August 1997.

36. Ibid.

37. "Mass Funeral for 44," *The Times*, 27 August 1944.

38. Ibid.

39. Cambridge American Cemetery and Memorial, http://www.abmc.gov/cemeteries/cemeteries/ca.php (accessed 9 October 2011.

40. Scott, "BAD2 Recalls English Tragedy."

Chapter 8

1. Harry Holmes, *World's Greatest Air Depot* (Shrewsbury, UK: Airlife Publishing Ltd., 1998), 60–63.

2. War Department, U.S. Army Air Forces, Report of Aircraft Accident, AAF Station 582, Accident No. 104 (26 August 1944), Air Force Historical Research Agency, Maxwell Air Force Base, Alabama.

3. Accident report, data page.

4. Accident report, Greenwood statement, eyewitness.

5. Accident report, Cartmell statement, eyewitness.

6. Accident report, Allsup testimony, eyewitness.

7. David G. Mayor, "The Day Freckleton Wept," *BAD News*, vol. 2, no. 2 (March 1979), 5.

8. Accident report, Harper statement.

9. Ibid.

10. Accident report, Shaw statement.

11. Ibid.

12. Accident report, Zdrubek statement.

13. Ibid.

14. Ibid.

15. Accident report, Manassero statement.

16. Ibid.

17. Ibid.

18. Ibid.

19. Ibid.

20. Accident report, summary and recommendations.

21. Ibid.

22. David Cook, "Aircraft and Lightning," http://www.newton.dep.anl.gov/askasci/wea00/wea00024.htm (accessed 20 September 2011).

23. Wendell Bechtold, "Aircraft and Lightning," http://www.newton.dep.anl.gov/askasci/wea00/wea00024.htm (accessed 20 September 2011).

24. Edward J. Rupke, "What Happens When Lightning Strikes an Airplane," *Scientific American*, http://www.scientificamerican.com/article.cfm?id=what-happens-when-lightni (accessed 25 September 2011).

25. NASA Lightning Research conducted by NASA Storm Hazards Research Program, 1981–1986.

26. David G. Mayor, "The Day Freckleton Wept," *BAD News*, vol. 2, no. 2 (March 1979), 1.

27. Mayor, "The Day Freckleton Wept," 7

28. Ibid.

29. Ralph Scott to James Hedtke, 4 June 2008, "RE: Answers to Questions," personal email.

30. Holmes, *World's Greatest Air Depot*, 104.

Chapter 9

1. U.S. Air Force Records, BAD2 Daily Historical Report, September 1944.

2. Ibid.

3. Ibid.

4. "General Spaatz to Lord Derby and Freckleton," *Lancashire Daily Post*, 30 August 1944.

5. Ibid.

6. Ibid.

7. Bing Crosby and Peter Martin, *Call Me Lucky* (Cambridge, MA: Da Capo Press, 2001), 4–20.

8. Ibid., 81–102.

9. BAD2 historical report, 1 September 1944.

10. Ralph Scott, "BAD2 Recalls English Tragedy," *Stars and Stripes*, 3 January 1985.

11. Ibid.

12. Sandy Roach, "A Very Special Rose," *West Chatham and Effingham Closeup*, 4 May 2000. Also see Andrew Loudon, "The Day a Village Died in Flames," *Daily Mail*, 18 December 2000.

13. William Bone to James Hedtke, personal letter, 19 June 2008.

14. BAD2 daily historical report, 13 September 1944.

15. BAD2 Daily historical report, 25 September 1944.

16. For more information on Dr. McIndoe, see Leonard Mosely, *Faces from the Fire: The Biography of Sir Archibald McIndoe* (London: Weidenfeld and Nicolson, 1962).

17. "Remembering the Freckleton Air Disaster," *Lancashire Evening Post*, 23 May 2007.

18. Bone letter.

19. David G. Madden, "A Day I've Remembered," *BAD News*, vol. 33, no. 1 (January, 2009), 4.

20. Valerie Whittle, school survivor, interview with author, 9 February 2012.

21. Ibid.

22. Ibid.

23. Ibid.

24. Harry Holmes, *World's Greatest Air Depot* (Shrewsbury, UK: Airlife Publishing Ltd., 1998), 89.

25. Ibid., 102.

26. BAD2 daily historical report, 5 October 1944.

27. Holmes, *World's Greatest Air Depot*, 105.

28. Ibid.

29. Ralph Scott to James Hedtke, personal letter, 8 August 2008.

30. John Toland, *Battle: The Story of the Bulge* (Lincoln, NE: Bison Books, 1999), 365–378.

31. Holmes, *World's Greatest Air Depot*, 105.

32. Ibid.

33. Ibid., 109–115.

34. Ibid., 105–111.

35. Joseph P. Lash, *Eleanor and Franklin*

(New York: W.W. Norton and Company, Inc., 1971), 918–935.

36. Ibid.

37. Holmes, *World's Greatest Air Depot*, 121.

38. Ibid.

39. Ibid., 123.

40. Ibid.

Chapter 10

1. Harry Holmes, *World's Greatest Air Depot* (Shrewsbury, UK: Airlife Publishing Ltd., 1998), 123.

2. Ibid., 125.

3. Ibid., 128.

4. Ralph Scott to James Hedtke, personal letter, 8 August 2008.

5. Par Henningsson, "American Internees in Sweden 1943–1945," *Sweden After the Flak*, vol. 1, no. 1 (Winter 1999), 5–6.

6. Ibid.

7. Ibid.

8. Ibid.

9. Thomas Miller to James Hedtke, personal letter 7 August 2008.

10. Ibid.

11. Ibid.

12. Ibid.

13. Ibid.

14. Holmes, *The World's Greatest Air Depot*, 128–130.

15. Stephane Groueff, *Manhattan Project: The Untold Story of Making the Atomic Bomb* (Lincoln, NE: iUniverse, 2000), 8–45.

16. Ibid.

17. Merle Miller, *Plain Speaking: An Oral Biography of Harry S. Truman* (New York: Berkley Medallion Books, 1974), 244–250.

18. Groueff, *Manhattan Project*, 362–365.

19. Ibid.

20. Holmes, *World's Greatest Air Depot*, 130.

21. "Memorial Is Dedicated," *The New York Times*, 21 August 1945.

22. "Freckleton Monument Dedicated," *Lancashire Daily Post*, 20 August 1945.

23. Ibid.

24. Holmes, *World's Greatest Air Depot*, 131–132.

25. Ibid., 142.

26. Ibid., 133.

Chapter 11

1. John Keegan, *The Second World War* (New York: Penguin Books, 1989), 591–593.

2. Ibid.

3. Stephen Daggett, "Cost of Major U.S. Wars," *CRS Report for Congress* (Washington, DC: Congressional Research Service, 29 June 2010), 1.

4. Harold G. Vatter, "The War's Consequences," *History of the U.S. Economy Since World War II*, eds. Harold G. Vatter and John F. Walker (New York: M.E. Sharpe, Inc., 1996), 3–11.

5. United States Census Bureau, 2010 Census.

6. Roger Middleton, *The British Economy Since 1945* (New York: Palgrave McMillan, 2000), 10–23.

7. "Clash of Ideas over Freckleton Memorial," *Lancashire Daily Post*, 10 September 1944.

8. "Dedication and Unveiling of the Memorial to the Victims of the Aeroplane Disaster," program from the memorial ceremony, 24 May 1947.

9. "Clash of Ideas Over Freckleton Memorial."

10. Ibid.

11. Ibid.

12. Ibid.

13. Ibid.

14. Dedication Program.

15. Ibid.

16. Ibid

17. Ibid.

18. Ibid.

19. Ibid.

20. Ibid.

21. Joyce Turner, *The Freckleton Tragedy, 1944* (Blackpool, UK: Landy Publishing, 2007), 52.

22. Richard Spencer, *Reminiscences of*

Freckleton (Preston, UK: G.W. Whitehead, Ltd., no date), 32.

23. "Freckleton Village Memorial Hall Charity." http://www.charitiesdirect.com/charities/freckleton-village (accessed 9 December 2011).

24. Andrew Loudon, "The Day a Village School Died in Flames and a Feud Was Born," *Daily Mail*, 18 December 2000.

25. Andrew Loudon, "Cash Feud that Started in War End in Peace," *Daily Mail*, 27 December 2001.

26. Ibid.

27. *BAD News*, Statement of Purpose.

28. Richard McClune to Valerie Whittle, personal letter in author's possession, 9 August 1986.

29. Ibid.

30. Shelagh Iredale, "US War Veterans' Gift to Church," *Blackpool Gazette*, 23 September 1993.

31. Anna Thompson, "We Will Never Forget You," *Lytham–St. Anne's Express*, 25 August 1994.

32. Ibid.

33. Ibid.

34. Audrey Woods, "English Tombstones Can Honor Parents, But Not Dad, Mum," *Seattle Times*, 28 August 1994.

35. Shelagh Iredale, "Rain Lashed Tribute," *Lytham–St. Anne's Express*, 25 August 1994.

36. Ibid.

37. Ralph Scott, keynote address delivered at BAD2 memorial garden dedication at the Eighth Air Force Heritages Museum, Pooler, Georgia, 23 August 1997.

38. Ibid.

39. Ibid.

40. Official program of BAD2 memorial garden dedication, Eighth Air Force Heritage Museum, Pooler, Georgia, 23 August 1997.

41. "Rob Stocks, Tearful Tribute," *Blackpool Gazette*, 24 August 2004.

42. Lisa Ettridge, "Tribute to Victims of Village Crash," *Blackpool Gazette*, 23 May 2007.

43. Official program of the memorial service to mark the 65th anniversary of the Freckleton air disaster, 23 August 2009.

44. Ibid.

45. Ibid.

46. For the complete story of the Aberfan disaster, see Tony Austin, *Aberfan: The Story of a Disaster* (London: Hutchinson Publishing, 1967).

47. To learn more about the Lockerbie bombing, see Rodney Wallis, *Lockerbie: The Story and the Lessons* (Westport, CT: Praeger Publishers, 2001).

Chapter 12

1. Office of National Statistics for the United Kingdom, 2001 Census information for Freckleton.

2. Ibid.

3. Ibid.

4. Ibid.

5. Ibid.

6. Ibid.

7. Ibid.

8. "Schools in Freckleton," http://www.freckleton.org/amenities/schools.html (accessed 5 April 2012).

9. Peter Shakeshaft, *History of Holy Trinity Freckleton* (Lancaster, UK: Scotforth Books, 2012), 37.

10. BAe Systems website, www.baesystems.com (accessed 3 March 2012).

11. Robert Skelton, "Jobs Loss at BAe Systems to Devastate Towns," http://www.wsws.org/en/articles/2011/10/baes-o18.html (accessed 5 April 2012).

12. Ralph Scott to James Hedtke, personal letter, 8 August 2008.

13. Ralph Scott obituary, *Iosco County News-Herald*, 11 February 2010.

14. Ralph Scott, personal letter to Valerie Whittle, in the author's possession, 12 August 1986.

15. Thomas Miller to James R. Hedtke, personal letter, 7 August 2008.

16. Thomas Miller, interview with author, 25 June 2008.

17. Miller letter.

18. William Bone to James Hedtke, personal letter, 19 June 2008.

19. Ibid.

20. Margaret Mary Bone obituary, http:

//obits.dignitymemorial.com (accessed 10 April 2012).

21. Bone letter.

22. Kenneth Shenton, "Doris Gardiner: The Teacher Who Survived the Wartime Freckleton Air Disaster," *The Independent,* 25 August 2010.

23. Ibid.

24. "Village Recalls Day of Horror," *Blackpool Gazette,* 23 August 2004.

25. Valerie Whittle, school survivor, interview with author, 8 February 2012.

26. Ibid.

27. Ibid.

28. "Day Death Fell Out of the Sky: The Survivors," *Lancashire Evening Post,* 21 August 2004.

29. "Still Haunted by Tragic Deaths of School Playmates," *Lancashire Evening Post,* 24 August 2011.

30. Ruby Currell, infants' school survivor, interview with author, 12 February 2012.

31. Ibid.

32. "Village Recalls Day of Horror."

33. Ibid.

Epilogue

1. "Freckleton Fire: Teen Arrested on Suspicion of Murder," *BBC News Lancashire,* 11 January 2012.

2. Ibid.

3. "Freckleton Fire: Thousands of Alarms Checked," *Active Fire Management* http://www.activefiremanagement.co.uk/ resources/news/456-freckleton-fire (accessed 3 April 2012).

4. "Freckleton Fire," *Blackpool Gazette,* 2 February 2012.

5. Ibid.

6. "Inquest Opens in Tragedy," *Blackpool Gazette,* 10 February 2012.

7. "Funeral Takes Place for Freckleton House Fire Siblings," *BBC News Lancashire,* 16 February 2012.

8. Ibid.

Bibliography

Books

Ambrose, Stephen E. *The Wild Blue.* New York: Simon & Schuster, 2001.

Auston, Tony. *Aberfan: The Story of a Disaster.* London: Hutchinson, 1967.

Ayres, Travis L. *The Bomber Boys: Heroes Who Flew the B-17s in World War II.* New York: Penguin Group, 2005.

Bak, Richard. *Joe Louis: The Great Black Hope.* Dallas: DaCapo Press, 1998.

Birdsall, Steve. *Log of Liberators.* New York: Doubleday, 1973.

Bowman, Martin. *The Mighty Eighth at War.* Barnsky, UK: Pen and Sword, 2010.

Carigan, William. *Ad Lib: Flying the B-24 Liberator in World War II.* Manhattan, KN: Sunflower University Press, 1988.

Cotter, Jarrod. *North American P-51 Mustang.* Somerset, UK: Haynes, 2001.

Craven, Wesley Frank, and Jame Lea Cate, eds. *The Army Air Forces in World War II,* vol. 6, *Men and Planes.* Chicago: University of Chicago Press, 1955.

Crosby, Bing, and Peter Martin. *Call Me Lucky.* Cambridge, MA: DaCapo Press, 2001.

Dodson, James. *Final Rounds.* New York: Bantam, 1996.

Ethell, Jeffrey L. *World War II Nose Art in Color.* St. Paul, MN: MBI, 1993.

Freeman, Roger. *The Might Eighth: A History of Units, Men and Machines of the U.S. 8th Air Force.* London: Cassell and Company, 2000.

Gardiner, Juliet. *Overpaid, Oversexed and Over Here: The American GI in World War II Britain.* New York: Abbeville, 1992.

Goebel, Robert. *Mustang Ace: Memoirs of a P-51 Fighter Pilot.* London: Zenith Press, 2004.

Groueff, Stephanie. *Manhattan Project: The Untold Story of the Making of the Atomic Bomb.* Lincoln, NE: iUniverse, 2000.

Holmes, Harry. *The World's Greatest Air Depot.* Shrewsbury, UK: Airlife, 1998.

_____. *Warton in Wartime.* Stroud, UK: Tempus, 2001.

Keegan, John. *The Second World War.* New York: Penguin Group, 1989.

Keller, O. B. *The Bobby Jones Story: The Authorized Biography.* Chicago: Triumph, 2003.

Kennedy, Paul F. *Billy Conn: The Pittsburgh Kid.* Bloomington, IN: Author House, 2007.

Lash, Joseph P. *Eleanor and Franklin.* New York: W.W. Norton, 1971.

Logan, Ian and Henry Nield. *Classy Chassy, American Aircraft "Girl Art" 1942–1953.* Miami, FL: AW, 1977.

Mayhew, E. R. *The Reconstruction of Warriors: Archibald McIndoe, the Royal Air Force and the Guinea Pig Club.* Barnesly, UK: Greenhill, 2004.

Middleton, Roger. *The British Economy since 1945.* New York: Palgrave McMillan, 2001.

Miller, Donald. *Masters of the Air*. New York: Simon & Schuster, 2006.

Miller, Merle. *Plain Speaking: An Oral Biography of Harry Truman*. New York: Berkley Medallion Books, 1974.

Mireless, Anthony J. *Fatal Army Air Force Aviation Accident in the United States 1941–1945*. Jefferson, NC: McFarland, 2006.

Morgan, Robert, with Ron Powers. *The Man Who Flew the Memphis Belle: Memoir of a World War II Bomber Plot*. New York: Dutton, 2001.

Morison, Samuel L., and Henry S. Commager. *The Growth of the American Republic*, vol. 2. New York: Oxford University Press, 1962.

Mosley, Leonard. *Faces from the Fire: The Biography of Sir Archibald McIndoe*. London: Weidenfeld and Nicolson, 1962.

Nanney, James S. *Army Air Forces Medical Services in World War II*. Washington, DC: Air Force History and Museum Program, 1998.

Parnell, Ben. *Carpetbaggers: America's Secret War in Europe*. Waco, TX: Eakin Press, 1987.

Ross, Stewart. *Evacuation (At Home in World War II)*. Ibadan, Nigeria: Evans Brothers, 2007.

Scutts, Jerry. *Republic P-47 Thunderbolt: The Operational Record*. St. Paul, MN: MBI, 1998.

Shakeshaft, Peter. *The History of Freckleton*. Lancaster, UK: Carnegie, 2001.

Simon, George T. *Glenn Miller and His Orchestra*. Dallas: DaCapo Press, 1974.

Spencer, Richard. *Freckleton in Old Picture Postcards*. Zaltbommel, Netherlands: European Library, no publishing date.

_____. *Reminiscences of Freckleton*. Preston, UK: G. W. Whitehead, no publishing date.

Thernstrom, Stephen, and Abigal Thernstrom. *America in Black and White*. New York: Simon & Schuster, 1997.

Toland, John. *Battle: The Story of the Bulge*. Lincoln, NE: Bison, 1999.

Turner, Joyce. *The Freckleton Tragedy, 1944*. Blackpool, UK: Landy, 2007.

Vatter, Harold, and John F. Walker, eds.

History of the U.S. Economy since 1945. New York: M. E. Sharpe, 1996.

Vickers, John A., eds. *A Dictionary of Methodism in Britain and Ireland*. London: Epworth, 2000.

Wagner, Ray. *Mustang Designer: Edmund Schmeud and the P-51*. Washington, DC: Smithsonian Institution Press, 1990.

Wallis, Rodney. *Lockerbie: The Story and the Lessons*. Westport, CT: Praegar, 2001.

Documents

Freckleton War Memorial Committee Minute Book. Lancashire Record Office, Preston, UK, Reference #PR501018.

National Archives and Records Administration. *U.S. World War II Army Enlistment Records, 1938–1946* [database online]. Provo, UT: The Generations Network, Inc., 2006

National Cemeteries Administration. *U.S. Veterans Gravesites, ca. 1775–2006* [database online]. Provo, UT: Generations Network, Inc., 2006.

Office of National Statistics, United Kingdom. Census Information for Freckleton, 2001.

U.S. Army Air Forces Records. Military Administrative Division. *BAD #2 Daily Log, August through October 1944*. Maxwell Air Force Base, Alabama.

U.S. Army Air Forces Records. Military Administrative Division. *BAD #2 Historical Reports for August and September 1944*. Maxwell Air Force Base, Alabama.

U.S. Bureau of the Census. 2010 Census.

War Department. *Instructions for American Servicemen in Britain*. Washington, DC, 1942.

War Department. U.S. Army Air Forces Report of Aircraft Accident. Accident No. 104, A. A. F. Station 582, 26 August 1944. Maxwell Air Force Base, Alabama.

Electronic Sources

Army Air Corps Flight Training in WWII. *National Museum of the United States Air*

Force. http://scharch.org/Dick_Baer/_RFB%20AAF%20Training/AAF.htm (accessed 1 February 2012).

BAe Systems website. www.baesystems.com (accessed 12 December 2011).

Band of Hope. *About Us.* http://www.hopeuk.org/Aboutus/ (accessed 17 January 2012).

Cambridge American Cemetery and Memorial. http://www.abmc.gov/cemeteries/cemeteries/ca.php (accessed 9 October 2011).

Crosby, Allan, and Peter Shakeshaft. *History of a Village: Freckleton.* June 8–9, 2013. http://www.bbc.co.uk/history/trail/local_history/village/history_of_a_village_01.shtml (accessed 12 September, 2011).

Dwyer, Larry. *The Aviation History Online Museum.* http://www.aviation-history.com (accessed 2 February 2012).

Freckleton Brass Band. *History.* http://www.freckletonband.co.uk/History.php (accessed 20 November 2010).

The Freckleton Disaster—B-24 42-50291- 23rd August 1944. http://web.UKonline.co.uk/Liat/site/B-24%2042-50291.htm (accessed 23 May 2007). [link is broken]

Freckleton in 1934. http://www.amounderness.co.uk/freckleton_guide_1934.html (accessed 12 January 2012).

Freckleton Village website. http://www.Freckleton.org (accessed 20 November 2010).

Freckleton War Memorial. http://freckletonmemorial.webs.com (accessed 30 November 2011).

George Baker. http://sadsack.org/GBaker.htm (accessed 29 February 2012).

History of the Mighty Eighth and Eighth Air Force Historical Society. http://www.8thAfhs.org/ourhistory.htm (accessed 26 January 2012).

Inquests after a Disaster. *When Disaster Strikes.* http://www.disasteraction.org.uk/support/da_guide13.htm (accessed 10 March 2012).

Rupke, Edward J. "What Happens When Lightning Strikes an Airplane." *Scientific American.* http://www.scientificamerican.com/article.cfm?id=what-happens-when-lightni (accessed 25 September 2011).

Schools in Freckleton. http://www.freckleton.org/amenities/schools.html (accessed 5 April 2012).

The Ship Inn. http://theshipinnFreckleton.co.uk (accessed 12 January 2012).

Skelton, Robert. "Job Losses at BAE Systems to Devastate Towns." *World Socialist Web Site.* http://www.wsws.org/en/articles/2011/10/baes-o18.html (accessed 5 April 2012).

Emails

Armitage, Julie, to James Hedtke. "RE: Hodgson Institute," 13 January 2012, personal email.

Carr, David, to James Hedtke. "RE: Freckleton Air Disaster," 24 April 2012, personal email.

Scott, Ralph, to James Hedtke. "RE: Freckleton Air Disaster," 20 May 2008, personal email.

_____. "RE: Answers to Questions," 4 June 2008, personal email.

_____. "RE: BAD2 Association," 8 August 2008, personal email.

_____. "RE: Freckleton," 19 August 2008, personal email.

Interviews and Letters

Bloemendal, Ernest. Interview by author, 12 June 2008.

Bone, William to James Hedtke. Personal letter, 19 June 2008.

Cottam, Irene. Interview by author, 5 February 2012.

Currell, Ruby. Interview by author, 12 February 2012.

Dollin, Elise. Interview by author, 10 February 2012.

Hall, Barbara. Interview by author, 4 February 2012.

McClune, Richard, to Valerie Whittle. Personal letter, 9 August 1986.

Miller, Thomas. Interview by author, 25 June 2008.

_____. to James Hedtke. Personal letter, 7 August 2008.

Richardson, Joan. Interview by author, 7 February 2012.

Scott, Ralph, to Valerie Whittle. Personal letter, 12 August 1986.

_____, to James Hedtke. Personal letter, 20 May 2008.

_____. Personal letter, 8 August 2008.

_____. Personal letter, 12 August 2008.

Whittle, Valerie. Interview by author, 8 February 2012.

Newpapers

Blackpool Gazette. September 1992–January 2012.

Daily Mail. December 2000–December 2001.

Dayton Daily. July 2007.

The Guardian. January 2012.

The Independent. August 2010.

Iosco County News-Herald. March 2010.

The Lancashire Daily/Evening Post. August 1944–January 2012.

Lytham St. Anne's Express. August 1944–January 2012.

The New York Times. August 1944–February 1959.

Savannah Morning News. August 1997.

Seattle Times. August 1994.

The Southwest Daily Times. June 1999.

The Stars and Stripes. January 1985.

The Times. August 1944–December 1955.

West Chatham and Effingham Closeup. May 2000.

Periodicals

Brack, Allan. "Friendly Freckleton." Lancashire Life (January 1985): 23–25.

Ferrara, Harold. "A Personal Story." Sweden after the Flak, vol. 1, no. 1 (Winter 1999): 4.

Henningson, Par. "American Internees in Sweden 1943–1945!" Sweden after the Flak, vol. 1, no.1 (Winter 1999): 5–6.

Madden, David. "A Day I've Remember." BAD News, vol. 33, no. 1 (January 2009): 1–5.

Mayor, David G. "The Day Freckleton Wept." BAD News, vol. 2, no. 2 (March 1979): 1–7.

Melin, Ingemar. "Bulltofta, June 20–21, 1944." Sweden after the Flak, vol. 1, no. 1 (Winter 1999): 1–3.

Shakeshaft, Peter. A Short History of Holy Trinity Church. Published in aid of the Church Restoration Fund, 1977.

"U.S. Soldiers Carry Coffins of 36 Infants," Lancashire Daily Post, 26 August 1944.

West, Fred. "Classy Chassis II." The Dropzone, vol. 4, no. 1 (April 2006): 9–12.

Supporting Sources

Base Air Depot No. 2. Memorial Garden Dedication Ceremony Program. 23 August 1997.

BBC One. "Freckleton Air Disaster." Documentary. Inside-Out Northwest. 26 January 2007.

Carr, David. "My Grandmother, Mrs. Agnes Carr." Unpublished essay. September 2006.

_____. "The Freckleton Air Disaster." Unpublished poem. December 2006.

Memorial Service Program for the 65th Anniversary of the Freckleton Air Disaster. Freckleton, UK. 23 August 2009.

Scott, Ralph. Unpublished address delivered at the BAD2 Memorial Garden Dedication Ceremony. Eighth Air Force Heritage Museum. Pooler, Georgia. 23 August 1997.